KB086978

Let's Study!

The Grammar School 3

Iambooks

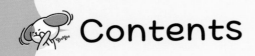

Contents

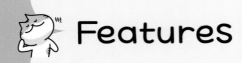

Features

새로운 중학교 교과 과정 반영
자기주도 학습을 통한 내신 완벽 대비
내신 기출문제 분석
명확한 핵심 문법 해설
Workbook – 다양하고 풍부한 문법문제 수록

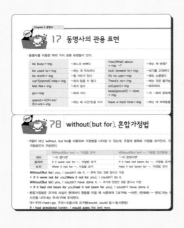

Unit 문법 설명

· 새로운 교과 과정이 반영된 교과서를 분석하여 꼭 알아야 할 문법 사항을 예문과 함께 정리하였습니다.

· 쉬운 설명으로 문법의 기초를 다질 수 있습니다.

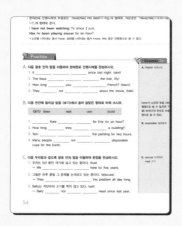

Practice

· 다양한 주관식 문법 문제를 통해 배운 문법 사항을 문제로 풀어보며 익히도록 하였습니다.

· 핵심 문법 설명을 토대로 배운 문법 사항을 Practice를 통해 확실하게 점검할 수 있습니다.

Review Test

· 해당 Chapter에서 배운 문법 사항을 통합하여 다양한 주관식 문제를 통해 복습하며 점검하도록 하였습니다.

· 학습 내용을 바탕으로 문제를 해결하며 응용력을 키울 수 있도록 하였습니다.

Chapter Test

· 해당 Chapter에서 배운 내용들을 학교 시험 유형으로 구성하였으며 출제 비율이 높은 문제를 선별하여 종합 문제로 제시하였습니다.

· 학교 시험에 나올만한 내신 대비 문제와 주관식 문제를 수록하여 내신을 완벽하게 대비하도록 하였습니다.

· 종합문제를 통해 자신의 실력을 점검하도록 하였습니다.

Workbook

· 해당 Chapter에서 배운 문법 사항과 관련된 추가 문법 문제로 구성하였습니다.

· 주관식 문제를 대폭 수록하여 많은 문제를 풀어보며 실력을 쌓을 수 있도록 하였습니다.

문법 용어 정리

가정법 사실이 아닌 것을 가정하거나 상상하여 나타내는 표현법. 동사의 형태에 따라 가정법 과거, 가정법 과거완료, 가정법 미래로 나타낸다.

가주어 문장의 주어가 부정사구이거나 that절일 경우 문장의 균형을 맞추기 위해 그 주어를 대신하여 it을 쓰는데, 이때의 it을 가주어라고 한다.

간접의문문 「의문사/if[whether]+주어+동사」의 형태. 의문문이 다른 문장의 일부분이 될 때 이것을 간접의문문이라고 한다.

간접화법 다른 사람의 말을 자신의 말로 고쳐서 전달하는 방법이다.

감탄문 문장 끝에 감탄 부호(!)를 붙이며 기쁨, 슬픔, 놀람 등의 감정을 나타내는 문장. what으로 시작하는 형태와 how로 시작하는 형태가 있다.

과거분사 「동사원형+-ed」의 형태를 원칙으로 하며 불규칙 동사는 불규칙적으로 변한다. 명사 앞, 뒤에서 명사를 수식하며 완료나 수동의 의미를 담고 있다.

관계대명사 「접속사+대명사」의 역할. 앞에 오는 명사(사람, 사물, 동물)를 꾸며 주는 문장을 이끌어 준다.

관계부사 「접속사+부사」의 역할. 앞에 오는 명사(장소, 시간, 이유, 방법)를 꾸며 주는 문장을 이끌어 준다.

관사 a(n), the를 관사라고 하는데 이들은 항상 명사 앞에 쓰이므로 마치 단어(명사)에 모자를 씌운 것 같다 하여 관사라고 부른다.

구 「주어+동사」의 형태를 포함하지 않고 2개 이상의 단어가 모여 하나의 품사 역할을 하는 것을 말한다.

능동태 '…이 ~을 하다'라는 주어가 목적어에게 행위를 가하는 문장을 말한다.

대동사 앞에 나온 동사(구)가 반복적으로 나오는 것을 피하기 위해 do나 does와 같은 말을 대신 사용하는데 이를 대동사라고 한다.

도치 문장은 일반적으로 「주어+동사+목적어/보어」의 어순이 되는데, 이와 같은 어순에서 동사나 목적어/보어 등이 주어 앞에 놓이는 것을 도치라고 한다. 의문문, 감탄문이 그 대표적인 예인데 평서문에서도 도치가 되는 경우가 많다.

독립부정사 보통 문장의 앞부분에 쓰여 문장 전체를 수식하는 부사구 역할을 하며 관용적 표현이 많다.

독립분사구문 분사구문의 의미상 주어와 문장의 주어가 다를 경우 분사구문의 주어를 생략하지 않고 분사 앞에 그대로 둔다.

동명사 「동사원형+-ing」의 형태. 동사가 형태를 바꾸어 명사 역할을 한다는 뜻으로 붙여진 이름이다. 동사의 성질을 그대로 갖고 있어 그 자체의 목적어, 보어, 수식어구를 취한다.

동사원형 동사의 기본형(원형). 조동사 뒤에 쓰이거나 명령문의 동사로 사용한다.

등위접속사 단어와 단어, 구와 구, 절과 절을 대등한 관계로 연결시켜 주는 역할을 한다.

명령문 명령, 요구, 금지 등을 나타내는 문장이며 보통 주어 You를 생략하고 동사원형으로 시작한다.

명사절 접속사, 의문사, 관계대명사(what)가 이끄는 절. 문장에서 명사 역할(주어, 보어, 목적어 역할)을 한다.

문장 요소 문장을 이루는데 반드시 필요한 주요소(주어, 동사, 목적어, 보어)와 주요소를 꾸미는 수식 요소가 있다.

복문 「주어+동사」 형태의 절이 둘 이상인 문장. 그 중 하나의 절이 의미상 중요한 절이 되며 나머지 절이 그 절에 종속되어 있는 문장이다.

부대상황 분사구문의 한 종류로서, 주절의 동작과 동시에 일어나는 동작이나 사건이 잇따라 일어나는 경우를 나타낸다.

부분 부정 all, both, every가 부정문에 사용되면 일부분만 부정하는 말이 되는데 이를 부분 부정이라고 한다.

부사절 「접속사+주어+동사」 형태. 문장에서 장소, 시간, 원인, 목적, 결과, 조건, 양보 등의 의미를 나타내는 부사 역할을 하는 절을 말한다.

부정대명사 some, any, one, other, another과 같은 단어가 특정한 사람이나 사물을 가리키지 않고 막연히 어떤 사람이나 사물 또는 수량을 가리키는 대명사를 말한다.

부정사 부정사는 품사가 정해지지 않았다는 말로 「to+동사원형」의 형태가 일반적이지만, to가 없는 부정사도 있다. 부정사는 동사 본래의 성질을 가지고 있으므로 그 자체의 목적어, 보어, 수식어구를 취하며 문장에서 명사, 형용사, 부사의 역할을 한다.

분사구문 때, 이유, 조건, 양보 등을 나타내는 부사절을 분사로 시작하는 분사구로 간결하게 나타내는 구문을 말한다.

비교급 형용사나 부사는 원급, 비교급, 최상급으로 변하는데 비교급은 '더 ~한, 더 ~하게'의 뜻으로 원급에 -er를 붙이는 규칙 변화와 그렇지 않은 불규칙 변화가 있다.

비인칭 주어 it 시간, 거리, 요일, 명암, 날씨 등을 나타낼 때 문장의 주어로 it이 사용된다. '그것'이라고 해석되는 대명사 it과는 다르다.

빈도부사 동사를 수식하여 얼마만큼 자주 행해지는가를 나타내는 부사. be동사나 조동사 뒤에, 일반동사 앞에 놓인다.

사역동사 '…에게 ~을 시키다'라는 의미를 가진 동사로 let, make, have 등이 있다.

상관 접속사 단어와 단어, 구와 구, 절과 절을 연결하는 말로 전후 두 요소가 짝이 되어 쓰이는 접속사이다.

선택의문문 두 개 이상 중에서 상대방의 선택을 묻는 의문문이며 Yes나 No를 사용하여 대답하지 않는다.

선행사 「접속사+대명사」의 역할을 하는 관계대명사나 「접속사+부사」의 역할을 하는 관계부사가 수식하는 앞 문장의 명사나 대명사를 말한다.

수동태 「be동사+과거분사」의 형태. 능동태의 목적어를 주어로 삼아 '~이 되다' 또는 '~되어 있다'라고 해석되며, 주어가 어떤 일을 당한다는 의미의 문장을 말한다.

수여동사 '…에게 ~을 주다'라는 의미를 지닌 동사로 목적어 2개를 취하는 4형식 문장을 만든다.

시제 동사가 나타내는 동작 또는 상태가 일어난 시간적 위치. 시제는 크게 기본시제(현재, 과거, 미래), 완료시제(현재완료, 과거완료, 미래완료), 진행시제(현재진행, 과거진행, 미래진행, 현재완료진행, 과거완료진행, 미래완료진행)로 나눌 수 있다.

원급 형용사나 부사는 원급, 비교급, 최상급으로 변하는데 원급은 다른 것과 비교하지 않는 형용사, 부사의 원래 형태를 말한다.

원형부정사 to가 붙지 않은 부정사를 말한다. 주로 지각동사나 사역동사의 목적격보어로 쓰인다.

의미상 주어 to부정사는 동사의 성질을 가지고 있기 때문에 내용상 주어(=의미상 주어)가 필요하며 보통 「for+목적격」으로 나타낸다. 단, 사람의 성격을 나타내는 형용사와 뒤에는 「of+목적격」을 사용한다.

의지미래 주어의 강한 의지나 고집을 나타낼 때 사용하는 시제이며 조동사 will을 사용한다.

이중소유격 소유격은 a(n), the, this, that, any, every, some, no 등과 나란히 사용할 수 없으므로 소유의 관계를 나타내는 전치사 of를 함께 써서 「of+소유대명사」의 형태로 나타낸다.

재귀대명사 인칭대명사의 소유격 또는 목적격에 -self나 -selves를 붙여서 '~ 자신'이라는 뜻을 나타내는 대명사이다.

준동사 동사의 본래의 기능을 가지고 있으면서 다른 품사의 구실을 하는 동사형을 준동사라고 한다. 준동사에는 부정사, 동명사, 분사가 있다.

지각동사 '보다, 듣다, 냄새를 맡다' 등의 감각 기관을 통하여 대상을 인식함을 나타내는 동사이다.

진주어 to부정사나 명사절과 같이 문장이 길 때에는 그 자리에 대신 It을 쓰고 to부정사나 명사절을 문장 뒤에 두기도 하는데, 이때의 to부정사나 명사절을 진주어라고 한다.

최상급 형용사나 부사는 원급, 비교급, 최상급으로 변하는데 최상급은 '가장 ~한, 가장 ~하게'의 뜻으로 원급에 -est를 붙이는 규칙 변화와 그렇지 않은 불규칙 변화가 있다.

형용사절 「접속사+대명사」의 역할을 하는 관계대명사와 「접속사+부사」의 역할을 하는 관계부사가 이끄는 문장을 형용사절이라고 한다.

to부정사는 어떤 역할을 하는가?

to부정사는 「to+동사원형」의 형태로 문장에서 명사, 형용사, 부사의 역할을 한다.

▶ 명사적 용법: 주어, 목적어, 보어의 역할을 한다.

▶ 형용사적 용법: 「명사[대명사]+to부정사+(전치사)」의 형태로 명사나 대명사를 수식한다.

▶ 부사적 용법: ~하기 위해(목적), ~하니(원인), ~해서 …하다(결과) 등의 의미를 나타낸다.

to부정사의 주어는 어떻게 나타내는가?

to부정사의 의미상 주어가 일반인이거나 문장 전체의 주어 또는 목적어와 같으면 생략한다. 그 외에 의미상의 주어를 쓸 때는 일반적으로 「for+목적격」으로 표현하고, 사람의 성격이나 태도를 나타내는 형용사가 오면 「of+목적격」으로 표현한다.

Chapter 1. 부정사

01 | 명사처럼 쓰이는 to부정사

- to부정사는 명사처럼 문장에서 주어, 목적어, 보어로 쓰인다. to부정사가 주어로 쓰일 때는 보통 가주어 It을 써서 「It ~ to부정사」로 나타내는 것이 자연스럽다.

  To master English in a year is not easy. = It is not easy to master English in a year. (가주어 It)

  I hope **to take a trip** to France someday. (목적어)

  His goal is **to publish** a new novel. (보어)

- to부정사의 부정은 「not[never]+to부정사」의 형태로 쓴다.

  Max decided **not to accept** her invitation.

Practice

A. 다음 괄호 안에서 알맞은 것을 고르시오.

1. (Understand / To understand) other cultures is important.

2. Jessie planned (losing / to lose) 3kg in a month.

3. My dream is (to be / to being) a movie director.

4. He expected (to won / to win) the marathon race.

5. The player decided (to leave not / not to leave) his team.

B. 다음 두 문장이 같은 뜻이 되도록 빈칸에 알맞은 말을 쓰시오.

1. To go out alone at night is dangerous.

   = _____ is dangerous _____ _____ out alone at night.

2. To use these tools is very convenient.

   = _____ is very convenient _____ _____ these tools.

3. To ride a bike is good for health.

   = _____ is good for health _____ _____ a bike.

C. 다음 우리말과 같도록 괄호 안의 말을 이용하여 문장을 완성하시오.

1. 가장 중요한 것은 최선을 다하는 것이다. (do)

   → The most important thing is _____ _____ your best.

2. 그녀는 그녀의 개를 산책시키기를 원하니? (walk)

   → Does she want _____ _____ her dog?

3. Tony는 그 꽃병을 만지지 않기로 약속했다. (touch)

   → Tony promised _____ _____ _____ the vase.

4. 새로운 친구들을 사귀는 것은 흥미롭다. (make)

   → _____ _____ new friends is exciting.

Grammar Tip

to부정사의 부정은 to부정사 앞에 not을 써서 나타내는데, 좀 더 강한 부정을 나타낼 때는 never를 쓴다.

A. culture 문화
   movie director 영화감독
   expect 기대하다

to부정사가 주어로 쓰일 때는 주어 자리에 가주어 It을 쓰고, 진주어인 to부정사구는 뒤로 보내는 것이 자연스럽다.

B. tool 연장, 도구
   convenient 편리한

C. walk one's dog
   ~의 개를 산책시키다
   vase 꽃병

02 의문사＋to부정사

- 「의문사＋to부정사」는 명사처럼 쓰이며 문맥에 맞게 what, how, where, when, who 등을 써서 표현한다.

  Let me know **when to leave**.

  She asked me **how to raise** an iguana.

- 「의문사＋to부정사」는 「의문사＋주어＋should＋동사원형」으로 바꿔 쓸 수 있다.

  Judy couldn't decide **what to wear** for the party.

  = Judy couldn't decide **what she should wear** for the party.

Practice

A. 다음 〈보기〉에서 알맞은 말을 골라 문장을 완성하시오.

〈보기〉 what to buy   how to use   where to put   when to order

1. Do you know _____ this machine?
2. I forgot _____ food.
3. He asked me _____ the key.
4. Did you decide _____ for Anne's birthday?

B. 다음 두 문장이 같은 뜻이 되도록 빈칸에 알맞은 말을 쓰시오.

1. Nobody advised me what to do.

   = Nobody advised me _____ _____ _____ _____.

2. Jessica doesn't remember where to find her luggage.

   = Jessica doesn't remember _____ _____ _____ _____ her luggage.

3. I'm not sure when to leave.

   = I'm not sure _____ _____ _____ _____.

4. He doesn't know how to feed the dog.

   = He doesn't know _____ _____ _____ _____ the dog.

C. 다음 우리말과 같도록 빈칸에 알맞을 말을 쓰시오.

1. 그는 어디에 앉아야 할지 궁금했다.

   → He wondered _____ _____ _____ on.

2. 그들은 누구를 초대할지 정하지 않았다.

   → They didn't decide _____ _____ _____.

3. 언제 멈춰야 할지 내게 말해 줘.

   → Please tell me _____ _____ _____.

4. Sarah는 자전거 타는 법을 배우고 싶어 한다.

   → Sarah wants to learn _____ _____ _____ a bike.

Grammar Tip

의문사 why 뒤에는 to부정사를 사용할 수 없다.

A. machine 기계

「의문사＋to부정사」를 「의문사＋주어＋should＋동사원형」으로 바꿀 때, 주절과 주어가 달라지는 경우에 유의한다.

Can **you** tell me where to park my car?
→ Can you tell me where I should park my car?

B. luggage 수하물
feed 먹이를 주다

C. sit on 앉다
ride 타다

Unit 03 형용사처럼 쓰이는 to부정사

· to부정사가 형용사처럼 쓰일 때는 앞의 명사나 대명사를 수식하는 역할을 하며, '~할', '~하는'으로 해석한다.

I need a book to read for bedtime.

Do you have any questions to ask me?

· to부정사가 수식하는 명사가 전치사의 목적어인 경우에는 뒤에 반드시 전치사를 써야 하며, 전치사에 따라 의미가 달라지는 것에 유의한다.

Peter is looking for a roommate to live with. (함께 살 ~)

Sweden is a good country to live in. (~에서 살)

Practice

A. 다음 괄호 안에서 알맞은 것을 고르시오.

1. Kevin is looking for a pencil (to write / to write with).

2. Please give me a chance (for explain / to explain) why I was late.

3. The chair isn't strong enough (to sit / to sit on).

4. We had an opportunity (working / to work) abroad.

B. 다음 괄호 안의 말을 바르게 배열하여 문장을 완성하시오.

1. We booked _____. (stay, at, to, hotel, a)

2. It's _____.
(phone, to, time, my, charge)

3. She brought up _____.
(important, about, talk, an, topic, to)

4. What is _____?
(new, way, a, to, best, language, the, learn)

C. 다음 우리말과 같도록 괄호 안의 말을 이용하여 문장을 완성하시오.

1. 그 아이들은 가지고 놀 장난감들이 좀 필요하다.
→ The children need some toys _____ _____ _____. (play)

2. Mike는 반지를 살 돈이 없다.
→ Mike doesn't have _____ _____ _____ a ring. (buy)

3. Marie Currie는 노벨상을 받은 최초의 여성이다.
→ Marie Currie was the _____ _____ _____ _____ the Nobel Prize. (win)

4. 나의 책들을 보관할 공간이 없다. (store)
→ There is no _____ _____ _____ my books.

Grammar Tip

A. explain 설명하다
opportunity 기회
abroad 해외에, 해외로

B. charge 충전하다
bring up (화제를) 꺼내다
topic 주제

일반적인 장소를 나타내는 space, place 등의 경우에는 보통 전치사를 쓰지 않는다.

C. win 획득하다, 타다
space 공간
store 보관하다

04 | be동사+to부정사

· be동사 뒤에 to부정사가 오면 여러 가지 의미를 나타낼 수 있다.

예정	~할 예정이다	We **are to travel** abroad during the vacation.
의무	~해야 한다	He **is to finish** his work by nine.
가능	~할 수 있다	Many stars **were to be** seen in the sky.
운명	~할 운명이다	He **was to become** King when he grew up.
의지	~하려고 하다	If she **is to pass** the exam, she has to study hard.

Practice

A. 다음 〈보기〉에서 단어를 골라 알맞은 형태로 빈칸에 쓰시오.

〈보기〉　open　　win　　observe　　enter

1. If we are _____ the game, we must start training now.
2. They were never _____ the palace without permission.
3. We are _____ the traffic rules.
4. The new store is _____ next Friday.

B. 다음 빈칸에 「be+to부정사」를 이용하여 문장을 완성하시오.

1. She is going to depart for Mexico tomorrow morning.
   → She _____ _____ _____ for Mexico tomorrow morning.
2. They were destined to get married.
   → They _____ _____ _____ married.
3. You should submit the report by tomorrow.
   → You _____ _____ _____ the report by tomorrow.
4. If you want to be a pianist, practice more.
   → If you _____ _____ _____ a pianist, practice more.

C. 다음 우리말과 같도록 괄호 안의 말을 이용하여 문장을 완성하시오.

1. Beth는 이번 수요일에 그 책을 반납해야 한다. (return)
   → Beth _____ _____ _____ the book this Wednesday.
2. 마지막 강연은 6시에 시작할 예정이다. (start)
   → The last lecture _____ _____ _____ at six.
3. 비가 올 때 운전을 하면 안 된다. (drive)
   → You _____ _____ _____ when it is raining.
4. 방에서 오직 그의 목소리만 들을 수 있었다. (hear)
   → Only his voice _____ _____ _____ in the room.

Grammar Tip

「be+to부정사」의 부정은 to부정사 앞에서 not이나 never를 쓴다.

A. permission 허가, 허락
　observe 준수하다
　train 훈련하다

to부정사의 보어 역할은 주어의 의미를 설명하고, 「be+to부정사」는 예정, 의무 등의 의미를 나타낸다.
· His aim is **to be** a president. (보어 역할)
· The two leaders **are to meet** in Chicago. (예정)

B. depart 떠나다, 출발하다
　destined ~할 운명인
　submit 제출하다

C. lecture 강연
　be heard 들리다

unit 05 부사처럼 쓰이는 to부정사

· to부정사가 부사처럼 쓰일 때는 목적, 원인, 결과, 조건, 근거 등의 의미를 나타낸다.

목적	~하기 위해서	We shouted **to warn** everybody of the danger.
원인	~해서, ~하게 되어	I was pleased **to get** a gift.
결과	~해서 …하다	Emma grew up **to be** a cook.
조건	~한다면	You may be surprised **to see** it.
근거	~하다니, ~하는 것을 보니	He must be rich **to have** an amazing car.
형용사 수식	~하기에	The question is difficult **to answer**.

Practice

A. 다음 밑줄 친 부분을 우리말로 해석하시오.

1. He would be upset <u>to know the truth</u>. _____

2. We were happy <u>to see her at the party</u>. _____

3. She must be intelligent <u>to speak four languages</u>.

   _____

4. They need more time <u>to make a decision</u>.

   _____

B. 다음 괄호 안의 말을 바르게 배열하여 문장을 완성하시오.

1. They went to the bakery, _____.
   (to, closed, find, only, it)

2. Leave _____ the bus. (early, miss, to, not)

3. I don't think this book is _____.
   (to, easy, understand)

4. I was _____ the news. (hear, sorry, to)

C. 다음 〈보기〉에서 골라 알맞은 형태로 빈칸에 쓰시오.

〈보기〉 climb   wash   pass   be

1. My grandma lived _____ eighty.

2. This mountain is very dangerous _____.

3. Peter practiced a lot, only _____ the audition.

4. You'd better use this brush _____ the dishes.

Grammar Tip

A. intelligent 똑똑한
make a decision 결정하다

to부정사 앞에 only나 never가 쓰여 결과의 의미를 나타내기도 한다. 이때는 '~하지만 …하다'로 해석한다.

B. ill 아픈

목적의 의미로 쓰인 to부정사는 「in order to부정사」 또는 「so as to부정사」로 바꿔 쓸 수 있다.
I need some money **to buy** new shoes.
= I need some money **in order to[so as to] buy** new shoes.

C. had better ~하는 게 낫다

14

Unit 06 | too ~ to, enough to

- 「too+형용사[부사]+to부정사」는 '~하기에 너무 …한'의 뜻으로, too는 보통 부정의 의미를 나타낸다.
  「so+형용사[부사]+that+주어+can't+동사원형」으로 바꿔 쓸 수 있다.
  He is **too** hungry **to** walk fast.
  = He is **so** hungry **that he can't** walk fast.
- 「형용사[부사]+enough to부정사」는 '~할 만큼 충분히 …하다'의 뜻을 나타낸다.
  「so+형용사[부사]+that+주어+can+동사원형」으로 바꿔 쓸 수 있다.
  Jessica is rich **enough to** buy an expensive ring.
  = Jessica is **so** rich **that she can** buy an expensive ring.

Practice

A. 다음 두 문장이 같은 뜻이 되도록 빈칸에 알맞은 말을 쓰시오.

1. You are clever enough to complete the mission.
   = You are _____ _____ _____ you _____ _____ the mission.
2. My laptop was so heavy that I couldn't carry it.
   = My laptop was _____ _____ for me _____ _____.
3. The problem is so easy that they can solve it.
   = The problem is _____ _____ for them _____ _____.

B. 다음 상황에 맞도록 괄호 안의 말을 바르게 배열하시오.

1. I couldn't stay in the room. It was too cold.
   → The room was _____. (stay, too, cold, to)
2. He can reach the switch. He is very tall.
   → He is _____ the switch.
   (to, enough, tall, reach)
3. Don't run here. The road is too icy.
   → The road is _____. (icy, to, too, run)

C. 다음 우리말과 같도록 괄호 안의 말을 이용하여 문장을 완성하시오.

1. 이 커피는 너무 뜨거워서 마실 수 없다. (hot)
   → This coffee is _____.
2. 그 도로는 너무 좁아서 두 대의 차가 지날 수 없다. (narrow)
   → The road is _____ for two cars _____ each other.
3. 그의 목소리는 모든 사람이 듣기에 충분히 크다. (loud)
   → His voice is _____ for everyone _____.
4. 어떤 원숭이들은 도구를 사용할 만큼 똑똑하다. (smart)
   → Some monkeys are _____ tools.

Grammar Tip

to부정사의 주체와 문장의 주어가 다를 때는 to부정사 앞에 「for[of]+목적격」의 형태로 to부정사의 의미상의 주어를 쓴다.

A. mission 임무
laptop 휴대용 컴퓨터

B. stay 머무르다
reach 닿다
icy 얼음에 뒤덮인

C. narrow 좁은
tool 도구

A. 다음 <보기>에서 단어를 골라 알맞은 형태로 쓰시오.

<보기> tell   return   become   preserve

1. Salt is used _____ food longer.
2. His dream is _____ a great actor.
3. Anna is not a person _____ the rumor.
4. They were never _____ their home again.

B. 다음 밑줄 친 부분을 바르게 고치시오.

1. The pie is <u>enough big</u> to share together.   _____
2. She moved to Chicago <u>see</u> his parents more often.

    _____
3. Those stools are not safe for kids <u>to sit</u>.   _____
4. If you <u>are succeed</u>, you have to try harder.   _____

C. 다음 우리말과 같도록 괄호 안의 말을 이용하여 문장을 완성하시오.

1. 어젯밤에는 너무 추워서 잠을 잘 수 없었다. (cold)
   → It was _____ _____ _____ _____ well last night.

2. 그는 내일 생일 파티를 열 예정이다. (have)
   → He _____ _____ _____ his birthday party tomorrow.

3. 그 소녀가 그 문제를 풀다니 똑똑한 게 틀림없다. (solve)
   → The girl is must be smart _____ _____ the problem.

4. 언제 그것을 보내야 할지 알려 줘. (send)
   → Let me know _____ _____ _____ it.

D. 다음 두 문장이 같은 뜻이 되도록 빈칸에 알맞은 말을 쓰시오.

1. The young man will finish the project.
   = The young man _____ _____ _____ the project.

2. The language is so complicated that I couldn't learn it.
   = The language is _____ _____ _____ _____ .

3. I don't know how I should get to the post office.
   = Tell me _____ _____ _____ to the post office.

Grammar Tip

A. salt 소금
   actor 배우
   rumor 소문
   preserve 보존하다

be동사 뒤에 to부정사가 오면 예정, 의무, 의지 등 다양한 의미를 가질 수 있다.

B. share 나누다, 공유하다
   stool
   (등받이와 팔걸이가 없는) 의자

C. throw a party 파티를 열다

D. project 프로젝트, 업무
   complicated 복잡한

07 to부정사의 의미상의 주어

- to부정사의 주체가 문장의 주어와 다를 때는 의미상의 주어를 쓴다. to부정사의 의미상의 주어는 일반적으로 「for +목적격」으로 쓰고, 사람의 성격이나 태도를 나타내는 형용사가 오면 「of+목적격」으로 쓴다.

  The manual is difficult **for me** to understand.

  It was <u>clever</u> **of her** to teach herself.

- to부정사의 의미상의 주어가 일반인이거나 문장의 주어나 목적어와 같은 경우에는 생략한다.

  It is not good to eat too much fatty food.

  She is too young to drive a car.

  He told me to walk the dog.

Practice

A. 다음 괄호 안의 말을 이용하여 문장을 완성하시오.

1. It is not easy _____ _____ _____ _____ cookies.
   (she, bake)

2. It was careless _____ _____ _____ _____ such a thing.
   (he, say)

3. It was natural _____ _____ _____ _____ the law.
   (they, obey)

4. He reminded _____ _____ _____ Laura tomorrow. (I, call)

B. 다음 밑줄 친 부분을 바르게 고치시오.

1. It was very nice <u>for you</u> to serve food for the poor.
   _____

2. We wish <u>for Julie</u> to exercise regularly.   _____

3. It is common <u>of her</u> to make that mistake.   _____

4. Some words are too difficult <u>of me</u> to translate.   _____

C. 다음 우리말과 같도록 괄호 안의 말을 이용하여 문장을 완성하시오.

1. 나는 네가 진실을 말하기를 원한다. (tell)
   → I want _____ _____ _____ the truth.

2. 이 재킷은 너무 비싸서 내가 살 수가 없다. (buy)
   → This jacket is too expensive _____ _____ _____ _____.

3. Jay는 내가 그의 가게 앞에 주차하는 것을 허락하지 않았다. (park)
   → Jay doesn't allow _____ _____ _____ in front of his shop.

4. 나를 집까지 데려다 주다니 그는 친절하다. (take)
   → It was kind _____ _____ _____ _____ me home.

Grammar Tip

사람의 성격이나 태도를 나타내는 형용사에는 kind, bad, wrong, stupid, smart, careless, crazy, wise, silly 등이 있다.

A. law 법
   obey 따르다
   remind 상기시키다

to부정사의 의미상의 주어가 문장 전체의 주어나 목적어와 같으면 생략한다.

B. regularly 규칙적으로
   translate 번역하다

C. allow 허락하다

unit 08 to부정사의 시제

- to부정사의 행위가 문장 전체의 시제와 같으면 「to+동사원형」을 쓴다.

  It appears that the man likes Eva.
  = The man appears **to like** Eva.

- to부정사의 행위가 문장 전체의 시제보다 먼저 일어났으면 「to+have+p.p」형태의 완료형을 쓴다.

  It seems that you caught a cold.
  = You seem **to have caught** a cold.

Practice

A. 다음 두 문장이 같은 뜻이 되도록 빈칸에 알맞은 말을 쓰시오.

1. It seems that he enjoys his new hobby.
   = He seems _____ _____ his new hobby.

2. I think that they had plenty of money.
   = I think them _____ _____ _____ plenty of money.

3. It appears that she is nervous before the audience.
   = She appears _____ _____ nervous before the audience.

B. 다음 괄호 안의 말을 이용하여 문장을 완성하시오.

1. We expect him _____ _____ the exam. (pass)

2. I feel lucky _____ _____ _____ abroad before. (be)

3. He seems _____ _____ _____ ill yesterday. (be)

4. I'm happy _____ _____ _____ him then. (meet)

C. 다음 우리말과 같도록 괄호 안의 말을 이용하여 문장을 완성하시오.

1. 너는 많은 사람을 아는 것처럼 보인다. (know)
   → You seem _____ _____ a lot of people.

2. 그의 차는 도로에서 고장이 났던 것처럼 보인다. (break down)
   → His car seems _____ _____ _____ _____
   in the road.

3. 그 소녀는 자주 나를 못 본 척한다. (see)
   → The girl often pretends not _____ _____ me.

4. 그 화재는 저 난로에서 시작됐던 것처럼 보인다. (start)
   → The fire seems _____ _____ _____ in that stove.

Grammar Tip

A. plenty of 많은
   audience 청중, 관중

문장 전체의 시제가 현재일 때, 과거를 나타내는 부사구가 쓰이면 to부정사는 완료형으로 쓴다.

B. abroad 해외에
   ill 아픈

C. break down 고장 나다
   pretend ~인 척하다

09 원형부정사

- make, have, let 등의 사역동사는 목적격보어로 원형부정사를 쓴다.

  His parents <u>let</u> him **go** to the party.

  Hot and humid weather <u>makes</u> me **feel** tired.

- see, watch, hear, feel, smell, notice 등의 지각동사는 목적격보어로 원형부정사를 쓴다.

  She <u>saw</u> children **cross** the street.

  ＊지각동사의 목적격보어로 진행 중인 동작을 강조할 때는 현재분사를 쓰기도 한다.

  Can you <u>smell</u> something **burn**?

  Can you <u>smell</u> something **burning**?

Practice

A. 다음 괄호 안에서 알맞은 것을 고르시오.

1. I didn't see anybody (pass / to pass) in the hallway.

2. Can you help me (get / getting) dinner ready?

3. Her parents wouldn't let her (travel / to travel) alone.

4. I felt something (to crawl / crawling) up my leg.

B. 다음 밑줄 친 부분을 바르게 고치시오. (가능한 모든 정답을 쓰시오.)

1. They felt the house <u>shakes</u> because of the earthquake.

   _____

2. They helped me <u>carrying</u> the luggage.   _____

3. Let me <u>to finish</u> the painting for you.   _____

4. I could hear air <u>to leak</u> from the balloon.   _____

C. 다음 우리말과 같도록 괄호 안의 말을 이용하여 문장을 완성하시오.

1. 너는 그 사고가 일어나고 있는 것을 봤니? (happen)

   → Did you see _____ _____ _____?

2. 그는 오랫동안 나를 밖에 서 있게 했다. (stand)

   → He made _____ _____ outside for a long time.

3. 엄마는 내가 여동생에게 사과하도록 시키셨다. (apologize)

   → My mom had _____ _____ to my sister.

4. 우리는 그가 아래층으로 가는 것을 알아챘다.

   → We noticed _____ _____ downstairs.

Grammar Tip

지각동사의 목적격보어로 원형부정사를 쓰는데, 진행의 의미를 강조할 때는 현재분사를 쓸 수 있다.

A. get dinner ready
   저녁을 준비하다
   crawl 기다, 기어가다

help의 목적격보어로 동사가 올 때는 원형부정사나 to부정사 둘 다 쓸 수 있다.

B. earthquake 지진
   luggage 짐
   leak 세다

C. apologize 사과하다
   notice 알아채다
   downstairs 아래층으로

10 대부정사와 독립부정사

· 같은 동사의 반복을 피하기 위하여 to부정사의 to만 쓰는 것을 대부정사라고 한다.

Justin continued to sing loudly although I told him not **to**. (to = to sing loudly)

She wanted us to wear a pink shirt, but we didn't agree **to**. (to = to wear a pink shirt)

· 독립된 의미를 가지고 문장 전체를 수식하는 to부정사를 독립부정사라고 한다.

to be frank[honest] with you	솔직히 말하면	to be sure	확실히
to begin with	우선, 먼저	to tell the truth	사실대로 말하면
to make matters worse	설상가상으로	so to speak	말하자면
strange to say	이상하게도	that is to say	즉, 다시 말하면
not to mention	~은 말할 것도 없이	needless to say	말할 필요도 없이

Practice

A. 다음 밑줄 친 to 뒤에 생략된 말을 찾아 쓰시오.

1. The doctor advised him to exercise, but he didn't want <u>to</u>.

_____

2. Try on this coat if you want <u>to</u>. _____

3. She wanted to order Chinese food, but I didn't allow her <u>to</u>.

_____

B. 다음 우리말과 같도록 〈보기〉에서 골라 문장을 완성하시오.

〈보기〉 to be honest with you	to be sure
to make matters worse	not to mention

1. _____, I don't think I can make it. (솔직히 말하면)
2. We got lost in the woods. _____, it is getting dark. (설상가상으로)
3. _____, Fred is good humored. (확실히)
4. She can speak Spanish, _____, English.
   (말할 것도 없이)

C. 다음 우리말과 같도록 괄호 안의 말을 이용하여 문장을 완성하시오.

1. 말하자면, 그것은 요즘 가장 인기 있는 노래이다. (speak)
   → _____, it is the most popular song now.
2. 우선, 우리는 주제를 골라야 한다. (begin)
   → _____, we have to pick a topic.
3. 이상하게도, 그는 컴퓨터 게임을 좋아하지 않는다. (strange)
   → _____, he doesn't like computer games.

Grammar Tip

A. advise 충고하다
order 주문하다

독립부정사를 문장 앞에 쓸 때는 그 뒤에 comma(,)를, 중간에 쓸 때는 앞뒤로, 마지막에 쓸 때는 바로 앞에 붙인다.

B. get lost 길을 잃다
good humored 유쾌한
Spanish 스페인어

C. pick 고르다, 뽑다
topic 주제

 **Review Test**

A. 다음 두 문장이 같은 뜻이 되도록 빈칸에 알맞은 말을 쓰시오.

1. I'm sorry that I kept you waiting.
   = I'm sorry _____ _____ _____ you waiting.

2. It seems that John was a genius.
   = John seems _____ _____ _____ a genius.

3. It is clever that you find out the answer.
   = It is clever _____ _____ _____ find out the answer.

4. She wants that I send a parcel to Max.
   = She wants _____ _____ _____ a parcel to Max.

B. 다음 밑줄 친 부분을 바르게 고치시오.

1. I've never seen him to wear shorts. _____

2. It is silly for the boy to give up the test. _____

3. I made her promises that she wouldn't be late again.

   _____

4. Bill appears to spend his childhood in Asia. _____

C. 다음 괄호 안의 말을 바르게 배열하여 문장을 완성하시오.

1. He warned _____ statues in the gallery.
   (to, us, touch, not)

2. He _____ on the shoulder. (somebody, touch, felt)

3. This pattern was, _____, the trend of last year.
   (to, speak, so)

4. He _____ his telescope. (me, to, allowed, use)

D. 다음 우리말과 같도록 괄호 안의 말을 이용하여 문장을 완성하시오.

1. 그녀는 고양이를 키울 계획이었지만, 그들은 허락하지 않으셨다. (allow)
   → She planned to raise a cat, but they _____ _____ _____.

2. Kevin은 항상 나를 웃게 만든다. (laugh)
   → Kevin always _____ _____ _____.

3. 설상가상으로 비가 내리기 시작했다. (worse)
   → _____ _____ _____ _____, it started to rain.

4. 그는 전에 유명한 배우였던 것 같다. (be)
   → He appears _____ _____ _____ a famous actor.

Grammar Tip

A. genius 천재
   parcel 소포

to부정사의 행위가 문장 전체의 시제보다 앞서 일어났으면 완료형 to부정사를 쓴다.

B. shorts 반바지
   silly 어리석은
   childhood 어린 시절

C. statue 조각상
   somebody 누군가
   trend 유행
   telescope 망원경

D. raise (식물·동물 등을) 기르다
   famous 유명한

[1-2] 다음 빈칸에 알맞은 것을 고르시오.

1.
Tom's hope is _____ on the national soccer team.

① play
② to play
③ to playing
④ plays
⑤ to be played

2.
Jill wants friends _____.

① to talk
② to talk in
③ to talk on
④ to talk with
⑤ to talk about

3. 다음 중 not이 들어갈 위치로 알맞은 것은?

We should ① promise ② to ③ use bad languages ④ to our friends ⑤.

4. 다음 중 밑줄 친 부분의 쓰임이 다른 하나는?
① He bought some books to read.
② Brian is the only one to arrive on time.
③ I need a few days to think about that.
④ The actress wanted some bodyguards to protect her.
⑤ Hellen shouted to warn people of the danger.

5. 다음 우리말을 바르게 영작한 것은?

그녀의 엄마는 그녀를 좀 쉬게 했다.

① Her mom made her takes some rest.
② Her mom made her take some rest.
③ Her mom made her to take some rest.
④ Her mom made her taking some rest.
⑤ Her mom to make her take some rest.

6. 다음 중 어법상 어색한 것은?
① I need something to open this bottle with.
② He felt the building shaking yesterday.
③ He advised me not to read too much comic books.
④ I heard someone crying in the distance.
⑤ I'm sorry to be late for last class.

[7-8] 다음 문장과 뜻이 같은 것을 고르시오.

7.
This backpack is very expensive, so I can't buy it.

① This backpack is too expensive to buy.
② This backpack is expensive enough to buy.
③ This backpack isn't too expensive to buy.
④ This backpack is cheap to buy.
⑤ This backpack is too expensive not to buy.

8.
You are not to tease other people.

① You must tease other people.
② You are teased by other people.
③ You may not tease other people.
④ You don't have to tease other people.
⑤ You should not tease other people.

9. 다음 문장의 빈칸에 들어갈 알맞은 것을 두 개 고르면?

Please tell me _____ to leave.

① where
② when
③ what
④ why
⑤ which

10. 다음 빈칸에 들어갈 말이 나머지와 다른 것은?

① It is kind _____ him to carry the box.

② It's unusual _____ her to get so angry.

③ The house was too small _____ us to live in.

④ It is impossible _____ my brother to get a driver's license.

⑤ This book is not easy _____ me to under understand.

11. 다음 빈칸에 알맞지 않은 것은?

> The man _____ the boys clean up after the meeting.

① had　　　　　② made
③ helped　　　　④ saw
⑤ asked

12. 다음 대화의 빈칸에 가장 알맞은 것은?

> A: Why do you look so tired?
> B: It was too hot today. _____ the air conditioner in my office was broken.

① So to speak
② To tell the truth
③ To be sure
④ To make matters worse
⑤ Strange to say

[13–14] 다음 두 문장의 뜻이 같도록 빈칸에 알맞은 말을 쓰시오.

13.

> It seems that the festival took place in September.

= The festival seems _____ _____ _____ place in September.

14.

> Jake was so thirsty that he drank up the milk.

= Jake was _____ _____ _____ drink up the milk.

15. 다음 밑줄 친 부분 중 어법상 어색한 것은?

> Diana wanted ①to take a long trip ②alone, but her parents ③told ④her ⑤not.

16. 다음 문장의 뜻이 같지 않은 것은?

① I don't know how I should spend money wisely.
= I don't know how to spend money wisely.

② It appears that he is a wealthy man.
= He appears to have been a wealthy man.

③ We came here in order to enter a competition.
= We came here to enter a competition.

④ The people are going to visit Europe next week.
= The people are to visit Europe next week.

⑤ To stop the car suddenly can be very dangerous.
= It is very dangerous to stop the car suddenly.

17. 다음 빈칸에 공통으로 알맞은 것은?

> · His wish is _____ stay healthy.
> · If you are _____ invite some friends, send the invitation cards.

① to　　　　　② for
③ about　　　　④ of
⑤ on

18. 다음 <보기>의 밑줄 친 부분과 쓰임이 같은 것은?

<보기>
They were shocked <u>to hear</u> the news.

① It is difficult <u>to master</u> English in a short time.
② He gets lonely if there is nobody <u>to talk</u> to.
③ He decided not <u>to go</u> out because of the the heavy snow.
④ William wants <u>to make</u> a good impression at the interview.
⑤ This soup is spicy for children <u>to eat</u>.

19. 다음 우리말과 같도록 할 때, 빈칸에 알맞은 말을 쓰시오.

솔직히 말하면, 너는 그의 생각을 알지 못하고 알려고 노력하지도 않는다.

→ To be frank with you, you don't know his thought, and you don't try _____.

20. 다음 빈칸에 들어갈 말이 바르게 짝지어진 것은?

· Show me _____ to peel the fruit.
· It is careless _____ to be late again.

① how – you
② where – for you
③ how – of you
④ how – for you
⑤ what – of you

<서술형 문제>

21. 다음 괄호 안의 말을 이용하여 우리말을 영작하시오.

여기에서 그 상자들을 보관할 장소를 찾는 것은 쉽지 않다. (easy, find, a place, store, the boxes)

→ _____

22. 다음 우리말과 같은 뜻이 되도록 빈칸에 알맞은 말을 쓰시오.

이상한 이야기지만, 나는 전에 꿈에서 여기를 와 본 적이 있는 것 같다.

→ _____,
I think I've been here before in a dream.

23. 다음 두 문장이 같은 뜻이 되도록 빈칸에 알맞은 말을 쓰시오.

It seems that she had a lot of friends.

= She seems _____.

24. 다음 대화의 내용에 맞게 to부정사를 이용하여 문장을 완성하시오.

Fred: Where are you going for summer vacation?
Emma: I haven't made up my mind yet. There are so many places to visit.

→ Emma haven't decided _____ _____ _____ for summer vacation.

25. 다음 밑줄 친 부분 중 어법상 어색한 것을 찾아 바르게 고쳐 쓰시오.

Sarah <u>was to have</u> her birthday party. She didn't know <u>what to do</u>. Her sister, Julia helped Sarah. They decided to buy food first. They spent a lot of time <u>to prepare</u> snacks for the party. Sarah told her friends <u>not to bring</u> any birthday presents. She just will make them <u>to have</u> a lot of fun.

_____ → _____

동명사는 어떤 역할을 하는가?

동명사는 「동사원형+-ing」의 형태로 문장에서 주어, 목적어, 보어의 역할을 한다.

– 주어 역할 : ～하는 것은, ～하기는

– 목적어 역할 : ～하는 것을

– 보어 역할 : ～하는 것(이다)

동명사와 to부정사를 목적어로 취하는 동사에는 무엇이 있는가?

– 동명사를 목적어로 취하는 동사 : enjoy, finish, give up …

– to부정사를 목적어로 취하는 동사 : want, decide, hope …

– 동명사와 to부정사를 목적어로 취하는 동사 : like, love, start …

Chapter 2. 동명사

unit 11 주어, 보어로 쓰이는 동명사

- 동명사가 주어로 쓰일 때는 일반적으로 문장의 맨 앞에 온다. 이때 동명사는 단수 취급하며, to부정사로 바꿔 쓸 수 있다.

  Taking a walk regularly is good for your health.

  = To take a walk regularly is good for your health.

- 동명사가 보어로 쓰일 때는 보통 be동사 뒤에 오며, to부정사로 바꿔 쓸 수 있다.

  My favorite activity in summer is **swimming**.

  = My favorite activity in summer is to swim.

- 동명사의 부정은 동명사 앞에 not 또는 never를 쓴다.

  Not wasting time is a good habit.

Practice

A. 다음 〈보기〉에서 알맞은 말을 골라 문장의 빈칸에 동명사로 쓰시오.

〈보기〉 watch	eat	travel	protect

1. _____ the environment is very important.
2. My goal is _____ foreign movies without subtitles.
3. _____ around the world can be very exciting.
4. His biggest problem is not _____ vegetables.

B. 다음 괄호 안의 말을 바르게 배열하여 문장을 완성하시오.

1. His job _____. (vehicles, is, repairing)
2. _____ one of my favorite hobbies.
   (to, music, listening, is, classical)
3. Judy's job _____. (is, characters, designing)
4. _____ common these days.
   (e-books, becoming, is, reading)

C. 다음 우리말과 같도록 괄호 안의 말을 이용하여 문장을 완성하시오.

1. 밤에 운전을 빨리 하는 것은 매우 위험하다. (drive)
   → _____ _____ is very dangerous at night.
2. 이번 주말의 내 계획은 낚시하러 가는 것이다 (go)
   → My plan for this weekend is _____ _____.
3. 충분한 잠을 자지 않는 것은 너를 피곤하게 만들 것이다. (get)
   → _____ _____ enough sleep will make you feel tired.

Grammar Tip

A. protect 보호하다
   environment 환경
   subtitle 자막

동명사가 주어로 쓰일 때는 단수 취급하여 동사도 단수형이 와야 한다.

B. vehicle 차량
   common 흔한

동명사의 부정은 동명사 앞에 not이나 never를 쓴다.

C. go fishing 낚시하러 가다
   get enough sleep 충분한 잠을 자다

unit 12 목적어로 쓰이는 동명사

· 동명사는 enjoy, finish, avoid, quit, give up, admit, mind, imagine, consider, suggest와 같은 동사의 목적어로 쓰인다.

Do you <u>enjoy</u> **eating** out? (→ to eat ×)

Jake <u>gave up</u> **learning** ballet.

· 전치사 다음에는 명사나 대명사가 올 수 있으며 동사가 올 때는 항상 동명사 형태로 써야 한다.

He's proud <u>of</u> **winning** to the marathon race.

Sarah is good <u>at</u> **playing** the piano.

Practice

A. 다음 괄호 안의 말을 이용하여 문장을 완성하시오.

1. I think it's better to avoid _____ them this week. (meet)

2. Would you mind _____ the volume down? (turn)

3. She has a dream of _____ a famous actress. (be)

4. He's worried about _____ a written test next week. (take)

B. 다음 밑줄 친 부분을 바르게 고치시오.

1. Can you imagine <u>to live</u> without water? _____

2. Sam is considering <u>purchase</u> new shoes. _____

3. We had to put off <u>leave</u> until tomorrow. _____

4. How about <u>come</u> to my house for dinner? _____

C. 다음 우리말과 같도록 괄호 안의 말을 이용하여 문장을 완성하시오.

1. Jack은 영화를 보러 가자고 제안했다. (go)
   → Jack suggested _____ to the movies.

2. 매일 아침 물을 마시는 것의 장점이 무엇이니? (drink)
   → What are the advantages of _____ water every morning?

3. 많은 나라들이 우주 탐험에 관심을 갖고 있다. (explore)
   → Many countries are interested in _____ space.

4. 그들은 운동장에서 축구를 하는 것을 즐겼다. (play)
   → They enjoyed _____ soccer at the playground.

Grammar Tip

avoid, mind, imagine, suggest 등의 동사와 전치사 뒤에 동사가 올 때는 동명사 형태로 쓴다.

A. volumn 음량, 볼륨
written test 필기시험

B. consider 고려하다
purchase 구입하다
put off 연기하다

C. advantage 장점
explore 탐험하다
space 우주, 공간

13 동명사의 의미상의 주어

Unit

- 동명사의 주어가 문장 전체의 주어와 일치하지 않을 때는 동명사 앞에 소유격이나 명사의 형태 그대로 의미상의 주어를 쓴다.

  Max's mom doesn't like <u>his</u> **eating** too much sweets.

  We can't stand <u>Bill</u> **telling** lies.

- 동명사의 주체가 일반인이거나, 문장 전체의 주어나 목적어와 같으면 의미상의 주어는 생략한다.

  Taking care of babies requires a lot of patience.

  I thanked you for **sharing** your information.

Practice

A. 다음 괄호 안에서 알맞은 것을 고르시오.

1. They hate (he / his) driving a truck.

2. My mom is proud of (my / mine) being a volunteer.

3. I'm sure of (her / hers) preparing dinner.

4. (They / Their) missing embarrassed the people.

B. 다음 괄호 안의 말을 바르게 배열하여 문장을 완성하시오.

1. They dislike _____ at night.
   (staying, late, Chris, up)

2. He doesn't mind _____.
   (the, throwing away, old, clothes, her)

3. I was angry at _____.
   (rude, your, being, so)

4. We can't forgive _____.
   (killing, people, for, animals, fun)

C. 다음 우리말과 같도록 괄호 안의 말을 이용하여 문장을 완성하시오.

1. 그 손님들은 너무 시끄럽게 떠든 것에 대해 사과했다. (make)
   → The guests apologized for _____ so much noise.

2. 나는 그가 친구와 다투는 것을 상상할 수 없다. (quarrel)
   → I can't imagine _____ _____ with his friends.

3. Greg은 그의 학생이 규칙을 어겼다는 것을 인정했다. (break)
   → Greg admitted _____ _____ _____ the rules.

4. 나의 엄마는 내가 시험에 떨어진 것을 부끄러워했다. (fail)
   → My mom was ashamed of _____ _____ the test.

Grammar Tip

구어체에서는 동명사의 의미상 주어로 소유격 대신 목적격을 쓰기도 한다.

Would you mind **my[me]** opening the door?

A. volunteer 자원봉사자
   missing 실종
   embarrass 당황스럽게 만들다

B. rude 무례한
   for fun 재미로

C. apologize 사과하다
   quarrel 다투다
   be ashamed of ~을 부끄러워하다

14 동명사와 현재분사

- 동명사와 현재분사는 「동사원형+-ing」의 형태를 가지지만, 동명사는 용도나 목적의 명사적 역할을 하고, 현재분사는 동작, 상태의 형용사적 역할을 한다.

  a **dancing** room (동명사) = a room for dancing

  a **dancing** boy (현재분사) = a boy who is dancing

- 동명사는 '~하는 것'으로 해석하며 현재분사는 '~하고 있는'으로 해석한다.

  His hobby is **watching** sci-fi movies. (동명사)

  He is **watching** a sci-fi movie. (현재분사)

Practice

A. 다음 밑줄 친 부분이 동명사인지 현재분사인지 쓰시오.

1. a. Brad needs a <u>sleeping</u> bag for camping. _____
   b. Brad is <u>sleeping</u> under the tree. _____

2. a. She showed me a <u>washing</u> machine. _____
   b. My mom is <u>washing</u> her pants. _____

B. 다음 문장을 우리말로 해석하시오.

1. Going skiing at night is very dangerous.
   → _____

2. They know the man walking with his dog.
   → _____

3. Our plan is opening a shop downtown.
   → _____

C. 다음 우리말과 같도록 괄호 안의 말을 이용하여 문장을 완성하시오.

1. Hellen은 할머니께 지팡이를 사 드렸다. (walk)
   → Hellen bought his grandma a _____ _____.

2. 그는 독서용 안경을 찾고 있다. (read)
   → He is looking for his _____ _____.

3. 모래를 가지고 노는 것은 아이들에게 좋다. (play)
   → _____ _____ _____ is good for kids.

4. 노란색 야구 모자를 쓰고 있는 소년이 Sam이다. (wear)
   → The boy _____ _____ _____ _____ is Sam.

Grammar Tip

A. sleeping bag 침낭
washing machine 세탁기

명사 뒤에서 수식하는 현재분사는 현재분사 앞에 「주격 관계대명사+be동사」가 생략된 형태로 볼 수 있다.
the bird **singing** on the tree
→ the bird (**which is**) singing on the tree

B. downtown 시내에

C. walking stick 지팡이
look for ~을 찾다

unit

15 동사의 목적어 1(동명사, to부정사 동사)

· 동명사만을 목적어로 취하는 동사

> enjoy, finish, avoid, admit, quit, consider, keep, mind, practice, suggest, deny, give up, put off, imagine ...

Henry enjoys **watching** baseball more than **playing**.

Have you ever considered **building** a house for yourself?

· to부정사만을 목적어로 취하는 동사

> want, hope, need, wish, decide, promise, plan, expect, agree, learn, choose, afford ...

We don't want **to sell** the old car.

He really expects **to see** the great tower.

Practice

A. 다음 괄호 안에서 알맞은 것을 고르시오.

1. The doctor suggested (doing / to do) yoga.
2. How old were you when you learn (skating / to skate)?
3. Here are some tips to avoid (catching / to catch) a cold.
4. The man should quit (shaking / to shake) his legs.

B. 다음 우리말과 같도록 괄호 안의 말을 이용하여 문장을 완성하시오.

1. Peter는 규칙을 지키기로 다시 약속했다. (keep)
   → Peter promised _____ _____ the rules again.
2. 소년들 중 한 명이 그 창문을 깬 것을 인정했다. (break)
   → One of the boys admitted _____ the window.
3. 그녀는 내가 말할 때 계속 방해한다. (interrupt)
   → She keeps _____ me when I'm talking.
4. 우리는 너의 결정을 받아들이기로 동의했다. (accept)
   → We agreed _____ your decision.

C. 다음 〈보기〉에서 골라 알맞은 형태로 빈칸에 쓰시오.

〈보기〉 apply	raise	remember	read

1. Have you finished _____ the long story?
2. Why did you give up _____ for the job?
3. I didn't expect _____ that mistakes.
4. They plan _____ money through the campaign.

Grammar Tip

A. tip 조언
shake the legs 다리를 떨다

동명사를 목적어로 취하는 동사는 보통 현재나 과거의 의미가 담겨 있고, to부정사를 목적어로 취하는 동사는 주로 소망, 계획, 의도 등의 의미가 담겨 있다.

B. interrupt 방해하다

C. apply for ~에 지원하다
raise (자금 등을) 모으다
campaign 캠페인

16 동사의 목적어 2(모두 쓰는 동사)

· 동명사와 to부정사를 목적어로 취하는 동사 ← 의미의 변화가 없음

> begin, start, like, hate, love, dislike, continue ...

We should start **working[to work]** out.

· 동명사와 to부정사를 목적어로 취하는 동사 ← 의미의 변화가 있음

> remember, forget, try, regret ...

I clearly remember **locking** the window. (동명사는 '~하는 것을'이라는 뜻으로 과거의 의미)
I clearly remember **to lock** the window. (to부정사는 '~할 것을'이라는 뜻으로 미래의 의미)
She tried **knitting** gloves. ('~을 시험 삼아 해 보다'의 의미)
She tried **to knit** gloves. ('~을 노력하다'의 의미)

Practice

A. 다음 밑줄 친 부분에 유의하여 문장을 우리말로 해석하시오.

1. a. He <u>forgot to send</u> the package. _____
   b. He <u>forgot sending</u> the package. _____

2. a. They <u>tried to make</u> spaghetti. _____
   b. They <u>tried making</u> spaghetti. _____

B. 다음 괄호 안의 말을 알맞은 형태로 바꿔 빈칸에 쓰시오.

1. I believe what I said was true. I don't regret _____ it. (say)

2. She remembered _____ on her first day of school. (cry)

3. Don't forget _____ your password at next logon. (change)

C. 다음 우리말과 같도록 괄호 안의 말을 이용하여 문장을 완성하시오.

1. 나는 그 결정을 내린 것을 후회한다. (make)
   → I regret _____ the decision.

2. 너는 식사 후에 약 먹는 것을 잊어서는 안 된다. (take)
   → You should not forget _____ some medicine after meals.

3. 춥게 느껴지면 따뜻한 차를 한 잔 마셔 봐. (drink)
   → If you feel cold, try _____ hot tea.

4. 그녀는 잠자기 전에 TV를 끄는 것을 기억한다. (turn)
   → She remembers _____ off TV before she goes to bed.

Grammar Tip

A. package 소포

「regret+동명사」는 '~했던 것을 후회하다'라는 뜻이고, 「regret+to부정사」는 '~하게 되어 유감이다'의 뜻을 나타낸다.

B. password 암호
   logon 로그온

C. make the decision 결정하다
   medicine 약

17 동명사의 관용 표현

· 동명사를 이용한 여러 가지 관용 표현들이 있다.

be busy+-ing	~하느라 바쁘다	How[What] about +-ing ~?	~하는 게 어때?
be used to+-ing	~하는 게 익숙하다	look forward to+-ing	~하기를 고대하다
be worth+-ing	~할 가치가 있다	It's no use+-ing	~해도 소용없다
can't[cannot] help+-ing	~하지 않을 수 없다	There's no+-ing	~하는 것은 불가능하다
feel like+-ing	~하고 싶다	on[upon]+-ing	~하자마자
go+-ing	~하러 가다	keep[prevent] ~ from +-ing	~가 …하지 못하게 하다
spend+시간(+in)/ 돈(+on)+-ing	~하는 데 시간/돈을 쓰다	have a hard time+-ing	~하는 데 어려움을 겪다

Practice

A. 다음 괄호 안에서 알맞은 것을 고르시오.

1. When was the last time you went (comping / to camp)?
2. I don't feel like (watching / to watch) movies today.
3. We are looking forward to (see / seeing) the ancient sculpture.
4. She is so busy (prepare / preparing) for the seminar.

B. 다음 〈보기〉에서 골라 알맞은 형태로 빈칸에 쓰시오.

〈보기〉 admire	skip	hear	read

1. On _____ the radio news, they shouted with joy.
2. I can't help _____ your encourage.
3. I think this novel is worth _____ many times.
4. Sue is used to _____ breakfast.

C. 다음 우리말과 같도록 빈칸에 알맞은 말을 쓰시오.

1. 그녀를 설득하려고 노력해 봐도 소용없다.
   → It is _____ _____ _____ to persuade her.
2. Sue는 쇼핑하는 데 너무 많은 시간을 쓴다.
   → Sue _____ too much _____ _____ shopping.
3. 우리의 휴가를 다음 달까지 연기하는 게 어때?
   → _____ _____ _____ our vacation until next month?

Grammar Tip

A. ancient 고대의
   sculpture 조각상
   seminar 세미나

「be used to+-ing」는 '~하는 게 익숙하다'라는 뜻이고, 「used to+동사원형」은 '~하곤 했다'의 뜻으로 과거의 규칙적인 습관을 나타낸다.

B. with joy 기뻐서
   encourage 용기
   novel 소설
   skip 거르다

C. persuade 설득하다
   postpone 연기하다

A. 다음 밑줄 친 부분을 바르게 고치시오.

1. Chloe enjoys <u>to eat</u> local food when she travels. _____

2. My teacher is proud of <u>we</u> getting the award. _____

3. Don't forget <u>watering</u> this plant once a week. _____

4. I look forward to <u>receive</u> a letter from the boy living in Africa.

_____

Grammar Tip

A. local food 지역 음식
award 상
receive 받다

B. 다음 괄호 안의 말을 알맞은 형태로 바꿔 빈칸에 쓰시오.

1. It is no use _____ with her. (argue)

2. I am sure of his _____ the speech contest. (win)

3. The boys hope _____ to the amusement park. (go)

4. Nick tried _____ the exam, but he couldn't make it. (pass)

B. argue 논쟁하다
amusement park 놀이공원

C. 다음 괄호 안의 말을 바르게 배열하여 문장을 완성하시오.

1. They _____. (using, plastic bags, stopped)

2. He is worried about _____.
(address, Lucy, forgetting, his)

3. My brother doesn't _____.
(give, up, time machine, inventing, the)

4. _____ can be very dangerous.
(wearing, seat belts, not)

동명사의 주체가 문장의 주어와 다를 때는 소유격이나 명사 그대로의 형태인 의미상의 주어를 쓴다.

C. plastic bag 비닐봉지
skip 거르다
seat belt 안전벨트

D. 다음 우리말과 같도록 괄호 안의 말을 이용하여 문장을 완성하시오.

1. 그녀는 치즈를 먹는 것에 익숙하지 않다. (eat)
→ She is not _____ _____ _____ cheese.

2. 내일 내게 전화하는 거 기억해. (call)
→ _____ _____ _____ me tomorrow.

3. 나는 곧 당신을 방문하기를 기대한다. (visit)
→ I look _____ _____ _____ you soon.

4. 이 잡지들은 모아둘 가치가 있다. (collect)
→ These magazines _____ _____ _____.

동명사는 목적, 용도를 나타내는 명사적 역할을 한다.

D. magazine 잡지

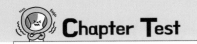 

[1-2] 다음 빈칸에 알맞은 것을 고르시오.

1.
_____ vegetables every day is good for our health.

① Eat　　　　② Eats
③ Eating　　　④ To eating
⑤ To be eating

2.
Henry gave up _____ Chinese.

① learn　　　　② learning
③ learned　　　④ to learning
⑤ to have learned

3. 다음 중 밑줄 친 부분의 쓰임이 다른 하나는?
① Where is the fitting room?
② Eva bought new dancing shoes.
③ That singing girl is my sister.
④ Does this restaurant have a smoking section?
⑤ The waiting room was very chilly.

[4-5] 다음 우리말을 바르게 영작한 것을 고르시오.

4.
나의 할머니는 문자를 보내는 것에 익숙하지 않으시다.

① My grandma is used send a text message.
② My grandma is not used to send a text message.
③ My grandma is not used sending a text message.
④ My grandma is not used to sending a text message.
⑤ My grandma is used to not sending a text message.

5.
우리는 그가 하루 종일 컴퓨터 게임하는 것을 걱정한다.

① We are worried about he playing computer games all day.
② We are worried about his playing computer games all day.
③ We are worried about him to play computer games all day.
④ We are worried about playing computer games all day.
⑤ We are worried about his play computer games all day.

6. 다음 밑줄 친 부분 중 어법상 어색한 것은?

My mom ① doesn't like ② we ③ wasting water, so we tried ④ to use less water when ⑤ we take a shower.

[7-8] 다음 문장과 뜻이 같은 것을 고르시오.

7.
I want to take a rest in my free time.

① I feel like take a rest in my free time.
② I feel like to take a rest in my free time.
③ I feel like to taking a rest in my free time.
④ I feel like taking a rest in my free time.
⑤ I don't feel like taking a rest in my free time.

8.
It is useless to regret your mistake.

① It is no use to regret your mistake.
② It is no use regret your mistake.
③ It is no use regretting your mistake.
④ It is use regretting your mistake.
⑤ It is use not regretting your mistake.

9. 다음 밑줄 친 부분 중 어법상 어색한 것은?

① I'm considering stopping using straws.

② We avoid eating junk food.

③ Being rich is not the most important in life.

④ Your problem is hurting other people's feelings.

⑤ He decided entering a music school.

10. 다음 중 어법상 옳은 것은?

① He stopped to laugh when I came into the room.

② Do you remember to watch the musical before?

③ They didn't expect seeing her here.

④ Would you mind to carry this box?

⑤ What about watching a movie tonight?

11. 다음 빈칸에 알맞지 않은 것은?

> Diana _____ walking her dog in the evening.

① enjoys   ② loves
③ plans   ④ considers
⑤ keeps

12. 다음 빈칸에 들어갈 말이 바르게 짝지어진 것은?

> · I couldn't help _____ when he told funny story.
> · She tried _____ patient all the time.

① laugh – be   ② laughing – being
③ to laugh – to be   ④ to laugh – being
⑤ laughing – to be

[13-14] 다음 두 문장을 한 문장으로 바꿔 쓸 때 빈칸에 알맞은 말을 쓰시오.

13.
> You should take this medicine before each meal. Don't forget about it.

= Remember _____ _____ this medicine before each meal.

14.
> I often forget to lock the door. My mom dislike it.

= My mom dislike _____ _____ to lock the door.

15. 다음 중 어법상 어색한 곳을 찾아 바르게 고치시오.

> We look forward to have a Halloween party this Saturday.

_____ → _____

16. 다음 <보기>의 밑줄 친 부분과 쓰임이 같은 것은?

> <보기>   What were you doing last night?

① I thanked you for inviting me.

② Visiting new countries is very exciting.

③ Have you ever thought about becoming a chef?

④ Maria regrets telling him the news that she was in the hospital.

⑤ The swimming boy is very famous in his school.

17. 다음 빈칸에 공통으로 알맞은 것은?

· I was kept _____ for you all day.
· His performance is worth _____ for.

① wait
② waits
③ to wait
④ waiting
⑤ waited

18. 다음 우리말과 뜻이 같도록 빈칸에 알맞은 것은?

우리는 그가 화석을 찾을 것이라고 확신했다.
→ We were sure of _____ fossils.

① him discover
② he discovers
③ his discovering
④ him to discover
⑤ he discovering

19. 다음 대화의 빈칸에 가장 알맞은 것은?

A: Will you come to my house for dinner?
B: Sorry, I can't. I'm very busy _____ for the seminar next week.

① prepare
② preparing
③ to prepare
④ prepared
⑤ to be preparing

20. 다음 (A), (B), (C)의 각 네모 안에서 어법에 맞는 것을 골라 바르게 짝지어진 것은?

· The girls denied (A) [telling / to tell] lies.
· Did you agree (B) [buying / to buy] the car at a low price?
· He admitted (C) [doing not / not doing] our best in the competition.

	(A)	(B)	(C)
①	telling	buying	doing not
②	telling	to buy	doing not
③	telling	to buy	not doing
④	to tell	buying	not doing
⑤	to tell	to buy	doin not

〈서술형 문제〉

21. 다음 우리말과 같도록 괄호 안의 단어들을 바르게 배열 하시오.

그 화제들에 대해 토론하는 것이 필요하다.
(is, topics, necessary, discussing, the)

→ _____

22. 다음 우리말과 같도록 괄호 안의 말을 이용하여 문장을 완성하시오.

그는 네가 그 뮤지컬에 출연하는 것을 자랑스러워 한다. (appear)

→ He is proud of _____ _____ in the musical.

23. 다음 두 문장이 같은 뜻이 되도록 빈칸에 알맞은 말을 쓰시오.

It is impossible to live without electricity.

= There _____ _____ _____ without electricity.

24. 다음 괄호 안의 말을 이용하여 우리말을 영작하시오.

우리는 강에 쓰레기 버리는 것을 멈춰야 한다.
(stop, throw, should, trash, river)

→ _____

25. 다음 밑줄 친 부분 중 어법상 어색한 것을 찾아 바르게 고쳐 쓰시오.

I remember going to Canada last year. When I saw Niagara Falls, I could not help shouting. I wanted to take a lot of pictures, but the batteries in my cell phone went dead. I forgot charging my cell phone! It was stupid of me to make such a mistake.

_____ → _____

분사란 무엇인가?
분사는 동사의 성격을 가지면서 문장 내에서 형용사의 역할을 하며, 진행형, 완료형, 수동태, 분사구문 등을 만들 수 있다. 분사에는 현재분사(동사원형+-ing)와 과거분사(동사원형+-ed/불규칙형태)가 있다.
Mr. Green is **driving** the car. (현재분사)
I have **seen** that man once. (과거분사)

분사구문이란 무엇인가?
분사구문은 부사절을 분사로 시작하는 분사구로 간단하게 나타낸 것으로 시간, 이유, 조건, 양보 등의 의미로 쓰인다.
Talking on the phone, she drank some water.
(시간의 분사구문)

Chapter 3. 분사

Unit 18 분사의 역할

- 동사의 성격을 가지면서 형용사의 역할을 하는 분사에는 현재분사와 과거분사가 있다.

종류	형태	의미
현재분사	동사원형+-ing	능동 · 진행의 의미(~하는, ~하고 있는)
과거분사	「동사원형+-ed」 / 불규칙형태	수동 · 완료의 의미(~해진, ~하게 된)

- 분사는 문장에서 형용사와 동일하게 한정적 용법과 서술적 용법이 있다.

한정적 용법	명사의 앞이나 뒤에서 명사를 수식함	The man lying on the grass is Carl. (명사 뒤에서 수식)
		I found a broken vase. (명사 앞에서 수식)
서술적 용법	문장에서 주격 보어나 목적격 보어로 쓰임	We were shocked at the rumor. (주격 보어)
		I saw a woman crossing the road. (목적격 보어)

Practice

A. 다음 밑줄 친 분사의 역할을 고르시오.

1. You look very tired. (한정적 용법 / 서술적 용법)

2. This is a castle built in the 1700s. (한정적 용법 / 서술적 용법)

3. I heard my dog barking at someone. (한정적 용법 / 서술적 용법)

4. It was one of the most exciting games. (한정적 용법 / 서술적 용법)

B. 다음 괄호 안의 말을 알맞은 형태로 바꿔 빈칸에 쓰시오.

1. We can see _____ stars tonight. (fall)

2. Alex's lecture made his audience _____. (bore)

3. I read the novel _____ by Hemingway. (write)

4. The woman _____ glasses is my aunt. (wear)

C. 다음 우리말과 뜻이 같도록 괄호 안의 말을 이용하여 문장을 완성하시오.

1. 나는 무언가 내 팔을 기어오르고 있는 것을 느꼈다. (crawl)
   → I felt something _____ up _____.

2. 그 영화는 매우 만족스러웠다. (satisfy)
   → The film was _____ _____.

3. Peter는 지난 달에 이 중고차를 샀다. (use)
   → Peter bought this _____ _____ last month.

4. 캐나다에서 말해지는 언어는 영어와 프랑스어이다. (speak)
   → The languages _____ _____ _____ are
   English and French.

Grammar Tip

명사를 수식하는 분사가 다른 수식어구와 함께 쓰일 때는 명사 뒤에 위치한다.

A. bark 짖다

감정을 표현하는 동사는 능동의 의미일 때는 현재분사를, 수동의 의미일 때는 과거분사를 쓴다.

B. lecture 강연
   audience 청중

지각동사의 목적격 보어는 원형부정사와 분사를 둘 다 쓰는데, 진행 중인 동작을 나타낼 때는 현재분사를, 수동이나 상태를 나타낼 때는 과거분사를 쓴다.

C. crawl 기어오르다, 기다
   film 영화
   satisfy 만족시키다

19 | 분사구문

- 분사구문은 부사절을 분사로 시작하는 부사구를 간단하게 나타낸 것이다.
  - 분사구문을 만드는 법
    ① 부사절의 접속사를 생략한다.
    ② 부사절과 주절의 주어가 같으면 부사절의 주어를 생략한다.
    ③ 부사절과 주절의 시제가 같으면 동사를 -ing 형태로 고친다.

    <u>Because</u> <u>I</u> <u>felt</u> tired, <u>I</u> came back home early.
      ↓   ↓ ↓
      ✕   ✕ **Feeling** tired, I came back home early.

- 분사구문의 부정은 분사 앞에 not이나 never를 붙인다.

  Not knowing her phone number, I couldn't contact her.

Practice

A. 다음 두 문장이 같은 뜻이 되도록 빈칸에 알맞은 말을 쓰시오.

1. After he finished the work, he met his friend.
   = _____ the work, we met his friend.

2. When she saw the strange man, she was frightened.
   = _____ the strange man, she was frightened.

3. As he heard the accident, he turned pale.
   = _____ the accident, he turned pale.

4. Because he doesn't have enough money, he can't buy the car.
   = _____ _____ enough money, he can't buy the car.

B. 다음 괄호 안의 말을 알맞은 형태로 바꿔 빈칸에 쓰시오.

1. _____ busy, I couldn't drive you to the station. (be)
2. She read a newspaper, _____ to music. (listen)
3. _____ left, you will find a gas station. (turn)
4. _____ the room, I saw my brother sleeping. (enter)

C. 다음 우리말과 같도록 빈칸에 알맞을 말을 쓰시오.

1. 밝게 웃으면서 그는 우리를 환영했다.
   → _____ brightly, he welcomed us.

2. 기분이 좋지 않았기 때문에 나는 파티에 가지 않았다.
   → _____ _____ well, I didn't go to the party.

3. 부상을 당했지만 그는 마라톤을 완주했다.
   → _____ injured, he finished the marathon.

Grammar Tip

A. frightened 겁먹은, 무서워하는
turn pale 창백해지다

분사구문을 만들 때 의미를 분명히 하기 위해서 접속사를 생략하지 않을 수도 있다.
While shopping at the mall, I met Cindy.

B. gas station 주유소

C. welcome 환영하다
injure 부상을 입다
marathon 마라톤

unit 20 분사구문의 의미 1(시간, 이유, 조건)

· 시간을 나타내는 분사구문은 '~할 때(when)' '~하는 동안(while)' '~하기 전에(before)' '~한 후에(after)' 등으로 해석한다.

Watching TV, he fell asleep.

→ While he was watching TV, he fell asleep.

· 이유를 나타내는 분사구문은 '~ 때문에(because)', '~이므로(since, as)' 등으로 해석한다.

Having a fever, I saw a doctor.

→ Because I had a fever, I saw a doctor.

· 조건을 나타내는 분사구문은 '~하면(if)'으로 해석한다.

Leaving right now, you will catch the train.

→ If you leave right now, you will catch the train.

Practice

A. 다음 괄호 안의 말을 알맞은 형태로 바꿔 빈칸에 쓰시오.

1. _____ too fast, I had stomach trouble. (eat)
2. _____ interested in insects, he reads books about it. (be)
3. _____ a taxi, you'll get there in ten minutes. (take)
4. _____ the car accident, they tried to rescue the driver. (see)

B. 다음 두 문장이 같은 뜻이 되도록 주어진 접속사를 이용하여 바꿔 쓰시오.

1. Doing your best, you'll win the game. (if)
   → _____, you'll win the game.

2. You should look out for cars crossing the street. (when)
   → You should look out for cars _____.

3. Playing soccer, he hurt his leg. (while)
   → _____, he hurt his leg.

4. Not receiving an email, he called her again. (because)
   → _____, he called her again.

C. 다음 우리말과 같도록 괄호 안의 말을 이용하여 문장을 완성하시오.

1. 좋은 팀워크를 가진다면 우리는 프로젝트를 끝낼 수 있다. (have)
   → _____ good teamwork, we can finish the project.

2. 음악을 듣고 있어서 그는 전화벨 소리를 듣지 못했다. (listen)
   → _____ to music, he didn't hear the phone ringing.

3. 옷을 갈아입은 후에, 그녀는 무대에 올랐다. (change)
   → _____ her clothes, she came on stage.

Grammar Tip

A. stomach trouble 배탈
insect 곤충
rescue 구조하다

분사구가 주절 앞에 올 때는 분사구 뒤에 콤마(,)를 넣고, 주절 뒤에 올 때는 콤마(,)를 따로 쓰지 않는다.

B. look out for ~을 조심하다
receive 받다

C. teamwork 팀워크
come on stage 무대에 오르다

21 분사구문의 의미 2(양보, 동시, 연속)

· 양보를 나타내는 분사구문은 '비록 ~일지라도(though, although)'로 해석한다.

Being young, she is wiser than her sister.

→ **Though** she is young, she is wiser than her sister.

· 분사구문의 동작이 주절의 동작과 동시에 일어나는 동시동작은 '~ 하면서(as)'로 해석한다.

Waiting for him, I read a book.

→ **As** I waited for him, I read a book.

· 주절의 동작 다음에 분사구문의 동작이 연속해서 일어나는 연속동작은 '~하고 나서, 그리고 ~하다(and)'로 해석한다.

A stone flew into the house, **breaking** the window.

→ A stone flew into the house **and** broke the window.

Practice

A. 다음 괄호 안의 말을 알맞은 형태로 바꿔 빈칸에 쓰시오.

1. _____ the station, I called her up. (approach)

2. _____ invited to the party, he didn't come after all. (be)

3. _____ his hand, he got on the train. (wave)

4. I turned on the computer, _____ her email. (check)

B. 다음 두 문장이 같은 뜻이 되도록 주어진 접속사를 이용하여 바꿔 쓰시오.

1. Being rich, he doesn't waste money at all. (though)

→ _____, he doesn't waste money at all.

2. The bus left Seoul at four, arriving here at nine. (and)

→ The bus left Seoul at four _____.

3. Drinking hot coffee, she talked to the manager. (as)

→ _____, she talked to the manager.

4. He took out his purse, paying for dinner. (and)

→ He took out his purse _____.

C. 다음 우리말과 같도록 괄호 안의 말을 이용하여 문장을 완성하시오.

1. 운전을 하면서 그는 콧노래를 불렀다. (drive)

→ _____ his car, he hummed a song.

2. 비록 그들의 옆집에 살지만, 나는 그들과 거의 이야기하지 않는다. (live)

→ _____ next door to them, I seldom talk with them.

3. 그녀는 불을 끄고 일찍 잠자리에 들었다. (go)

→ She turned off the lights, _____ to bed early.

Grammar Tip

연속동작을 나타내는 분사구문은 보통 주절 다음에 온다.

A. approach 다가가다
after all 결국에는
wave 흔들다

B. waste 낭비하다
pay for ~을 지불하다

C. hum 콧노래를 부르다
next door 옆집
seldom 거의 ~않다

A. 다음 괄호 안에서 알맞은 것을 고르시오.

1. The concert was (exciting / excited) and we were (exciting / excited).

2. She ordered a (baking / baked) potato and the soup of the day.

3. Bella eats some (boiling / boiled) eggs after she works out.

4. Many people saw the sun (rising / risen) in the sky.

B. 다음 우리말과 같도록 빈칸에 알맞은 말을 쓰시오.

1. 너는 매우 들떠 보인다. (excite)
→ You look very _____.

2. 많은 외국인들이 한국에서 만들어진 TV 프로그램들을 좋아한다. (make)
→ Many foreigners like TV programs _____ in Korea.

3. 비록 유명하지 않지만 그는 매우 독창적인 예술가이다. (be)
→ _____ _____ famous, he is a very creative artist.

4. 청소를 끝낸 후에 나는 낚시하러 갔다. (finish)
→ _____ cleaning, I went fishing.

C. 다음 분사구문은 부사절이 되도록, 부사절은 분사구문이 되도록 문장을 완성하시오.

1. Arriving at the library, we found it closed.
→ _____ at the library, we found it closed.

2. If you hold on to your dream, you can do it.
→ _____ on to your dream, you can do it.

3. Not feeling well, he came home earlier.
→ _____ well, he came home earlier.

4. As she listened to the radio, she wrote something down.
→ _____ to the radio, she wrote something down.

D. 다음 우리말과 같도록 괄호 안의 말을 이용하여 문장을 완성하시오.

1. 나는 뭔가 타는 냄새를 맡았다. (burn, something)
→ I smelled _____.

2. 헤밍웨이가 쓴 그 소설들은 매우 인기 있다. (novels, write)
→ _____ Hemingway are popular.

3. 우주에 관심이 있어서 그녀는 우주비행사가 되기로 결심했다.
(space, interest)
→ _____, she decided to be an astronaut.

Grammar Tip

사람의 감정을 나타내는 분사는 분사가 직접 수식하거나 보충 설명하는 명사가 감정을 유발하는 원인일 때는 현재분사를, 감정을 느끼는 주체일 때는 과거분사를 쓴다.

A. boil 끓이다, 삶다
rise (해, 달이) 뜨다

B. go fishing 낚시하러 가다

C. hold on to 고수하다, 지키다

D. astronaut 우주비행사

22 완료형 분사구문

- 부사절의 시제가 주절의 시제보다 앞설 때는 완료형 분사구문 「having+p.p.」의 형태로 쓴다.
  Because she <u>has seen</u> the movie before, she <u>didn't want</u> to see it again.
  → **Having seen** the movie before, she didn't want to see it again.

- 부사절의 시제가 주절의 시제를 앞서고 또한 수동의 의미일 때는 「having+been+p.p.」의 형태로 쓴다.
  Since I <u>was raised</u> in New York, I <u>can</u> speak English.
  → **Having been raised** in New York, I can speak English.

 Practice

A. 다음 괄호 안에서 알맞은 것을 고르시오.

1. (Spending / Having spent) all his allowance, he can't buy what he wants.

2. (Having written / Having been written) 100 years ago, it has useful information.

3. (Losing / Having lost) the key, I can't enter the house.

4. (Not having heard / Having not heard) the alarm, I'm running late.

B. 다음 밑줄 친 부분을 바르게 고치시오.

1. <u>Having painted</u> in dark colors, it needs something bright.

2. Having <u>eaten not</u> anything, I don't feel hungry.

3. <u>Being born</u> in the UK, he lives in the USA now.

4. <u>Having meeting</u> him before, I recognized him at once.

C. 다음 우리말과 같도록 괄호 안의 말을 이용하여 문장을 완성하시오.

1. 기사를 읽었기 때문에 나는 그 사고에 대해 알고 있다. (read)
   → _____ _____ the article, I know about the accident.

2. 그것은 유리로 만들어졌기 때문에 깨지기 쉽다. (make)
   → _____ _____ _____ of glass, it is easy to break.

3. 폭탄으로 파괴되었기 때문에 다리가 다시 건설되었다. (destroy)
   → _____ _____ _____ by a bomb, the bridge was rebuilt.

4. 잠을 잘 못 잤기 때문에 나는 머리가 아프다. (sleep)
   → _____ _____ _____ well, I have a headache.

Grammar Tip

완료형 분사구문의 부정은 「not+having+p.p.」의 형태로 쓴다.

A. allowance 용돈
run late 늦다

부사절의 시제가 주절의 시제보다 앞설 때 완료형 분사구문으로 나타내는데 수동의 의미는 「having+been+p.p.」로 쓴다.

B. recognize 알아보다
at once 한 번에, 즉시

C. article 기사, 글
destroy 파괴하다
bomb 폭탄
rebuild 다시 짓다

Unit
23 being, having been의 생략

- 수동태가 쓰인 부사절을 분사구문으로 바꾸면 「being+p.p.」 또는 「having+been+p.p.」의 형태가 되는데 이때 분사구문에 처음 오는 being이나 having been은 생략할 수 있다.

Because he was shocked at the news, he couldn't say anything.
   ×   ×   ↓

    (Being) shocked at the news, he couldn't say anything.
      ×   ↓

    Shocked at the news, he couldn't say anything.

(Having been) Built in 1960, the building still looks modern.

Practice

A. 다음 문장이 같은 뜻이 되도록 빈칸에 알맞은 말을 쓰시오.

1. When she was given the gift, she jumped with joy.
= _____ _____ the gift, she jumped with joy.
= _____ the gift, she jumped with joy.

2. Though he was born in London, he can't speak English.
= _____ _____ _____ in London, he can't speak English.
= _____ in London, he can't speak English.

B. 다음 괄호 안의 말을 알맞은 형태로 바꿔 빈칸에 쓰시오.

1. _____ for beginners, this book is easy to understand. (publish)

2. _____ from the plane, the houses looked tiny. (see)

3. _____ by the mosquitoes, she felt itchy. (bite)

4. _____ from his city life, he wanted to move to a country. (tire)

C. 다음 우리말과 같도록 괄호 안의 말을 이용하여 문장을 완성하시오.

1. 유명한 가수에 의해 불려져서 그 노래는 인기 있었다. (sing)
→ _____ by a famous singer, the song was popular.

2. 밤에 촬영되어서 이 사진은 선명하지가 않았다. (take)
→ _____ at night, this photo was not clear.

3. 눈으로 덮여 있어서 그 산은 매우 아름다웠다. (cover)
→ _____ with snow, the the mountain was very beautiful.

4. 자동차 사고로 부상을 당해서 그녀는 병원에 있다. (injure)
→ _____ in the car accident, she is in the hospital.

Grammar Tip

being이나 having been이 생략된 분사구문은 형태는 같지만, 부사절로 바꿔 쓸 때 시제와 의미 등을 잘 판단해서 써야 한다.

A. with joy 기뻐서

B. publish 출판하다
tiny 아주 작은
bite 물다
itchy 가려운

C. clear 선명한
cover 덮다

24 | 독립분사구문, 비인칭 독립분사구문

- 분사구문의 의미상의 주어가 주절의 주어와 다를 때는 분사 앞에 의미상의 주어를 따로 쓰는데, 이것을 독립분사구문이라고 한다.

  As it was very cloudy, I had to take an umbrella just in case.

  It being very cloudy, I had to take an umbrella just in case.

- 독립분사구문의 의미상의 주어가 we, they, people, you 등과 같은 일반적인 사람을 나타낼 때는 주절의 주어와 일치하지 않더라도 주어를 따로 표시하지 않는다. 이것을 비인칭 독립분사구문이라고 한다.

  Generally speaking, dogs are more faithful than cats.

generally speaking	일반적으로 말해서	judging from	~로 판단하건대
frankly speaking	솔직히 말해서	considering	~을 감안하면
strictly speaking	엄밀히 말해서	speaking of	~ 이야기가 나왔으니 말인데
roughly speaking	대강 말하자면	talking of	~에 대해 말하자면

Practice

A. 다음 밑줄 친 부분을 분사구문으로 바꿔 쓰시오.

1. As there was no bus service, we had to take a taxi.
   → _____, we had to take a taxi.

2. When the sun had set, we stopped working.
   → _____, we stopped working.

3. Because it is a holiday, the bank is closed.
   → _____, the bank is closed.

B. 다음 괄호 안의 말을 바르게 배열하여 문장을 완성하시오.

1. _____, I went to bed. (11 o'clock, being, it)
2. _____, Lisa went out. (done, being, chores)
3. _____, we missed our flight.
   (being, a lot of, there, traffic)

C. 다음 우리말과 같도록 빈칸에 알맞은 말을 쓰시오.

1. 그녀의 말로 판단하건대, 그녀는 그녀의 일을 자랑스러워한다.
   → _____ _____ her words, she is proud of her job.

2. 일반적으로 말해서, 남자들이 여자들보다 스포츠를 더 좋아한다.
   → _____ _____, men like sports more than women.

3. 솔직히 말해서, 나는 그 공연이 만족스럽지 않았다.
   → _____ _____ I wasn't satisfied with the show.

Grammar Tip

독립분사구문에서 날씨, 시간, 요일 등을 나타낼 때는 비인칭 주어 it이 쓰이는 것에 유의한다.

A. bus service 버스 편
set (해, 달이) 지다

독립분사구문에서도 수동의 의미를 나타낼 때는 being 또는 having been을 생략할 수 있다.

B. chore 집안일

C. be proud of ~을 자랑스러워하다
be satisfied with ~에 만족하다

unit 25 | with+명사+분사

- 「with+명사+분사」는 '~한 채로', '~하면서'라는 뜻으로 동시동작을 나타내며 명사와 분사의 관계가 능동이면 현재분사를, 수동이면 과거분사를 쓴다.

She turned around and tears ran down her cheeks.
→ She turned around **with tears running down** her cheeks.

He waited his friends and his arms folded.
→ He waited his friends **with his arms folded**.

Practice

A. 다음 괄호 안에서 알맞은 것을 고르시오.

1. Hellen sat on the sofa with her legs (shaking / shaked).

2. I fell asleep with the radio (turning / turned) on.

3. He was brushing his teeth with water (run / running).

4. The kid came in with his pants (covering / covered) in mud.

B. 다음 두 문장의 뜻이 같도록 빈칸에 알맞은 말을 쓰시오.

1. She stared at me, and her legs were crossed.
   = She stared at me with her legs _____.

2. The girl approached me, and her hair flew in the wind.
   = The girl approached me with her hair _____ in the wind.

3. Fred practiced the cello, and his teacher watched him.
   = Fred practiced the cello with his teacher _____ him.

4. He went out, and the door was unlocked.
   = He went out with the door _____.

C. 다음 우리말과 같도록 괄호 안의 말을 이용하여 문장을 완성하시오.

1. 봄이 오자 꽃들이 피기 시작했다. (come)
   → Flowers began to bloom with spring _____.

2. Sally는 그녀의 손가락이 다친 채로 방에서 나왔다. (hurt)
   → Sally came out of the room with her finger _____.

3. 그 개는 혀를 늘어뜨린 채 그늘에 누워 있었다. (hang)
   → The dog lay in the shade with its tongue _____ out.

Grammar Tip

A. mud 진흙

B. stare 응시하다
approach 다가가다
unlock 열다

「with+명사+형용사/부사/전치사구」도 동시동작을 표현할 수 있다.
Don't speak **with your mouth full**.

C. bloom 꽃이 피다
hang 늘어뜨리다

A. 다음 두 문장이 같은 뜻이 되도록 빈칸에 알맞은 말을 쓰시오.

1. As they are imported, they are very expensive.
   → _____ _____, they are very expensive.

2. Because they haven't played a board game before, they don't know the rules.
   → _____ _____ _____ a board game before, they don't know the rules.

3. He leans against the wall, and his eyes are closed.
   → He leans against the wall with _____ _____ _____.

4. As it was sunny, we decided to ride bikes.
   → _____ _____ sunny, we decided to ride bikes.

B. 다음 밑줄 친 부분을 바르게 고치시오.

1. Building five years ago, it looks new.   _____

2. Losing my smartphone, I can't check text messages.
   _____

3. Having not reviewed the lesson, he got low grades.
   _____

4. He took a nap with the music turning on.   _____

C. 다음 괄호 안의 말을 알맞은 형태로 바꿔 빈칸에 쓰시오.

1. He worked out with sweat _____ down his face. (run)

2. _____ with the product, she bought it for me. (please)

3. _____ _____ Rome many times, we can find the way to the Colosseum. (visit)

4. _____ from her accent, he must be from Busan. (judge)

D. 다음 우리말과 같도록 괄호 안의 말을 바르게 배열하여 문장을 완성하시오.

1. 솔직히 말해서, 나는 그의 무례한 태도에 실망했다.
   (manner, speaking, disappointed, his, I'm, rude, frankly, at)
   → _____

2. 좌석이 없어서, 우리는 다음 기차를 기다렸다.
   (next, being, seats, for, train, waited, there, no, we, the)
   → _____

3. 그는 팔짱을 낀 채로 노래를 따라 불렀다.
   (folded, he, with, sang, arms, along, his)
   → _____

Grammar Tip

A. import 수입하다
   lean 기대다

수동의 의미를 나타내는 분사구문에서 being이나 having been은 생략할 수 있다.

B. text message 문자 메시지
   low grade 낮은 점수

C. product 제품
   Colosseum 콜로세움
   accent 억양

D. manner 태도
   seat 좌석

[1-2] 다음 빈칸에 알맞은 것을 고르시오.

1.
> The _____ leaves are spread all over the ground.

① fall   ② falling
③ fallen   ④ to fall
⑤ falls

2.
> _____ a movie, he fell asleep.

① Watch   ② Watching
③ To watch   ④ Watched
⑤ Being watched

[3-4] 다음 중 어법상 어색한 것을 고르시오.

3. ① Do you know the man standing at the door?
② She read a book written by Miller.
③ On New Year's Day, I saw the sun rising in the sky.
④ They were surprised at his behavior.
⑤ The wine producing in France is very famous.

4. ① The train leaves at five, arriving at nine.
② Not liking baseball, he did't join them.
③ Driving along the seashore, you will see a nice view.
④ Being lost the key, I can't open the drawer.
⑤ Being exhausted, he couldn't speak anything.

5. 다음 문장에서 어법상 틀린 부분을 찾아 바르게 고치시오.
> He is trying to thread a needle with one eye closing.

_____ → _____

6. 다음 밑줄 친 부분 중 생략할 수 없는 것은?
① <u>Being</u> painted by a girl, it looks perfect.
② <u>Having been</u> born in Chicago, he grew up in New York.
③ <u>Being</u> nervous, she began to bite her nails.
④ <u>Being</u> seen from above, it looks like a map of Korea.
⑤ <u>Having been</u> invited to a Halloween party, I dressed up as a witch.

7. 다음 빈칸에 들어갈 말이 바르게 짝지어진 것은?
> · I felt someone _____ on my shoulder.
> · I took a walk with my arms _____.

① touch - fold   ② touched - folded
③ touched - folding   ④ touching - folding
⑤ touch - folded

8. 다음 우리말을 바르게 영작한 것은?
> 비가 내려서 그녀는 비옷을 입었다.

① Rainy, she wore a raincoat.
② Being rainy, she wore a raincoat.
③ It being rainy, she wore a raincoat.
④ Having been rainy, she wore a raincoat.
⑤ It having been rainy, she wore a raincoat.

9. 다음 두 문장을 한 문장으로 바꿔 쓸 때, 빈칸에 알맞은 말을 쓰시오.
> A lady approached me.
> + And she asked for help.

→ A lady approached me, _____ for help.

10. 다음 문장과 뜻이 같은 것은?

> As he talked on the phone, he turned on the light.

① Talk on the phone, he turned on the light.
② Talking on the phone, he turned on the light.
③ Talked on the phone, he turned on the light.
④ Having talked on the phone, turned on the light.
⑤ Having been talked on the phone, he turned on the light.

11. 다음 대화의 빈칸에 가장 알맞은 것은?

> A: Do you want to go to a movie tonight?
> B: I'm afraid I can't. _____ well, I need to just relax.

① Feeling   ② Not feeling
③ Feeling not   ④ Not being feel
⑤ Not to feel

12. 다음 빈칸에 알맞은 것을 모두 고르면?

> _____ by the earthquake last year, the houses are rebuilding now.

① Destroy   ② Destroying
③ Destroyed   ④ Being destroyed
⑤ Having been destroyed

13. 다음 밑줄 친 부분 중 어법상 어색한 것은?

> Jessica is ① starting a new school next week. Jessica's mom is ② worried about her, ③ but she is quite ④ exciting that she can ⑤ make new friends.

14. 다음 밑줄 친 부분의 해석이 바르지 않은 것은?

① Frankly speaking, classical music is not to my taste. (솔직히 말해서)
② Considering his age, he looks very young. (~을 고려하면)
③ Strictly speaking, you need to do it again. (엄격히 말하자면)
④ Speaking of hobbies, I like learning sports dance. (~ 이야기가 나왔으니 말인데)
⑤ Judging from her uniform, she seems to be a police officer. (대강 말하자면)

[15-16] 다음 두 문장의 뜻이 같도록 빈칸에 알맞은 말을 쓰시오.

15.

> As I haven't ridden a horse before, I'm very nervous now.

= _____ _____ _____ a horse before, I'm very nervous now.

16.

> We left Seoul in the morning, reaching Paris at night.

= We left Seoul at night _____ _____ Paris at night.

17. 다음 밑줄 친 부분과 바꿔 쓸 수 있는 것은?

> Preparing dinner, I hurt my hand.

① If I prepared dinner
② While I prepared dinner
③ Since I prepared dinner
④ After I prepared dinner
⑤ Because I prepared dinner

18. 다음 (A), (B), (C)의 각 네모 안에서 어법에 맞는 것을 골라 바르게 짝지은 것은?

> · The girl (A) painted / painting on glass is my cousin.
> · The result made us (B) depressed / depressing.
> · The novel was (C) bored / boring, so I fell asleep.

	(A)	(B)	(C)
①	painted	depressed	bored
②	painted	depressing	bored
③	painting	depressed	boring
④	painting	depressed	bored
⑤	painting	depressing	boring

19. 다음 우리말과 같은 뜻이 되도록 빈칸에 알맞은 말을 쓰시오.

> 설탕이 없어서, 나는 대신 꿀을 사용했다.

→ _____ _____ no sugar, I used honey instead.

20. 다음 밑줄 친 부분 중 어법상 어색한 것을 찾아 바르게 고쳐 쓰시오.

> Getting dark, I went back home. Arriving at the bus stop, I heard someone calling my name. Turning around, I found Kate. She was smiling with her eyes shining. Not meeting her for two years, I was very surprised.

_____ → _____

<서술형 문제>

21. 다음 밑줄 친 부분을 부사절로 바꿔 쓰시오.

> Having heard the truth from her, I still don't believe it.

→ _____

22. 다음 <조건>에 맞게 우리말을 바르게 영작하시오.

> <조건>
> 1. know, road, lost, way 모두 이용하되, 필요시 어형을 바꿀 것.
> 2. 필요시 단어를 추가할 것.
> 3. 분사구문으로 쓸 것.

> 그 길을 몰랐기 때문에 그녀는 길을 잃었다.

→ _____

23. 다음 우리말과 같은 뜻이 되도록 빈칸에 알맞은 말을 쓰시오.

> 그는 다리를 꼰 채 구름 위로 날아가는 새들을 지켜보았다.

→ He is watching the birds _____ over the clouds _____ his legs _____.

24. 다음 두 문장의 뜻이 같도록 분사구문으로 바꿔 쓰시오.

> If you want to stay healthy, you should cut down on snacks.

= _____

25. 다음 두 문장을 한 문장으로 바꿔 쓸 때, 빈칸에 알맞은 말을 쓰시오.

> She watched the movie.
> + Her tears ran down her cheeks.
> → She watched the movie with _____ _____.

→ _____

시제란 무엇인가?
시제는 동사가 어떤 행동이나 사건이 일어난 시점을 나타내기 위해 동사의 형태를 변화시키는 것을 가리킨다.

완료시제란 무엇인가?
완료시제는 과거 이전의 일이 과거까지, 과거의 일이 현재의 한 시점까지, 미래의 어느 시점을 기준으로 그때까지 영향을 미치는 것을 표현한 시제이다.
When I arrived there, they **had** already **left**. (과거완료)
I **have been** to Europe twice. (현재완료)
Jay **will have finished** his work by that time. (미래완료)

Chapter 4. 시제

Unit 26 현재완료의 용법-완료, 결과

- 현재완료는 과거의 어느 시점에서 현재까지의 동작이나 상태를 나타내는 것으로, 「have[has]+p.p.」의 형태로 쓴다. 현재완료는 완료, 결과, 경험, 계속의 의미가 있다.
- 현재완료의 완료 용법은 과거에 시작된 동작이나 상태가 이제 막 완료되었음을 나타낸다. '지금 막 ~했다'로 해석하며 주로 just, already, yet 등과 함께 쓴다.
  She **has** just **finished** cleaning the room.
- 현재완료의 결과 용법은 과거에 했던 동작의 결과가 현재까지 남아 영향을 미칠 때 쓰며, '~해 버렸다(그 결과 지금은 ~하다)'로 해석한다.
  I **have lost** my favorite pen somewhere. (So I don't have it now.)

Practice

A. 다음 괄호 안에서 현재완료의 알맞은 용법을 고르시오.

1. She has gone to Busan. (완료 / 결과)

2. Has he done the dishes already? (완료 / 결과)

3. My car has been broken by the accident. (완료 / 결과)

4. I have just left for the station. (완료 / 결과)

B. 다음 괄호 안의 말을 이용하여 빈칸에 알맞은 말을 쓰시오.

1. I _____ _____ my homework. (submit)

2. The plane _____ already _____ from the airport. (depart)

3. He _____ _____ all his money on clothes. (spend)

4. Someone _____ _____ my purse. (steal)

C. 다음 우리말과 같도록 괄호 안의 말을 이용하여 문장을 완성하시오.

1. 나는 아직 언제 갈지 결정하지 못했다. (decided)
   → I _____ _____ yet when to go.

2. 그녀는 내가 준 시계를 잃어버렸다.(그 결과 지금은 없다.) (lose)
   → She _____ _____ the watch I gave.

3. Willy는 신문 읽는 것을 끝냈니? (finish)
   → _____ Willy _____ reading the newspaper?

4. 그는 미국으로 갔다.(그 결과 그는 여기 없다.) (go)
   → He _____ _____ to the US.

Grammar Tip

현재완료의 의문문 「Have[Has]+주어+p.p. ~?」로 나타낸다.

A. break 깨다, 부서지다

B. submit 제출하다
depart 출발하다
steal 훔치다

현재완료의 부정문은 「have[has]+not[never]+p.p.」로 나타낸다.

C. paper 종이, 신문

Unit 27 | 현재완료의 용법-경험, 계속

- 현재완료의 경험 용법은 과거부터 현재까지의 경험을 나타낸다. '~한 적이 있다'로 해석하며 주로 ever, never, before, once, twice 등과 함께 쓴다.

  Have you <u>ever</u> been to Japan?

- 현재완료의 계속 용법은 과거에 시작된 동작이나 상태가 현재까지 계속될 때 쓴다. '(계속) ~해 왔다'로 해석하며 주로 for나 since 등과 함께 쓴다.

  I **have taught** Japanese for three years.

  * for 뒤에는 일정 시간이나 기간을 나타내는 말이 오고, since 뒤에는 과거의 시점이나 시작점을 나타내는 말이 온다.

  Kevin **has taught** London <u>since</u> last year.

 **Practice**

A. 다음 괄호 안에서 현재완료의 알맞은 용법을 고르시오.

1. I have lived in New York for five years. (경험 / 계속)

2. She has not visited the old palace. (경험 / 계속)

3. Have you ever met him before? (경험 / 계속)

4. Emily has taken flute lessons since 2019. (경험 / 계속)

B. 다음 빈칸에 들어갈 말을 〈보기〉에서 골라 알맞은 형태로 바꿔 쓰시오.

〈보기〉 ride	read	be	sing

1. _____ you ever _____ a horse?

2. Daisy _____ _____ in the school choir.

3. Brad _____ never _____ a mistery novel.

4. Tattoos _____ _____ popular for many years.

C. 다음 우리말과 같도록 괄호 안의 말을 이용하여 문장을 완성하시오.

1. 우리는 작년부터 배고픈 아이들을 위해 기부해 오고 있다. (donate)
   → We _____ _____ for hungry children since last year.

2. Jones 씨는 전에 홍콩에 가 본 적이 있다. (be)
   → Mr. Jones _____ _____ to Hong Kong before.

3. 나는 Dean과 10년 동안 알고 지낸다. (know)
   → I _____ _____ Dean for ten years.

4. 나는 그녀로부터 아무것도 듣지 못하고 있다. (hear)
   → I _____ _____ anything from her.

Grammar Tip

A. flute 플루트

B. choir 합창단
mistery novel 추리 소설
tattoo 문신

「have been to+장소」: ~에 가 본 적이 있다(경험), ~에 다녀왔다(완료)
「have gone to+장소」: ~에 가버렸다(결과)

C. donate 기부하다

unit 28 현재완료 진행시제

- 현재완료 진행시제는 「have[has] been+-ing」의 형태로 쓴다. 과거의 어떤 시점부터 현재까지 진행 중인 동작의 계속을 나타내며 '계속 ~하고 있다'로 해석한다.

  My sister **has been sleeping** for two hours.

- 현재완료 진행시제의 부정문은 「have[has] not been+-ing」의 형태로, 의문문은 「Have[Has]+주어+been+-ing ~?」의 형태로 쓴다.

  I **have not been watching** TV since 3 p.m.

  Has he **been playing soccer** for an hour?

  * 소유를 나타내는 동사 have, 상태를 나타내는 동사 know, like 등은 진행형으로 쓸 수 없다.

Practice

A. 다음 괄호 안의 말을 이용하여 현재완료 진행시제를 완성하시오.

1. It _____ _____ _____ since last night. (rain)

2. The boys _____ _____ _____ the kite. (fly)

3. How long _____ you _____ _____ French? (learn)

4. They _____ not _____ _____ about the movie. (talk)

B. 다음 빈칸에 들어갈 말을 〈보기〉에서 골라 알맞은 형태로 바꿔 쓰시오.

〈보기〉 draw	wait	use	build

1. _____ Kate _____ _____ for Eric for an hour?

2. How long _____ they _____ _____ a building?

3. Tom _____ _____ _____ the painting for two hours.

4. Many people _____ not _____ _____ disposable cups for the Earth.

C. 다음 우리말과 같도록 괄호 안의 말을 이용하여 문장을 완성하시오.

1. 우리는 5년 동안 여기에 살고 있는 중이다. (live)
   → We _____ _____ _____ here for five years.

2. 그들은 하루 종일 그 문제를 논의하고 있는 중이다. (discuss)
   → They _____ _____ _____ the problem all day long.

3. Sally는 작년부터 고기를 먹지 않고 있다. (eat)
   → Sally _____ not _____ _____ meat since last year.

Grammar Tip

A. French 프랑스어

have가 소유의 뜻을 나타낼 때는 진행형으로 쓸 수 없지만 '먹다', '(시간을) 보내다'의 뜻으로 쓰일 때는 진행형으로 쓸 수 있다.

B. disposable 일회용의

C. discuss 논의하다
meat 고기

Unit

29 과거완료

- 과거완료는 과거의 어느 시점보다 더 먼저 일어난 동작이나 사건을 나타낸다.

  When I <u>arrived</u> at the station, the train **had** already **left**. (결과)

  I <u>wondered</u> if she **had taught** the students. (경험)

- 과거에 일어난 두 가지 일 중에서 먼저 일어난 일을 나타낼 때도 과거완료로 쓰는데, 이를 대과거라고 한다.

  I <u>lost</u> the bag which my dad **had bought** for me.

Practice

A. 다음 괄호 안에서 알맞은 것을 고르시오.

1. I returned the books that I (have borrowed / had borrowed) from the library.

2. She found the diary which she (have written / had written).

3. He (have gone / had gone) to LA when I called him.

4. When I entered the theater, the movie had already (began / begun).

B. 다음 괄호 안의 말을 이용하여 과거완료 시제를 완성하시오.

1. She _____ never _____ to Italy until he was 20 years old. (be)

2. We _____ _____ in Seoul before we moved here. (live)

3. He said he _____ _____ the film before. (see)

4. When I visited Jack, he _____ _____ a nap. (take)

C. 다음 우리말과 같도록 괄호 안의 말을 이용하여 문장을 완성하시오.

1. 나는 전날 온라인으로 주문한 코트를 받았다. (order)

   → I received the coat that I _____ _____ online the day before.

2. 그녀가 집에 왔을 때, 그녀의 가족은 저녁 식사를 이미 끝냈다. (finish)

   → When she came home, her family _____ already _____ dinner.

3. 그는 그의 친구에게 버스를 놓쳤다고 말했다. (miss)

   → He told his friend he _____ _____ the bus.

4. 그가 사 준 자전거가 고장 났다. (buy)

   → The bike which he _____ _____ broke down.

Grammar Tip

과거완료는 과거 이전의 일이 과거의 상황에 영향을 미칠 때 사용한다.

A. borrow 빌리다

B. film 필름

C. online 온라인의

the day before 전날

30 과거완료 진행시제와 미래완료

- 과거완료 진행시제는 「had been+-ing」의 형태로 과거 이전의 어느 시점의 동작이 과거까지 계속되는 것을 나타내며, '(계속) ~하고 있었다, ~하는 중이었다'로 해석한다.
  I **had been playing** the piano before they <u>arrived</u>.

- 미래완료는 「will+have+p.p.」의 형태로 미래의 어느 시점을 기준으로 그때까지 어떠한 상태나 동작의 완료, 결과, 경험, 계속을 나타낸다.
  The magic show **will have finished** before 9 p.m.

Practice

A. 다음 괄호 안에서 알맞은 것을 고르시오.

1. When I got there, he (had been waiting / will have waited).

2. She said she (had been writing / will have written) a novel.

3. By next week I (had been staying / will have stayed) here.

4. The pond (had been remaining / will have remained) by next month.

B. 다음 괄호 안의 말을 바르게 배열하여 문장을 완성하시오.

1. They _____ to Singapore twice if they go there again.
   (visited, have, will)

2. He _____ 50 portraits before he graduated.
   (had, drawing, been)

3. Next year, they _____ for 5 years.
   (been, will, married, have)

C. 다음 우리말과 같도록 괄호 안의 말을 이용하여 문장을 완성하시오.

1. Rachel은 올해까지 그 동아리에 속해 있을 것이다. (belong)
   → Rachel _____ _____ _____ to the club by this year.

2. 너는 다음 달이면 조종사로 얼마나 일하는 것이니? (work)
   → How long _____ you _____ _____ as a pilot by next month?

3. 내가 그녀를 만났을 때 그녀는 개를 산책시키는 중이었다. (walk)
   → She _____ _____ _____ her dog when I met her.

4. 그는 며칠 동안 몸이 좋지 않아서 휴식을 충분히 취했다. (feel, not)
   → He _____ _____ _____ _____ well for a few days, so he took a long rest.

Grammar Tip

A. remain 남아 있다

B. Singapore 싱가포르
portrait 자화상
graduate 졸업하다

과거완료 진행시제의 부정은 「had not been+-ing」의 형태로 쓴다.

C. belong to ~에 속하다

A. 다음 두 문장이 같은 뜻이 되도록 빈칸에 알맞은 말을 쓰시오.

1. He worked as a coach three years ago and is still working now.
   → He _____ _____ _____ as a coach for three years.

2. Gina lost her favorite sunglasses, and she doesn't have them.
   → Gina _____ _____ her favorite sunglasses.

3. They started waiting for Tom. He came 30 minutes later.
   → They _____ _____ _____ for 30 minutes before Tom came.

B. 다음 밑줄 친 부분을 바르게 고치시오.

1. They were close friends. They <u>will have known</u> each other for ten years.

2. Alex <u>has lived</u> alone for five years next year.

3. Judy is not here. She <u>had gone</u> to Italy.

4. They <u>have never seen</u> snow before they visited Korea.

C. 다음 우리말과 뜻이 같도록 괄호 안의 말을 바르게 배열하시오.

1. 너는 거기에 도착하기 전에 얼마나 오랫동안 운전을 했었니?
   → How long _____ before you got there.
   (been, had, driving, you)

2. 나는 다음 달까지 나의 과제를 끝낼 것이다.
   → I _____ my project by next month.
   (have, will, finished)

3. 그녀는 20살이 될 때까지 해외에 가 본 적이 없었다.
   → She _____ abroad until she was 20 years old.
   (never, had, been)

4. 그들은 세 시간 동안 방을 장식하고 있다.
   → They _____ the room for three hours.
   (have, decorating, been)

D. 다음 우리말과 같도록 괄호 안의 말을 이용하여 문장을 완성하시오.

1. 수세기 동안 사람들은 치료하기 위해 허브를 사용하고 있는 중이다. (use)
   → For centuries, people _____ _____ _____ herbs to heal.

2. 우리가 콘서트에 도착했을 때, 그 가수는 이미 노래 불렀다. (sing)
   → When we got to the concert, the singer _____ _____
   _____.

3. 내일 그 뮤지컬을 본다면 나는 그것을 두 번 보는 것이다. (watch)
   → I _____ _____ _____ the musical twice if I watch it
   tomorrow.

Grammar Tip

A. coach 코치

know, like, have(소유)와 같은 동사는 진행형으로 쓸 수 없다.

B. alone 혼자

완료시제의 부정은 have[has/had] 뒤에 not이나 never를 쓴다.

C. decorate 장식하다

D. herb 허브
heal 치료하다
twice 두 번

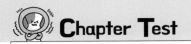 

[1-2] 다음 빈칸에 알맞은 것을 고르시오.

1.
> They _____ a new gym since March.

① build　　　　　② is building
③ have been building　④ will build
⑤ will have built

2.
> When I arrived home, my mom _____ in the room.

① sleeps　　　② slept
③ has slept　　④ had slept
⑤ will sleep

3. 다음 중 어법상 어색한 것은?
① I bought new gloves because I had lost my old ones.
② She said that she had not eaten meat.
③ He has taken a long trip fox six days.
④ They have finished the work by tomorrow.
⑤ I had left my smartphone at home, so I couldn't call you.

4. 다음 중 빈칸에 들어갈 말이 나머지와 다른 것은?
① I wondered if he _____ been to Spain before.
② I _____ been sick since last Friday.
③ This is the most expensive bag that I _____ ever bought.
④ They _____ gone to Italy to study design.
⑤ _____ you ever seen a singer in person?

5. 다음 밑줄 친 부분을 어법상 바르게 고쳐 쓰시오.
> I realized that I have left my umbrella on the bus.

_____ → _____

6. 다음 밑줄 친 부분 중 어법상 어색한 것은?
① The show had already started when he got to the hall.
② Dennis showed me photos that he had taken in Rome.
③ My parents will have been married for 25 years next month.
④ The boy has been crying before the police found him.
⑤ How long has she been waiting for him?

7. 다음 빈칸에 들어갈 말이 바르게 짝지어진 것은?
> The train _____ when we _____ to the platform.

① left − got　　　② left − had gotten
③ has left − got　④ had left − got
⑤ will have left − got

8. 다음 우리말을 바르게 영작한 것은?
> 지금까지 이틀 동안 비가 내리고 있는 중이다.

① It has raining for two days until now.
② It has been raining for two days until now.
③ It will have rained for two days until now.
④ It had been raining for two days until now.
⑤ It had rained for two days until now.

9. 다음 질문에 대한 대답으로 알맞은 것은?
> How long have you been living here?

① For two years ago.
② Since last year.
③ Before you arrived.
④ Until I was young.
⑤ After I graduate from school.

10. 다음 빈칸에 공통으로 알맞은 것은?

> · Noel _____ been preparing for dinner since six p.m.
> · She _____ just finished composing new music.

① has
② had
③ will
④ will have
⑤ have had

11. 다음 대화의 빈칸에 가장 알맞은 것은?

> A: How about visiting a science museum this afternoon?
> B: It _____ since last week because of a fire.

① closed
② had closed
③ has closed
④ will have closed
⑤ will close

12. 다음 괄호 안의 동사를 바르게 바꾼 것은?

> I (be) to London three times if I go there again.

① have been
② had been
③ had been being
④ will have been
⑤ will be

13. 다음 우리말과 같도록 괄호 안의 말을 바르게 배열한 것은?

> 내가 돌아왔을 때 Nancy는 아직 짐을 싸지 못했다.
> → Nancy (packed, suitcase, had, yet, her, not) when I returned.

① had packed not her suitcase yet
② had yet not packed her suitcase
③ had not packed her suitcase yet
④ yet had not packed her suitcase
⑤ not had packed her suitcase yet

[14-15] 다음 두 문장의 뜻이 같도록 빈칸에 알맞은 말을 쓰시오.

14.

> They began running an hour ago.
> They are still running.

= They _____ _____ _____ for an hour.

15.

> Cindy has stayed in Russia for two years.
> She will stay there a year more.

= Cindy _____ _____ _____ in Russia three years by next year.

16. 다음 밑줄 친 부분 중 어법상 어색한 것은?

> Hellen and I first ① met when I ② was in New York. She ③ was my roommate. We ④ have been knowing each other ⑤ since that time. She's my best friend.

17. 다음 (A), (B), (C)의 각 네모 안에서 어법에 맞는 것을 골라 바르게 짝지은 것은?

> · He (A) played / has played computer games an hour ago.
> · Lucy (B) has / will have lost weight by next month.
> · I returned the book that I (C) borrowed / had borrowed last week.

	(A)	(B)	(C)
①	played	has	borrowed
②	played	will have	borrowed
③	played	will have	had borrowed
④	has played	has	had borrowed
⑤	has played	has	borrowed

18. 다음 문장과 뜻이 같은 것은?

> My cousin went to India. He is not here.

① My cousin has gone to India.
② My cousin had gone to India.
③ My cousin has been to India.
④ My cousin has been going to India.
⑤ My cousin will have gone to India.

19. 다음 밑줄 친 부분의 쓰임이 <보기>와 같은 것은?

> <보기>
> He <u>has had</u> a toothache since last night.

① Someone <u>has stolen</u> my purse.
② <u>Have</u> you ever <u>tried</u> Vietnamese food?
③ I <u>have</u> already <u>booked</u> a ticket for Rome.
④ He <u>has worked</u> as a chef for two years.
⑤ The last bus <u>hasn't come</u> here yet.

20. 다음 두 문장을 한 문장으로 바꿔 쓸 때, 빈칸에 알맞은 것은?

> Karen spent all her money.
> + She doesn't have any now.
> → Karen _____ all her money.

① spends ② had spent
③ has spent ④ has been spending
⑤ will spend

<서술형 문제>

21. 다음 우리말과 뜻이 같도록 괄호 안의 말을 바르게 배열하시오.

> 그들은 지금까지 무지개를 본 적이 없다.
> (have, till, seen, rainbow, they, now,
> never, a)

→ _____

22. 다음 우리말과 뜻이 같도록 빈칸에 알맞은 말을 쓰시오.

> 나는 이 태블릿 PC가 고장 나기 전에 3년 동안
> 사용했었다.

→ I _____ _____ this tablet PC _____ three
years before it _____ down.

23. 다음 <조건>에 맞게 우리말을 바르게 영작하시오.

> <조건>
> 1. will, begin을 모두 이용하되, 필요시 어형을
>   바꿀 것.
> 2. 필요시 단어를 추가하여 8단어로 쓸 것.
> 3. 미래완료 시제로 쓸 것.

> 그 영화는 오후 5시 전에 시작하게 될 것이다.

→ _____

24. 다음 주어진 문장을 완료진행시제로 바꿔 문장을 완성하시오.

> He began to wear glasses when he was
> thirteen and is still wearing them now.

= He _____ he
was thirteen.

25. 다음 주어진 동사를 알맞은 형태로 바꿔 쓰시오.

> Henry ⓐ<u>learn</u> how to play tennis since
> April. He practices it hard every day. I
> think that he ⓑ<u>master</u> it by next year.

ⓐ _____

ⓑ _____

조동사란 무엇인가?
조동사는 동사 앞에 위치하여 동사의 의미를 보충하여 의도를 다
양하게 해 주는 역할을 한다.

조동사의 종류에는 어떤 것이 있는가?
조동사는 can, may, must, should, used to 등과 같이 가능, 추
측, 허가, 의무, 충고, 과거의 습관을 나타내는 조동사들이 있다.
He **can** speak Chinese fluently. (가능)
You **must** be home by midnight. (의무)
We **used to** live in Canada. (과거의 상태)

Chapter 5. 조동사

31 | can, could

- can은 '~할 수 있다(능력 = be able to)', '~해도 좋다(허락 = may)', '~일 수 있다(가능성)', '~일리 없다(추측)'의 의미를 나타낸다. 부정형은 cannot[can't]으로 쓰며, can을 이용하여 의문문을 만든다.

  Harry **can**[is able to] play the guitar. (능력)

  You **can**[may] use my smartphone. (허락)

  The store **can** be closed today. (가능성)

  She **cannot** be a liar. (추측)

  * 능력으로 쓰인 can의 미래시제는 will be able to로 나타낸다.

    You'll **be able to** pass the audition.

- could는 can의 과거형으로 쓰이거나, 정중한 부탁을 나타낼 때 쓰이기도 한다.

  I **couldn't** swim when I was a child. (can의 과거형)

  Could you say that again, please? (정중한 부탁)

 Practice

A. 다음 괄호 안에서 알맞은 것을 고르시오.

1. He (can / cans) get stamps from the post office.

2. You (can / can't) park here. It's a no parking zone.

3. (Could you / Are you able to) help me lift this box?

4. Sarah (can / could) solve the puzzle when she was ten.

B. 다음 괄호 안의 말을 바르게 배열하여 문장을 완성하시오.

1. I'm afraid I _____ Alex. He's busy now. (can't, see)

2. _____ some more cake? (I, have, can)

3. _____ the right road. (cannot, be, this)

4. She _____ English fluently. (to, be, speak, will, able)

C. 다음 우리말과 같도록 빈칸에 알맞은 말을 쓰시오.

1. 네가 벌써 배가 고플 리가 없다.
   → You _____ _____ _____ already.

2. 음악을 좀 줄여 주시겠어요?
   → _____ _____ _____ the music down a little, please?

3. 그 당시 나는 기타를 치지 못했다.
   → I _____ _____ the guitar at that time.

4. 그들은 오늘 오후에 도착할 수 있을 것이다.
   → They _____ _____ _____ _____ _____ this afternoon.

Grammar Tip

허락을 나타내는 can은 be able to로 바꿔 쓸 수 없다.

A. park 주차하다
zone 구역
lift 들어 올리다

B. fluently 유창하게

C. already 벌써
turn down 볼륨을 줄이다

Unit

32 | may, might

- may는 '~해도 좋다(허락＝can)', '~일지 모른다(불확실한 추측)'의 의미를 나타낸다.

  May[Can] I sit here? (허락)

  – Yes, you may[can]. / No, you may not[can not]. / No, you must not.

  They **may** be late, so don't wait for them. (불확실한 추측)

- might는 may의 과거형으로 쓰이거나, may보다 실현 가능성이 낮은 '추측'을 나타낸다.

  She hurried so that she **might** catch the bus. (may 과거형)

  She **might** want to meet the young man. (실현 가능성이 낮은 추측)

Practice

A. 다음 밑줄 친 부분에 유의하여 문장을 우리말로 해석하시오.

1. Joseph <u>may</u> be in the hospital.

   → _____

2. She <u>might be able to</u> watch a movie.

   → _____

3. You <u>may not</u> cross the street here.

   → _____

B. 다음 빈칸에 may를 넣어 문장을 다시 쓰시오.

1. I think she has a cold.
   → I think she _____ a cold.

2. There are some problems we don't know about.
   → There _____ some problems we don't know about.

3. Do I use the coupon with my membership card?
   → _____ the coupon with my membership card?

4. She says Paul doesn't want to stay longer.
   → She says Paul _____ to stay longer.

C. 다음 우리말과 같도록 빈칸에 알맞을 말을 쓰시오.

1. 나는 그녀가 돌아올지도 모른다는 것을 들었다.
   → I heard that she _____ _____ back.

2. Nick은 그 선물을 좋아하지 않을지도 모른다.
   → Nick _____ _____ _____ the present.

3. 당신이 가지고 있는 것을 봐도 될까요?
   → _____ _____ _____ what you have?

4. 그 방법은 십대들에게 맞지 않을 수 있다.
   → The method _____ _____ _____ perfect for teenagers.

Grammar Tip

조동사는 두 개를 나란히 쓸 수 없으므로 might+can은 might be able to로 바꿔 쓴다.

A. cross 길을 건너다

B. coupon 쿠폰
membership 회원

C. method 방법
teenager 십대

33 | must, have to

- must는 '~해야 한다(필요, 의무 = have to)', '~임에 틀림없다(강한 추측)'의 의미를 나타낸다.

  All passengers **must**[have to] wear seat belts. (의무)

  Hellen **must** be upset with you. (강한 추측)

- 부정 표현인 must not은 '~해서는 안 된다(금지)'의 의미를 나타내고, don't have to(= don't need to)는 '~할 필요가 없다(불필요)'의 의미를 나타낸다.

  We **must not** break the promise. (금지)

  You **don't have to** tell me what happened. (불필요)

- must를 과거나 미래시제로 표현할 때는 had to, will have to로 나타낸다.

  He **had to** leave for London as soon as possible.

Practice

A. 다음 괄호 안에서 알맞은 것을 고르시오.

1. Sally (must / have to) wear a school uniform.

2. We will (must / have to) buy the ticket here.

3. I (have to / had to) do the laundry last evening.

4. Andy skipped breakfast. He (must / has to) be hungry.

B. 다음 밑줄 친 부분을 must나 have to를 넣어 다시 쓰시오.

1. She has been working all day. She <u>is</u> tired. _____

2. I will <u>study</u> more to achieve my goal. _____

3. We <u>don't work</u> on holidays. _____

4. You <u>don't eat</u> greasy food for your healthy. _____

C. 다음 우리말과 같도록 괄호 안의 말을 이용하여 문장을 완성하시오.

1. 여기에 쓰레기를 버려서는 안 된다. (throw)

   → You _____ _____ _____ garbage away here.

2. 나는 나아지고 있어서 약을 먹을 필요는 없다. (take)

   → I'm getting better, so I _____ _____ _____ _____ medicine.

3. 엔진에 뭔가 잘못된 것이 틀림없다. (be)

   → There _____ _____ something wrong with engine.

4. 그는 버스를 놓쳐서 집에 걸어가야만 했다. (walk)

   → He _____ _____ _____ home because he missed the bus.

Grammar Tip

A. school uniform 교복
   skip 건너뛰다
   laundry 빨래

불필요를 나타내는 don't have to는 don't need to로 바꿔 쓸 수 있다.

B. achieve 성취하다
   goal 목표
   greasy 기름기 많은

C. throw away 버리다
   get better 나아지다
   engine 엔진

unit

34 | should, ought to

- should와 ought to는 '~해야 한다(의무, 당연한 행위)'의 의미를 나타낸다.

  We **should[ought to]** keep our school rules.

- 부정형은 should not과 ought not to로 쓰고, '~해서는 안 된다'의 의미를 나타낸다.

  You **should not[ought not to]** eat too much Coke.

- suggest, order, insist, demand 등과 같은 명령이나 주장을 나타내는 동사 뒤에 오는 that절에서는 대개 should를 생략하고 동사원형만 쓴다.

  My mom <u>ordered</u> that I **(should)** always do my best.

Practice

A. 다음 〈보기〉에서 알맞은 것을 골라 should를 이용하여 문장을 완성하시오.

〈보기〉 offer	save	walk	wear

1. You _____ _____ a long-sleeve shirt in the temple.
2. We _____ _____ seats to the elderly.
3. He _____ _____ his dog in the evening.
4. You _____ _____ a little money each week.

B. 다음 괄호 안에서 알맞은 것을 고르시오.

1. Children ought (to not / not to) be allowed to play in the street.
2. You (should / ought) learn how to swim at school.
3. You (should not / may not) drive fast at night.
4. The doctor suggested that he (exercise / exercises) regularly.

C. 다음 우리말과 같도록 괄호 안의 말을 이용하여 문장을 완성하시오.

1. 너는 입구 앞에 주차해서는 안 된다. (park)
   → You _____ _____ _____ in front of the garage.
2. 그는 우리가 즉시 출발해야 한다고 주장했다. (start)
   → He insisted that we _____ at once.
3. 우리는 빈 병을 재활용해야 한다. (recycle)
   → We _____ _____ _____ empty bottles.
4. 너는 식사 전에 간식을 먹어서는 안 된다. (eat)
   → You _____ _____ _____ _____ nacks before meals.

Grammar Tip

A. long-sleeve 긴 소매의
elderly 연세가 드신

B. allow 허락하다
exercise 운동하다

should는 '~하는 게 좋겠다'라는 뜻의 충고를 나타낼 때 쓰기도 한다.
You look sick. You **should** go home early.

C. garage 차고
insist 주장하다
empty 빈

35 had better, would better

- had better는 '~하는 게 낫다, ~하는 게 좋겠다(= should)'의 충고의 의미를 나타낸다. 부정형은 had better not 으로 쓴다.

  You **had better** wear a coat when you go out. (You had better = You'd better)

  We **had better not** remain here any longer. (We had better = We'd better)

- would rather A than B는 'B하느니 차라리 A하는 편이 낫다'라는 의미로 선택을 나타낼 때 쓰며, than 이하는 생략 가능하다. 부정형은 would rather not으로 쓴다.

  I **would rather** walk (than take a taxi).

  I **would rather not** have coffee.

 Practice

A. 다음 괄호 안에서 알맞은 것을 고르시오.

1. I'm running late. I (had / would) better go and get ready.

2. We (had better / would rather) take a rest than practice.

3. It's cold. You'd (better not / not better) go for a walk.

4. He would rather leave now than (stay / stays) home.

B. 다음 〈보기〉에서 골라 괄호 안의 말을 이용하여 문장을 완성하시오.

〈보기〉 tell	admit	have	spend

1. He has a stomachache. He _____ _____ _____ _____ pizza. (not, would rather)

2. You _____ _____ _____ your mistake. (had better)

3. It's not a good idea. I _____ _____ _____ _____ Eric. (not, had better)

4. I _____ _____ _____ less money on shopping than food. (would rather)

C. 다음 우리말과 같도록 괄호 안의 말을 이용하여 문장을 완성하시오.

1. 그들은 기차보다는 비행기로 여행하는 편이 낫겠다. (travel)
   → They _____ _____ _____ by plane than train.

2. 너는 Helen에게 사과하는 게 좋겠다. (apologize)
   → You _____ _____ _____ to Helen.

3. 너는 온라인으로 그 물품을 사지 않는 게 좋겠다. (buy)
   → You _____ _____ _____ _____ the item online.

4. 나는 모자보다는 자외선 차단제를 바르는 게 더 낫겠다. (wear)
   → I _____ _____ _____ sunscreen than a hat.

Grammar Tip

A. run late 늦다
get ready 준비하다

B. admit 인정하다
mistake 실수

should는 일반적인 상황에서의 의무를 나타내고, had better는 should보다 충고의 의미가 강할 때 사용한다.

C. apologize 사과하다
online 온라인의
wear sunscreen
자외선 차단제를 바르다

36 used to, would

- used to는 과거의 계속된 습관(~하곤 했다, 늘 ~했다)이나 상태(전에는 ~이었다)를 나타낸다.

  I **used to** read a newspaper before breakfast.

  We **used to** live in Paris and I'm still fond of the place.

- would는 '~하곤 했다'의 의미로 과거의 불규칙한 습관을 나타낸다.

  He **would** sing with them on the stage.

 Practice

A. 다음 괄호 안에서 알맞은 것을 고르시오.

1. William used to (go / going) camping every weekend.

2. There (would / used to) be a small bakery here.

3. She (would / used) bite her nails when she was nervous.

4. My grandfather used to (be / was) a good soldier.

B. 다음 〈보기〉에서 골라 used to를 이용하여 문장을 완성하시오.

〈보기〉 ride	think	be	live

1. This gallery _____ a clothing factory.

2. Mike _____ a bike when he was young.

3. People _____ that the Earth is flat.

4. Emily _____ next door to us.

C. 다음 우리말과 같도록 빈칸에 알맞은 말을 쓰시오.

1. Amber는 수줍음이 많은 소녀였다.

   → Amber _____ _____ _____ a shy girl.

2. 나는 일요일에 영화를 보러 가곤 했었다.

   → I _____ _____ to the movies on Sunday.

3. 다리가 있었지만, 지금은 사라졌다.

   → There _____ _____ _____ a bridge, but it's gone.

4. 그들은 환자들을 위해 악기를 연주하곤 했다.

   → They _____ _____ musical instruments for patients.

Grammar Tip

과거의 상태를 나타낼 때는 used to 를 써서 표현하고, would는 쓸 수 없 다.

A. bite 물다
nail 손톱

B. clothing factory 의류 공장
flat 평평한
next door 옆집에

C. shy 수줍음을 많이 타는
musical instrument 악기
patients 환자

Unit 37 | 조동사 + have + 과거분사형

• 「조동사+have+과거분사(p.p.)」는 말하는 시점보다 과거의 일을 나타내며, 과거의 사실에 대한 추측, 후회, 유감 등을 나타낸다.

must+have+과거분사(p.p.)	과거의 사실에 대한 강한 추측('~했음에 틀림없다')을 나타낸다. It **must have rained** last night.
may[might]+have+과거분사(p.p.)	과거의 사실에 대한 약한 추측('어쩌면 ~했을지도 모른다')을 나타낸다. He **may[might] have left** his watch at home.
cannot[can't]+have+과거분사(p.p.)	과거의 사실에 대한 강한 의심('~했을 리가 없다')을 나타낸다. Lauren **cannot have lent** you too much money.
should+have+과거분사(p.p.)	과거의 사실에 대한 후회나 유감('~했어야 했는데 (못했다)')을 나타낸다. should는 ought to와 바꿔 쓸 수 있다. You **should have told[ought to have told]** me much eariler.

Practice

A. 다음 괄호 안에서 알맞은 것을 고르시오.

1. He looked upset. He (may / should) have had a problem with him.

2. She won the MVP award. She (can't / must) have practiced hard.

3. There is no seat inside. We (must have booked / should have booked) a restaurant yesterday.

4. Peter (cannot have told / should have told) a lie. He is very honest.

B. 다음 괄호 안의 말을 바르게 배열하여 문장을 완성하시오.

1. Someone _____ the button. (have, must, touched)

2. He _____ while he was driving. (have, asleep, can't, fallen)

3. I saw the statue. She _____ in Rome. (been, have, might)

C. 다음 우리말과 같도록 괄호 안의 말을 이용하여 문장을 완성하시오.

1. 그녀가 내게 이 편지를 썼을 리가 없다. (write)
   → She _____ _____ _____ this letter to me.

2. 너는 좀 더 조심했어야 했다. (be)
   → You _____ _____ _____ more careful.

3. 그의 눈이 충혈됐어. 그는 피곤했던 게 틀림없어. (feel)
   → His eyes were bloodshot. He _____ _____ _____ tired.

4. 그들은 길을 잃었을지도 모른다. (lost)
   → They _____ _____ _____ their way.

Grammar Tip

A. book 예약하다
award 상

「should+have+p.p.」의 부정형은 「should not[shouldn't]+have+p.p.」로 나타내고, '~하지 말았어야 했는데 (했다)'로 해석한다.

B. such 그러한

C. bloodshot 충혈된

A. 다음 괄호 안에서 알맞은 것을 고르시오.

1. She (can / could) speak Chinese when she was young.

2. You (ought to not / ought not to) drink so much soft drink.

3. He (can't / must) have recognized her. She was wearing a mask.

4. It's snowing a lot. You (had / would) rather stay at home.

B. 다음 밑줄 친 부분을 바르게 고치시오.

1. The building <u>would</u> be a supermarket when I was young.

2. You <u>must</u> go to bed early last night.

3. I <u>had better</u> study at home than go to the party.

4. He <u>should not make</u> such a silly mistake.

C. 다음 우리말과 뜻이 같도록 괄호 안의 말을 바르게 배열하시오.

1. 그들은 9시에 도착했어야 했다.
   → They _____ at nine a.m.
   (have, arrived, should)

2. 그가 나의 메시지를 잊었을 리가 없다.
   → He _____ my message.
   (have, forgotten, can't)

3. 너는 그 영화를 보지 않는 게 좋겠다.
   → You _____ the movie.
   (not, had, watch, better)

4. 그는 나를 역까지 태워다 줄 수 있을 것이다.
   → He _____ me a ride to the station.
   (able, give, will, to, be)

D. 다음 우리말과 같도록 괄호 안의 말을 이용하여 문장을 완성하시오.

1. Lisa는 그를 믿지 말았어야 했다. (believe)
   → Lisa _____ .

2. 너는 한국 식당에서는 팁을 줄 필요가 없다. (give a tip)
   → You _____ at restaurants in Korea.

3. 그녀는 이미 그녀의 엄마에게 전화했을지도 모른다. (call)
   → She _____ already.

Grammar Tip

A. soft drink 탄산음료
   recognize 알아보다

had better와 would rather는 대명사 뒤에서 보통 축약형으로 쓰이므로 had와 would를 잘 구분하도록 한다.
· You'd better[You had better] drink some water.
· I'd rather[I would rather] go to the beach.

B. silly 어리석은

C. give ~ a ride ~를 태워 주다

D. give a tip 팁을 주다

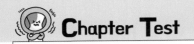

 31~37

[1-2] 다음 빈칸에 알맞은 것을 고르시오.

1.
> Ken isn't answering my call. He _____ be asleep.

① must   ② have to
③ might   ④ ought to
⑤ cannot

2.
> You _____ wear a coat. It's getting cold.

① may   ② would
③ had better   ④ should have
⑤ used to

[3-4] 다음 중 어법상 어색한 것을 고르시오.

3. ① He might have brought the bag.
② You ought to not quarrel with your brother.
③ I thought that he might feel lonely.
④ I will have to pay for it myself.
⑤ The news cannot be true. I don't believe it.

4. ① She ordered that we follow school rules.
② I would rather not say anything about the accident.
③ My mom used to work as a chef when she was young.
④ You had better to stop single food diet.
⑤ She doesn't have to keep working.

5. 다음 중 밑줄 친 부분의 의미가 나머지와 다른 것은?

① She may not want to join us.
② It may snow in this afternoon.
③ You may use this tablet PC anytime.
④ Polar bears may be in danger from global warming.
⑤ Chris has runny nose. He may have a flu.

6. 다음 밑줄 친 부분이 의미하는 것은?

> I should have accepted your advice.

① 추측   ② 강한 의심
③ 필요   ④ 후회
⑤ 허락

7. 다음 빈칸에 알맞지 않은 것은?

> _____ I ask you a favor?

① May   ② Can
③ Might   ④ Could
⑤ Had

[8-9] 다음 우리말을 바르게 영작한 것을 고르시오.

8.
> 우리는 휴가로 어디에 갈지 결정해야 했다.

① We had to decide where to go for vacation.
② We were able to decide where to go for vacation.
③ We had better decide where to go for vacation.
④ We might decide where to go for vacation.
⑤ We must decide where to go for vacation.

9.

> 너는 오히려 지하철을 타는 게 낫다.

① You would take a subway.
② You ought to take a subway.
③ You would rather take a subway.
④ You might take a subway.
⑤ You used to take a subway.

10. 다음 밑줄 친 부분을 어법상 바르게 고쳐 쓰시오.

> We <u>will can</u> catch up with the man.

→ _____

11. 다음 질문에 대한 대답으로 알맞은 것을 <u>모두</u> 고르면?

> May I take pictures in the museum?

① Yes, you may.
② No, you don't have to.
③ No, you must not.
④ Yes, you should.
⑤ No, you may not.

[12-13] 다음 두 문장의 뜻이 같도록 빈칸에 알맞은 말을 쓰시오.

12.

> It is not allowed to feed animals in the zoo.

= You _____ _____ _____ animals in the zoo.

13.

> I think he goes camping with Peter.

= He _____ _____ _____ with Peter.

14. 다음 빈칸에 공통으로 알맞은 것은?

> · I _____ watch the quiz show on TV.
> · We _____ rather eat pizza for lunch.

① should
② would
③ may
④ can
⑤ had

15. 다음 문장과 뜻이 같은 것은?

> It is our duty not to make noise during class.

① We should make noise during class.
② We should not make noise during class.
③ We may not make noise during class.
④ We ought to make noise during class.
⑤ We are able to make noise during class.

16. 다음 빈칸에 들어갈 말이 바르게 짝지어진 것은?

> · He _____ have written this music.
> He's only seven years old.
> · She _____ be a famous actress in Mexico.

① should – had better
② would – must
③ cannot – used to
④ might – would
⑤ must – ought to

17. 다음 우리말과 같도록 할 때 괄호 안의 말을 바르게 배열한 것은?

> 너는 밤 늦게 아무것도 먹지 않는 게 좋겠다.
> → You (not, eat, better, anything, had) late at night.

① had not better eat anything
② had eat better not anything
③ better not had eat anything
④ had eat anything better not
⑤ had better not eat anything

18. 다음 밑줄 친 부분 중 어법상 어색한 것은?

> We ① would live in the house near a park. Sometimes my sister and I ② used to play badminton in the park. I ③ cannot see the park anymore. A big mart ④ will be built there. I ⑤ should have visited before the park was gone.

19. 다음 대화의 빈칸에 가장 알맞은 것은?

> A: Did you hear that Dean bought a new car?
> B: Yes, I did. He _____ a lot of money.

① had better save
② must have saved
③ should have saved
④ cannot have saved
⑤ used to save

20. 다음 우리말과 같도록 할 때 빈칸에 알맞은 것은?

> 그녀의 남편은 그녀에게 며칠 쉬는 것을 제안했다.
> → Her husband suggested that she _____ for a few days.

① rest   ② rests
③ would rest   ④ may rest
⑤ has rested

〈서술형 문제〉

21. 다음 우리말과 뜻이 같도록 대화의 빈칸에 알맞은 말을 쓰시오.

> A: Can I eat something here?
> B: No, _____ _____ _____.
> (아니오, 안 됩니다.)

22. 다음 우리말과 같은 뜻이 되도록 빈칸에 알맞은 말을 쓰시오.

> 그것은 감옥이었지만 지금은 호텔이다.

→ It _____ _____ _____ a prison, but now it is a hotel.

23. 다음 〈조건〉에 맞게 대화의 밑줄 친 우리말을 바르게 영작하시오.

> 〈조건〉
> 1. work, out, better를 모두 이용하되, 필요시 어형을 바꿀 것.
> 2. 주어 You를 포함하여 총 6단어로 쓸 것.
> 3. 주어와 동사를 갖춘 완전한 문장으로 쓸 것.
> 4. 대·소문자와 구두점에 유의할 것.

> Max: I have gained weight these days.
> Laura: 너는 규칙적으로 운동을 하는 게 좋겠어.

→ _____

24. 다음 두 문장이 같은 뜻이 되도록 빈칸에 알맞은 말을 쓰시오.

> You didn't take a pill three times a day. I'm sorry for that.

= You _____ _____ _____ a pill three times a day.

25. 다음 괄호 안의 말을 알맞은 형태로 바꿔 빈칸에 쓰시오.

> I was going to meet Henry at the main square, but he hasn't come yet. He _____ about our appointment. (may, forget)

수동태란 무엇인가?

수동태는 주어가 어떤 행위를 당하는 것을 나타내며, '주어가 ～되다, ～당하다'로 해석한다.

Someone **broke** the window. (능동태)

The window **was broken** by someone. (수동태)

수동태는 언제 어떻게 쓰이나?

수동태는 행동의 주체보다는 행동을 받는 대상을 강조할 때 주로 쓰이며, be동사를 이용해 다양한 시제를 나타낸다.

The room **is cleaned** by Jim. (현재시제)

The room **was cleaned** by Jim. (과거시제)

The room **will be cleaned** by Jim. (미래시제)

The room **is being cleaned** by Jim. (현재진행 시제)

The room **has been cleaned** by Jim. (현재완료 시제)

Chapter 6. 수동태

Unit 38 단순 수동태

- 수동태는 「주어+be동사+p.p.+by+목적격」의 형태로 나타내며, be동사로 시제를 표현한다.

  The book **was written** by Miller. (과거 수동태)

- 행위자가 일반인이거나 분명하지 않거나 중요하지 않을 때 「by+목적격」은 생략할 수 있다.

  This bridge **was built** (by people) in 1980.

- 수동태의 부정문은 be동사 뒤에 not을 쓰고, 의문문은 be동사를 문장 앞에 쓴다.

  The backpack **is not bought** by him.

  Was the *Mona Lisa* **painted** by Leonardo Da Vinci?

Practice

A. 다음 괄호 안에서 알맞은 것을 고르시오.

1. The car (washed / is washed) by Jacob on weekend.

2. A lot of money was stolen (by / in) someone.

3. (Were / Did) these tables moved by Tim?

4. The package (not was / was not) delivered on time.

B. 다음 괄호 안의 말을 바르게 배열하여 문장을 완성하시오.

1. Many accidents _____.
   (caused, by, careless, are, driving)

2. Many people _____.
   (the, are, employed, by, company)

3. Tony _____.
   (invited, the, to, was, party, not)

4. How _____?
   (the, is, word, pronounced)

C. 다음 능동태 문장을 수동태 문장으로 바꿔 쓰시오.

1. A mosquito bit the man.
   → _____

2. The typhoon damaged the building.
   → _____

3. Does Anna paint the wall?
   → _____

Grammar Tip

A. steal 훔치다
package 소포
deliver 배달하다

B. cause ~을 초래하다
careless 부주의한
employ 고용하다
pronounce 발음하다

능동태 문장을 수동태 문장으로 바꿀 때 시제에 유의하여 be동사의 형태를 바꾼다.

C. mosquito 모기
bite 물다
typhoon 태풍
damage 훼손하다

39 조동사가 있는 수동태

- 조동사가 있는 문장의 수동태는 「주어+조동사+be+p.p.+by+목적격」의 형태로 나타낸다.
  Many teenagers will love this song.
  → This song **will be loved** by many teenagers.
- 부정문은 조동사 뒤에 not을 붙이고, 의문문은 조동사를 문장 앞에 쓴다.
  Stars **cannot be seen** in the sky.
  Will all flights **be canceled** because of fog?

Practice

A. 다음 괄호 안에서 알맞은 것을 고르시오.

1. This box (can be used / be can used) in many ways.

2. The food (should is / should be) cooked in an hour.

3. Your idea (may not be / may be not) accepted by them.

4. School rules (must be / be must) obeyed by students.

B. 다음 우리말과 같도록 괄호 안의 말을 이용하여 문장을 완성하시오.

1. 그 편지는 Amy에 의해 보내질 것이니? (send)
   → _____ the letter _____ _____ by Amy?

2. 그 차는 내일까지 수리되어야 한다. (repair)
   → The car _____ _____ _____ by tomorrow.

3. 그의 소설은 유럽에서 출판될지도 모른다. (publish)
   → His novel _____ _____ _____ in Europe.

4. 그 역사적 사실은 잊혀져서는 안 된다. (forget)
   → The historical facts _____ _____ _____ _____.

C. 다음 능동태 문장을 수동태 문장으로 바꿔 쓰시오.

1. You can not take food into the library.
   → _____

2. The waiter must serve the dissert soon.
   → _____

3. Will they sell a new computer?
   → _____

4. He may invent the engine.
   → _____

Grammar Tip

A. in many ways 여러모로
accept 받아들이다
obey 따르다

수동태 문장에서 행위자가 일반적이거나 중요하지 않을 때는 생략이 가능하다.

B. repair 수리하다
publish 출판하다
historical 역사적인

C. serve 제공하다
dessert 후식
engine 엔진

Unit 40 진행시제와 완료시제 수동태

- 진행시제의 수동태는 「주어+be동사+being+p.p.+by+목적격」의 형태로 나타내고, '~하게 되는 중이다, 되고 있는 중이다'로 해석한다.

  The man is drawing the big picture.

  → The big picture **is being drawn** by the man.

- 완료시제의 수동태는 「주어+have[has/had]+been+p.p.+by+목적격」의 형태로 나타낸다.

  The farmer has planted the flowers in the garden.

  → The flowers **have been planted** by the farmer in the garden.

  Have you found your socks in the drawer?

  → **Have** your socks **been found** by you in the drawer?

 Practice

A. 다음 괄호 안에서 알맞은 것을 고르시오.

1. The movie (is being filmed / is being filming) in France.

2. Some bread is (being baking / being baked) by Ellen.

3. The car (had been not / had not been) used very much.

4. The new highway (has been build / has been built).

B. 다음 괄호 안의 말을 바르게 배열하여 문장을 완성하시오.

1. _____ by you? (taken, the, have, photos)

2. The living room _____ by Serena.
   (being, decorated, was)

3. The garage _____ by Sam. (being, not, made, is)

4. Dinner _____ by my mom when I arrived.
   (been, prepared, had)

C. 다음 능동태 문장을 수동태 문장으로 바꿔 쓰시오.

1. David has helped the orphans.
   → _____

2. Are kids watching the magic show?
   → _____

3. We haven't found the missing dog yet.
   → _____

4. The policemen were chasing the thief.
   → _____

Grammar Tip

완료시제의 부정문은 have[has/had] 뒤에 not을 붙인다.

A. film 촬영하다
   highway 고속도로

B. decorate 장식하다
   garage 차고

C. orphan 고아
   missing 사라진
   chase 뒤쫓다

41 | 4형식 문장의 수동태

- 4형식 문장의 수동태는 간접목적어와 직접목적어를 각각 주어로 하는 2가지 형태의 수동태가 가능하다.
  She gave <u>her son</u> <u>gloves</u>.
  → Her son **was given** gloves by her. (주어가 간접목적어)
  → Gloves **were given to** her son by her. (주어가 직접목적어)

- write, read, sell, make, buy 등의 동사는 간접목적어를 주어로 하는 수동태를 만들 수 없다.
  Mike bought <u>her</u> <u>a beautiful ring</u>.
  → She was bought a beautiful ring by Mike. (×)
  → A beautiful ring **was bought for** her by Mike. (○)

 Practice

A. 다음 괄호 안에서 알맞은 것을 고르시오.

1. She (given / was given) a new wallet by her dad.
2. A story (told / was told) to us by his grandfather.
3. Some questions were asked (of / to) the actor by the reporter.
4. The pizza was made (to / for) children by him.

B. 다음 우리말과 같도록 괄호 안의 말을 이용하여 문장을 완성하시오.

1. 약간의 선물들이 Thomas에 의해 그녀에게 보내졌다. (send)
   → Some gifts _____ _____ _____ her by Thomas.

2. 나는 어느 누구에 의해서도 그 행사에 대해 듣지 못했다. (tell)
   → I _____ _____ _____ about the event by no one.

3. 그는 그들에 의해 새로운 직업을 제안받을 것이다. (offer)
   → He _____ _____ _____ a new job by them.

C. 다음 밑줄 친 부분을 주어로 하는 수동태 문장으로 바꿔 쓰시오.

1. He gives <u>us</u> lots of information in his blog.
   → _____

2. Her husband cooked her <u>special dinner</u>.
   → _____

3. The principal read students <u>the letter</u>.
   → _____

4. The foreigner asked <u>Ron</u> a question.
   → _____

 Grammar Tip

수동태 문장에서 직접목적어를 주어로 할 때 간접목적어 앞에 쓰이는 전치사의 종류는 동사에 따라 달라진다.
* to: give, tell, show, teach, send, lend, pay, bring ...
* for: make, buy, cook ...
* of: ask, require ...

A. reporter 기자

B. offer 제안하다

C. blog 블로그
   prinipal 교장 선생님

A. 다음 괄호 안에서 알맞은 것을 고르시오.

1. The Olympics (is held / is holding) every four years.

2. The poem (will posted / will be posted) by Brad tomorrow.

3. A new library has (built / been built) in my town.

4. The songs (were composing / were composed) by Harry.

B. 다음 밑줄 친 부분을 바르게 고치시오.

1. These shoes <u>can used</u> in water. _____

2. Has the engineer <u>being trained</u> for 6 months? _____

3. Many people were <u>be rescued</u> by firefighters. _____

4. A prize <u>will be give for</u> you in the competition. _____

C. 다음 우리말과 같도록 괄호 안의 말을 바르게 배열하시오.

1. 많은 영웅들이 우리에게 기억되고 있다.
   (us, been, have, by, remembered)
   → Many heroes _____.

2. 재미있는 엽서들이 Ben에 의해 내게 보여졌다.
   (me, shown, by, were, Ben, to)
   → Funny postcards _____.

3. 그 공이 소년에 의해 잡아졌다. (by, caught, boy, was, the)
   → The ball _____.

4. 그 동전들이 Maria에 의해 수집되고 있는 중이니?
   (being, coins, are, the, collected)
   → _____ by Maria?

D. 다음 우리말과 같도록 괄호 안의 말을 이용하여 문장을 완성하시오.

1. 그 스웨터는 나의 이모가 내게 사 주셨다. (buy)
   → The sweater _____ _____ _____ _____ by my aunt.

2. 꿀은 고대 시대부터 먹어져 왔다. (eat)
   → Honey _____ _____ _____ since ancient times.

3. 많은 돈이 너에 의해 지불되어야 한다. (pay)
   → A lot of money _____ _____ _____ by you.

Grammar Tip

tomorrow와 같이 시간이나 장소를 나타내는 말은 「by+목적격」 뒤에 쓴다.

A. hold 개최하다
   post 게시하다
   compose 작곡하다

B. engineer 기술자
   train 훈련하다
   competition 경쟁

C. hero 영웅
   postcard 엽서

D. ancient 고대의
   pay 지불하다

unit 42 | 5형식 문장의 수동태

- 5형식 문장의 수동태는 목적어를 수동태의 주어로 쓰고, 목적격보어는 「be동사+p.p.」 뒤에 쓴다.
  His parents named him "James."
  → He **was named** "James" by his parents.
- 지각동사와 사역동사의 수동태는 원형부정사를 to부정사로 바꿔 「be동사+p.p.」 뒤에 쓴다.
  We <u>saw</u> someone run to the store.
  → Someone **was seen to** run to the store. (지각동사의 수동태)
  She <u>made</u> them help the old man.
  → They **were made to** help the old man. (사역동사의 수동태)

Practice

A. 다음 괄호 안에서 알맞은 것을 고르시오.

1. He (elected / was elected) the leader by us.

2. The woman was heard (shouted / to shout) loudly.

3. I (was made / was making) happy by the mild weather.

4. She was told (turn / to turn) off the radio.

B. 다음 우리말과 같도록 괄호 안의 말을 이용하여 문장을 완성하시오.

1. 그 어린이들이 길을 건너는 것이 그들에 의해 보였다. (see)
   → The children _____ _____ _____ _____
   the street by them.

2. 그녀의 방은 그녀에 의해 깨끗하게 유지되었다. (keep)
   → Her room _____ _____ _____ by her.

3. 그 창문들은 그에 의해 열린 채로 놔두었다. (leave)
   → The windows _____ _____ _____ by him.

4. 그는 우리들에 의해 수퍼맨으로 불려진다. (superman)
   → He _____ _____ _____ by us.

C. 다음 능동태 문장을 수동태 문장으로 바꿔 쓰시오.

1. I saw him drive a bus.
   → _____

2. Bill made her follow the law.
   → _____

3. They named their baby Becky.
   → _____

4. She advised them to exercise regularly.
   → _____

Grammar Tip

A. leader 지도자
elect 선출하다
mild 온화한

B. cross 건너다
photographer 사진작가

5형식 문장은 「주어+동사+목적어+목적격보어」로 이루어진 문장이다.

C. advise 충고하다

Unit 43 | 동사구의 수동태

- 「동사+전치사/부사」의 동사구가 있는 문장을 수동태로 바꿀 때는 동사구를 하나의 동사처럼 취급하여 수동태를 만든다.

turn on/off	~을 켜다/끄다	bring up	양육하다
laugh at	~을 비웃다	call off	취소하다
run over	(차에) 치다	look after, take care of	~을 돌보다
look up to	~을 존경하다	look down on	~을 무시하다

I took care of my baby.
→ My baby **was taken care of** by me.

Practice

Grammar Tip

A. 다음 빈칸에 알맞은 말을 〈보기〉에서 골라 쓰시오.

> 〈보기〉   at   off   over   to

1. Ms. Davis is looked up _____ by many people.
2. The seminar was called _____ by the speaker.
3. Paul was laughed _____ by the other kids.
4. Sarah's dog is run _____ by the car.

B. 다음 우리말과 같도록 빈칸에 알맞은 말을 쓰시오.
1. 그 주제는 다음 수업에서 다뤄질 것이다.
   → The issue _____ _____ _____ _____ in the next class.
2. Amy는 그녀의 이모에 의해 양육되었다.
   → Amy _____ _____ _____ by her aunt.
3. 어느 누구도 다른 사람에 의해 무시당해서는 안 된다.
   → No one should _____ _____ _____ _____.
4. 그 시합은 내일까지 연기될 것이다.
   → The match will _____ _____ _____ until tomorrow.

C. 다음 능동태 문장을 수동태 문장으로 바꿔 쓰시오.
1. Daniel picked me up from the station.
   → _____

2. The robbery broke into my house.
   → _____

3. The staff turned off the lights in the hall.
   → _____

Grammar Tip

A. seminar 세미나, 토론

그 외 동사구
put off 연기하다
deal with ~을 다루다
put up with ~을 참다
pick up 태워 주다
break into 침입하다

B. issue 주제

C. robbery 강도

Unit 44 | 목적어로 쓰인 that절의 수동태

· 동사 think, say, know, believe, hope, suppose 등의 목적어로 쓰인 that절의 수동태는 「It is ~ that」의 형태로 쓴다. that절의 주어를 수동태의 주어로 쓰고, that절의 동사를 to부정사로 바꿀 수 있다.

Everyone <u>says</u> that she is the greatest scientist.

→ It **is said that** she is the greatest scientist.

→ She **is said to be** the greatest scientist.

Practice

A. 다음 괄호 안의 말을 바르게 배열하여 문장을 완성하시오.

1. _____ she was a spy. (was, that, believed, it)

2. _____ smoking is bad for health. (thought, that, is, it)

3. They _____ the project. (expected, finish, are, to)

4. _____ the company is in trouble. (that, it, said, is)

B. 다음 우리말과 같도록 빈칸에 알맞은 말을 쓰시오.

1. 그녀가 결백하다고 믿어지고 있다.
   → _____ _____ _____ that she is innocent.

2. Dean은 성실하다고들 말한다.
   → Dean _____ _____ _____ be diligent.

3. 그는 그 일을 잘 해낼 것이라고 생각되었다.
   → He _____ _____ _____ do the work well.

4. 그 계획은 비밀로 간주되었다.
   → It _____ _____ _____ the plan was a secret.

C. 다음 주어진 주어로 시작하는 수동태 문장으로 바꿔 쓰시오.

1. He said that Brian was on vacation.
   → It _____.

2. We found that Anna appeared on the show.
   → Anna _____.

3. They reported that many people were homeless after the flood.
   → It _____.

4. We hope that our team will win the game.
   → Our team _____.

Grammar Tip

A. spy 스파이
company 회사

B. innocent 결백한
diligent 성실한
be supposed 간주되다

that절의 주어를 수동태의 주어로 바꿔 쓸 때 시제가 미래시제인 경우에도 「to+동사원형」의 형태로 쓴다.

C. appear 나타나다
homeless 집을 잃은
flood 홍수

45 by 이외의 전치사가 쓰인 수동태

· 수동태에서 행위자는 「by+목적격」으로 나타내지만 by 대신에 다른 전치사를 쓰는 경우가 있다.

be interested in	~에 관심이 있다	be made of	~으로 만들어지다(물리적)
be covered with	~로 덮여 있다	be made from	~로 부터 만들어지다(화학적)
be pleased with	~에 기뻐하다	be known to	~에게 알려지다
be filled with	~으로 가득 차다	be known for	~으로 유명하다
be surprised at	~에 놀라다	be known as	~로서 알려지다
be worried about	~에 대해 걱정하다	be satisfied with	~에 만족하다

The Alps **is covered with** snow all year.

Practice

A. 다음 빈칸에 알맞은 말을 〈보기〉에서 골라 빈칸에 쓰시오.

〈보기〉 from   in   with   at

1. The ground was covered _____ fallen leaves.
2. Steel is made _____ iron.
3. We were surprised _____ his attitude.
4. Many of young people are not interested _____ politics.

B. 다음 괄호 안의 말을 이용하여 수동태 문장을 완성하시오.(단, 현재시제로 쓸 것)

1. We _____ _____ _____ her silence. (worry)
2. The balloon _____ _____ _____ helium. (fill)
3. They _____ _____ _____ their son's result. (please)
4. Her name _____ _____ _____ the whole world. (know)

C. 다음 우리말 뜻과 같도록 빈칸에 알맞은 말을 쓰시오.

1. 그 호텔은 훌륭한 요리로 유명하다.
   → The hotel _____ _____ _____ its excellent cuisine.
2. 그 사장은 진행에 만족했다.
   → The boss _____ _____ _____ the progress.
3. 그 바닥은 돌로 만들어져 있다.
   → The floors _____ _____ _____ stone.
4. 그는 위대한 예술가로 알려져 있다.
   → He _____ _____ _____ a great artist.

Grammar Tip

be made of는 형태의 변화만 있을 때 쓰고, be made from은 화학적 변화로 성질이 바뀔 때 쓴다.
The table **is made of** wood.
These cookies **are made from** rice.

A. steel 강철
attitude 태도
politics 정치

B. silence 침묵
helium 헬륨 가스

C. cuisine 요리
progress 진행, 과정

A. 다음 괄호 안의 말을 이용하여 수동태 문장을 완성하시오.

1. His office _____ by someone last night. (break into)

2. It _____ Joseph is an expert on China. (know)

3. Gwen _____ by his uncle when he was a child. (bring up)

4. The walls will _____ good pictures. (cover)

B. 다음 밑줄 친 부분을 바르게 고치시오.

1. The boys were made <u>wear</u> white sneakers. _____

2. Are you <u>interest at</u> space research? _____

3. The jacket <u>was buying to</u> me by my cousin. _____

4. He was never <u>saw eat</u> carrots. _____

C. 다음 두 문장의 뜻이 같도록 빈칸에 알맞은 말을 쓰시오.

1. We think that Sue is in Switzerland.
   = Sue _____ _____ _____ _____ in Switzerland.

2. Peter gave Julia a gold ring.
   = A gold ring _____ _____ _____ Julia by Peter.

3. We heard him play the guitar.
   = He _____ _____ _____ _____ the guitar.

4. They call the cat Sweetie.
   = The cat _____ _____ _____ by them.

D. 다음 우리말과 뜻이 같도록 괄호 안의 말을 이용하여 문장을 완성하시오.

1. 내 친구는 집에 오는 길에 차에 치였다.
   → My friend _____ a car on the way home.

2. 그는 그의 용기 때문에 모든 사람들에게 존경을 받는다.
   → He _____ by everyone because of his courage.

3. 모든 사람이 동등하다고 믿어진다.
   → _____ that all men are equal.

4. 나는 그에게 다시 전화를 해 달라는 부탁을 받았다.
   → I _____ him again.

Grammar Tip

A. expert 전문가

B. sneakers 운동화
   space 우주
   research 연구

that절을 목적어로 하는 동사 seem, happen, appear 등이 쓰인 문장은 수동태로 바꿔 쓸 수 없다.

C. Switzerland 스위스

D. on the way home
   집에 오는 길에
   courage 용기
   equal 동등한

[1-2] 다음 빈칸에 알맞은 것을 고르시오.

1.
> These pyramids _____ around 400 BC.

① build　　　　② built
③ are built　　④ were built
⑤ will be built

2.
> Paper _____ wood.

① makes　　　　　② made from
③ is made with　　④ is made of
⑤ is made from

3. 다음 중 어법상 옳은 것은?
① This soup can cooked anytime.
② The problem was explaining to the children.
③ We was never tell the real truth by him.
④ Dinner is being prepared by my mother.
⑤ The milk has been deliver every morning.

4. 다음 중 문장의 전환이 바르지 않은 것은?
① I bought her a backpack.
　→ A backpack was bought for her by me.
② We heard him sing a beautiful song.
　→ He was heard to sing a beautiful song.
③ I found that the task is impossible.
　→ The task was found be impossible.
④ Some boys laughed at Bob.
　→ Bob was laughed at by some boys.
⑤ She asked me to turn off the radio.
　→ I was asked to turn off the radio by her.

5. 다음 중 밑줄 친 부분이 어법상 틀린 것은?
① The car was given for me by her.
② Fred was elected a new leader by us.
③ It is said that she comes back soon.
④ The table is covered with dirt.
⑤ He was made to do the dishes by her.

6. 다음 대화의 빈칸에 알맞은 것은?

> A: When can I buy brand new shoes?
> B: They _____ this weekend.

① sell　　　　② will sell
③ will sold　　④ will be sold
⑤ will being sold

[7-8] 다음 우리말을 바르게 영작한 것을 고르시오.

7.
> 비밀은 그들에게 누설되어서는 안 된다.

① The secret must not disclose to them.
② The secret must not disclosed to them.
③ The secret must be not disclosed to them.
④ The secret must not be disclose to them.
⑤ The secret must not be disclosed to them.

8.
> 그녀는 최고의 영화감독이라고 말해진다.

① It says that she is the best movie director.
② It said that she is the best movie director.
③ It is said she to be the best movie director.
④ It is said that she is the best movie director.
⑤ It is said to she is the best movie director.

9. 다음 빈칸에 공통으로 알맞은 것은?

> · His face is filled _____ fear.
> · They were not satisfied _____ the service.

① in   ② at   ③ with
④ for   ⑤ by

10. 다음 괄호 안의 말을 알맞은 형태로 바꾼 것은?

> The man _____ jump over a fence last night. (see)

① saw   ② was seen
③ has seen   ④ was being seen
⑤ was seen to

11. 다음 밑줄 친 부분을 어법상 바르게 고쳐 쓰시오.

> He was made stay in his room.

→ _____

12. 다음 (A), (B), (C)의 각 네모 안에서 어법에 맞는 것을 골라 바르게 짝지은 것은?

> · The street (A) closed / is closed to the public.
> · His opinion was asked (B) of / for Sam by me.
> · We were surprised (C) at / in his answer.

	(A)	(B)	(C)
①	closed	of	at
②	closed	for	at
③	is closed	of	at
④	is closed	for	in
⑤	closed	for	in

13. 다음 빈칸에 들어갈 말이 바르게 짝지어진 것은?

> · All events were called _____ because of the snow.
> · Mozart is known _____ a composer.

① off – as   ② of – for
③ off – for   ④ with – as
⑤ off – by

14. 다음 질문에 대한 대답으로 알맞은 것은?

> Were the cups broken by you?

① Yes, I was.   ② No, I wasn't.
③ Yes, they were.   ④ Yes, I did.
⑤ No, they aren't.

15. 다음 문장을 수동태로 바르게 바꾼 것은?

> Lisa made me a waffle.

① I was made a waffle by Lisa.
② A waffle made for me by Lisa.
③ A waffle was made to me by Lisa.
④ A waffle was made Lisa for me.
⑤ A waffle was made for me by Lisa.

[16-17] 다음 두 문장이 같은 뜻이 되도록 빈칸에 알맞은 말을 쓰시오.

16.
> We are watching the movie.

= The movie _____.

17.
> The doctor advised him to quit smoking.

= He _____ by the doctor.

85

18. 다음 밑줄 친 부분 중 어법상 어색한 것은?

> A new restaurant ① has been built ② for seven months. It ③ is known to its delicious pasta. It ④ will be opened ⑤ next week.

19. 다음 우리말 뜻과 같도록 괄호 안의 말을 바르게 배열한 것은?

> 너의 장갑은 그 서랍에서 찾았니?
> → (your, have, been, gloves, found) in the drawer?

① Have your gloves found been
② Have your gloves been found
③ Have been found your gloves
④ Have found been your gloves
⑤ Have been your gloves found

20. 다음 문장을 능동태로 바르게 바꾼 것은?

> This program will be used for kids.

① We will use this program for kids.
② We will be use this program for kids.
③ We would use this program for kids.
④ We will used this program for kids.
⑤ We will be to use this program for kids.

〈서술형 문제〉

21. 다음 우리말과 같은 뜻이 되도록 빈칸에 알맞은 말을 쓰시오.

> 그 과학자는 많은 학생들에게 존경을 받는다.

→ The scientist _____ _____ _____
_____ _____ many students.

22. 다음 문장을 능동태로 바꿔 쓸 때 빈칸에 들어갈 적절한 말을 쓰시오.

> The city has not been visited by us yet.

→ We _____ _____ _____ _____
_____ yet.

23. 다음 〈조건〉에 맞게 괄호 안의 단어들을 이용하여 우리말을 바르게 영작하시오.

> 〈조건〉
> 1. 주어진 단어들을 모두 이용할 것.
> 2. 필요시 단어를 추가할 것.
> 3. 주어와 동사를 갖춘 완전한 문장으로 쓸 것.
> 4. 대·소문자 및 구두점에 유의할 것.

> 그의 이름이 종이에 쓰여지고 있다.
> (his name / write / on / paper)

→ _____

24. 다음 문장을 주어진 말로 시작하는 수동태로 바꿔 쓰시오.

> We think that James will travel to Europe.

(1) It _____.
(2) James _____.

25. 다음 ⓐ~ⓒ를 괄호 안의 말을 이용하여 알맞은 형태로 바꿔 쓰시오.

> It ⓐ (report) that many fish and sea animals eat plastic. They sometimes die from eating plastic. They must ⓑ (protect) by us. The garbage should not ⓒ (throw) away anymore.

ⓐ _____
ⓑ _____
ⓒ _____

비교구문이란 무엇인가?
비교구문은 둘 이상의 사람이나 사물의 성질, 상태 등의 정도 차이을 비교해서 나타내는 문장이다.
Mark is **stronger than** James.
She is **the busiest** woman in my office.

비교구문에는 어떤 것이 있는가?
형용사나 부사의 형태를 그대로 사용해서 원급을 이용하는 원급 비교가 있고, 형용사나 부사의 비교급이나 최상급을 이용하여 나타내는 비교급 비교와 최상급 비교가 있다.
That is **as big as** this. (원급 비교)
That is **bigger** than this. (비교급 비교)
That is **the biggest** of them. (최상급 비교)

Chapter 7. 비교구문

Unit 46 비교급과 최상급

· 형용사와 부사는 원급, 비교급, 최상급의 세 가지 변화형이 있다.

원급	형용사와 부사의 변화되지 않은 원래의 형태	tall 키가 큰
비교급	둘을 비교할 때 쓰는 말로 '더 ~한'의 뜻	taller 더 키가 큰
최상급	셋 이상을 비교할 때 쓰는 말로 '가장 ~한'의 뜻	tallest 가장 키가 큰

· 비교급과 최상급 만들기

규칙 변화	보통 원급에 -er을 붙여서 비교급을, -est를 붙여서 최상급을 만드는 것이 원칙이지만 -ly, -ing, -ful, -ous, -less 등으로 끝나는 단어와 3음절 이상의 단어는 「more, most+원급」의 형태로 만든다.	fast – faster – fastest large – larger – largest hot – hotter – hottest easy – easier – easiest famous – more famous – most famous
불규칙 변화	good[well] – better – best bad[ill] – worse – worst many[much] – more – most little – less – least	

Practice

A. 다음 단어의 비교급과 최상급의 형태를 쓰시오.

1. short – (   ) – (   )   2. big – (   ) – (   )

3. happy – (   ) – (   )   4. little – (   ) – (   )

5. useful – (   ) – (   )   6. good – (   ) – (   )

B. 다음 우리말을 참고하여 괄호 안의 단어를 알맞은 형태로 바꿔 쓰시오.

1. Summer is the (hot) season of four. (가장 더운) _____

2. She earns (much) money than you. (더 많은) _____

3. The Nile is the (long) river in the world. (가장 긴) _____

4. This is the (heavy) of the parcels. (가장 무거운) _____

C. 다음 우리말과 같도록 괄호 안의 말을 이용하여 문장을 완성하시오.

1. 이것이 이 가게에서 제일 싼 재킷이다. (cheap)
   → This is the _____ jacket in this store.

2. 축구가 야구보다 더 재미있다. (interesting)
   → Soccer is _____ _____ than baseball.

3. Kevin은 내가 기대했던 것보다 더 늦게 도착했다. (late)
   → Kevin arrived _____ than I expected.

4. 에베레스트 산이 세계에서 가장 높은 산이다. (high)
   → Mt. Everest is the _____ mountain in the world.

Grammar Tip

「단모음+단자음」으로 끝나는 단어는 자음을 한 번 더 쓰고 -er, -est를 붙이며 「자음+y」로 끝나는 단어는 y를 i로 고치고 -er, -est를 붙인다.

A. useful 유용한

비교급은 둘을 비교할 때 쓰고 최상급은 셋 이상을 비교할 때 쓴다.

B. season 계절
   parcel 소포

C. jacket 재킷
   expect 기대하다

Unit 47 | as + 원급 + as

- 원급 비교는 비교하는 대상이나 비교의 정도 차이가 비슷할 때 사용하는데, 형태를 변화시키지 않고 원급을 사용한다.

A ~ as+형용사/부사의 원급+as B	A는 B만큼 ~하다
A ~ not as[so]+형용사/부사의 원급+as B	A는 B만큼 ~하지 않다(못하다)
*「as+원급+as」는 동등비교를 나타내며, 「not as+원급+as」는 열등비교를 나타낸다.	
*「not as+원급+as」는 「not so+원급+as」로 바꿔 쓸 수 있다.	

Kate is 160cm. Her sister is 160cm, too.

→ Kate is **as tall as** her sister.

Kate is 160cm. Her brother is 165cm.

→ Kate is **not as tall as** her brother. (= Kate is **shorter than** her brother.)

Practice

A. 다음 괄호 안에서 알맞은 것을 고르시오.

1. Julia can swim as (well, better) as you.
2. John studies as (hard, harder) as Tom.
3. My bicycle is not as big as (your, yours).

B. 다음 두 문장을 한 문장으로 바꿔 쓸 때, 빈칸에 알맞은 말을 쓰시오.

1. Jamie goes to school early. + I go to school early.
   → Jamie goes to school _____ _____ _____ I do.
2. A rabbit is not dangerous. + A tiger is dangerous.
   → A rabbit is not _____ _____ _____ a tiger.
3. Carol is 175cm. + His father is 175cm, too.
   → Carol is _____ _____ _____ his father.
4. I have one thousand won. + She has one thousand won.
   → I have _____ _____ money _____ she does.

C. 다음 우리말과 같도록 빈칸에 알맞을 말을 쓰시오.

1. 이 베게는 저것만큼 부드럽다.
   → This pillow is _____ _____ _____ that.
2. 그는 보이는 것만큼 영리하지 않다.
   → He is _____ as _____ _____ he looks.
3. 이 강은 저것만큼 깊다.
   → This _____ _____ _____ _____ _____ that one.
4. 그것은 내가 생각한 것만큼 어렵지 않다.
   → It is _____ _____ _____ _____ _____ _____ _____ .

Grammar Tip

비교할 때 B의 어구가 A와 같은 것은 보통 생략한다. 또한 비교 대상은 문법적으로 같은 성격을 가진 것이어야 한다.

A. heavy 무거운

키를 나타낼 때는 tall을 사용하고 몸무게를 나타낼 때는 heavy를 사용한다. 돈이나 양을 나타낼 때는 much를 사용한다.

B. dangerous 위험한

C. pillow 베게
soft 부드러운
deep 깊은

48 원급 비교구문과 배수 비교구문

· 원급을 이용하여 다양한 비교 표현을 나타낼 수 있다.

as+원급+as possible = as+원급+as+주어+can[could]	가능한(할 수 있는 한) ~하게(하도록)
A ~ 배수+as+원급+as+B = A ~ 배수+비교급+than+B	A는 B보다 몇 배나 더 ~하다
* 「as+원급+as+주어+can[could]」에서 시제가 현재이면 can, 과거이면 could를 쓴다. * 배수는 '~ 배'를 나타내는 말로 twice(두 배)를 제외하고 '숫자+times'로 나타낸다.	

We drink water **as** much **as possible.** = We drink water **as** much **as we can.**

My purse is **twice as** expensive **as** hers. = My purse is **twice** more expensive **than** hers.

Practice

A. 다음 문장의 괄호 안에서 알맞은 것을 고르시오.

1. Send an email as soon as (possible, can).

2. I grow twice as (many, more) deer as he.

3. This house is three (time, times) as large as his.

4. Thomas jumped as high as he (can, could).

B. 다음 두 문장이 같은 뜻이 되도록 빈칸에 알맞은 말을 쓰시오.

1. He practiced as hard as he could to pass the audition.
   = He practiced as hard as _____ to pass the audition.

2. She donated three times as much as you.
   = She donated three times _____ _____ you.

3. Julie has fifty books. Nick has twenty-five books.
   = Julie has _____ _____ _____ books as Nick.

C. 다음 우리말과 같도록 괄호 안의 말을 이용하여 문장을 완성하시오.

1. 이 다리는 저것의 3배만큼 길다. (three, long)
   → This bridge is _____ as that one.

2. 그들은 가능한 빨리 집으로 돌아왔다. (soon, can)
   → They came back home _____.

3. 나의 점수는 너의 점수보다 2배만큼 높다. (twice, high)
   → My score is _____ as your score.

4. 그는 할 수 있는 한 음식을 많이 먹었다. (much, possible)
   → He ate food _____.

5. 나의 할머니는 나보다 4배 더 연세가 많다. (old, than)
   → My grandmother is _____ I am.

Grammar Tip

「as+원급+as+possible」은 「as+원급+as+주어+can」으로 바꿀 수 있는데 시제가 과거이면 could로 쓴다.

A. grow 기르다
   deer 사슴

B. audition 오디션
   donate 기부하다

「배수+as+원급+as」는 「배수+비교급+than」으로 바꾸어 나타낼 수 있다.

C. bridge 다리
   score 점수

Unit 49 | 비교급 + than

- 비교급 비교는 둘을 비교하여 둘 중 하나가 '더 ~한'것을 나타내는 표현이다.

A ~ 비교급+than B	A는 B보다 더 ~하다 → 형용사나 부사의 비교급과 than을 사용한다.

My brother is **taller than** my father (is).   Jonathan is **more creative than** he (is).

- much, even, still, far, a lot 등은 비교급 앞에서 비교의 의미를 강조한다.

The bike is <u>much</u> **cheaper** than the car.

This smartphone is <u>even</u> **better** than that one.

* very는 원급을 수식하여 원급 강조에 쓴다. → very는 비교급 문장에는 쓰지 않는다.

This is a <u>very</u> **useful** machine.

Practice

A. 다음 문장의 괄호 안의 단어를 알맞은 형태로 바꿔 빈칸에 쓰시오.

1. You are _____ than them. (angry)

2. The big ball falls _____ than the small ball. (fast)

3. She looked _____ than the rich people. (happy)

B. 다음 두 문장을 참고하여 한 문장으로 완성하시오.

1. This ruler is 10cm long. + That pencil is 12cm long.
   → That pencil is _____ _____ this ruler.

2. The book is large in size. + The paper is larger in size.
   → The paper is _____ _____ the book in size.

3. My mom gets up at six. + I get up at seven.
   → My mom gets up _____ _____ I.

4. Tom is ten years old. + Eric is twelve years old.
   → Tom is _____ _____ Eric.
   → Eric is _____ _____ Tom.

C. 다음 우리말과 같도록 괄호 안의 말을 이용항 문장을 완성하시오.

1. 표범은 고양이보다 더 위험하다. (dangerous)
   → Leopards are _____ cats.

2. 그는 그의 친구들보다 수학을 훨씬 더 열심히 공부한다. (even, hard)
   → He studies math _____ his friends.

3. 이 가방은 저 배낭보다 훨씬 더 무겁다. (still, heavy)
   → This bag is _____ that backpack.

4. 태양은 지구보다 훨씬 더 크다. (much, big)
   → The sun is _____ the earth.

Grammar Tip

-ful, -ous, -less 등으로 끝나는 단어와 3음절 이상의 단어는 「more+원급」의 형태로 비교급을 만든다.

두 가지 대상의 성질이나 특성을 비교할 때는 비교급을 이용한다.

B. ruler 자
   in size 크기에서

비교급을 강조할 때는 much, even, still, a lot 등을 사용하여 나타낸다.

C. leopard 표범
   dangerous 위험한

Unit 50 열등비교와 비교급 비교구문

- 열등비교는 '덜 ~하다'라는 뜻으로 직접 말하기보다는 우회적으로 표현할 때 많이 사용한다.

A ~ less+원급+than B = A ~ not as(so)+원급+as B	A는 B보다 덜 ~하다
*원급 앞에는 형용사의 음절 수에 상관없이 항상 less를 쓴다. *less는 little의 비교급이므로 다음에는 항상 원급이 와야 한다.	

Philip is **less tall than** Carol. = Philip is **not as(so)** tall as Carol.

→ Carol is **taller than** Philip.

- 비교급을 이용하여 다양한 비교 표현을 나타낼 수 있다.

비교급+and+비교급	점점 더 ~한(하게) 비교급이 「more+원급」인 경우에는 「more and more+원급」으로 쓴다.
the+비교급 ~, the+비교급 ~	~하면 할수록 점점 더 ~하다

It is getting **warmer and warmer**. **The higher** they go up, **the colder** it becomes.

Practice

A. 다음 두 문장이 같은 뜻이 되도록 빈칸에 알맞은 말을 쓰시오.

1. Amy is not as intelligent as her brother.
 → Amy is _____ _____ _____ her brother.

2. The actress is not as popular as the actor.
 → The actress is _____ _____ _____ the actor.

3. Mary plays the piano better than Harry.
 → Harry doesn't play the piano _____ _____ _____ Mary.

B. 다음 문장에서 <u>틀린</u> 부분을 찾아 바르게 고쳐 쓰시오.

1. Susan is less faster than her friends. _____

2. We don't feel as tired than our father. _____

3. My hometown is less larger than New York. _____

4. The hot the food is, the more we like it. _____

C. 다음 우리말과 같도록 괄호 안의 말을 이용하여 문장을 완성하시오.

1. Mike는 그의 형보다 덜 바쁘다. (busy)
 → Mike is _____ his elder brother.

2. 세계는 점점 더 작아지고 있다. (get, small)
 → The world is _____.

3. 우유가 신선하면 할수록 더 맛이 있다. (fresh, good)
 → _____ milk is, _____ it tastes.

Grammar Tip

「less+원급+than」=「not as(so)+원급+as」와 같으며 not은 동사와 주어의 인칭에 주의하여 부정문을 만든다.

A. intelligent 지적인, 영리한
 popular 인기가 있는

「비교급+and+비교급」에서 비교급이 「more+원급」인 경우에는 「more and more+원급」으로 쓴다.

B. tired 피곤한
 hometown 고향

C. elder 손위의, 연장의
 fresh 신선한

Unit 51 | 최상급 비교구문

· 최상급은 셋 이상을 비교하는 것으로 '가장 ~한'것을 나타내는 표현이다.

A ~ the+최상급+in(+단수명사) of(+복수명사)	A는 ~ 중에서 가장 ~하다 → 형용사의 최상급 앞에는 반드시 the를 쓴다.
one of the+최상급+복수명사	가장 ~한 ~들 중의 하나

That is **the most interesting** book in the library.

He is **the busiest** man of the people.

Alice is **one of the best English speakers** in my school.

· 최상급에 the를 붙이지 않는 경우

① 부사의 최상급에는 the를 붙이지 않기도 함. : I like Lisa **best** in my class.

② 동일 사람이나 사물을 비교할 때 : The lake is **deepest** at this point.

* 최상급의 강조 : much, even, quite, by far 등을 쓴다.

It is <u>even</u> **the most challengable** job.

Practice

A. 다음 문장의 괄호 안에서 알맞은 것을 고르시오.

1. Seoul is the (larger, largest) in Korea.

2. Mt. Everest is the highest (in, of) all the mountains.

3. Monet is one of the most famous (artist, artists).

4. Australia is the smallest continent (in, of) the world.

B. 다음 문장에서 밑줄 친 부분을 바르게 고쳐 쓰시오.

1. Bill Gates is one of the richest <u>man</u>. _____

2. Yesterday was <u>worse</u> moment in my life. _____

3. He is <u>far</u> the tallest boy in our class. _____

4. It is the <u>more</u> unique jacket I've ever seen. _____

C. 다음 우리말과 같도록 괄호 안의 말을 이용하여 문장을 완성하시오.

1. 2월은 모든 달 중에서 가장 짧다. (short)
   → February is _____ _____ _____ all the months.

2. 흰긴수염고래는 바다에서 가장 큰 동물이다. (large)
   → The blue whale is _____ _____ animal _____ the ocean.

3. 다이아몬드는 모든 돌들 중에서 가장 아름답다. (beautiful)
   → A diamond is _____ _____ _____ _____ all stones.

4. 그녀는 그 클럽에서 가장 활발한 소녀 중 하나이다. (lively)
   → She is _____ _____ _____ _____ girls in the club.

Grammar Tip

「the+최상급+in」 뒤에는 단수명사(범위)가 오고 「the+최상급+of」 뒤에는 복수명사(대상)가 온다.

A. mountains 산맥
   continent 대륙

B. moment 순간
   unique 독특한

C. blue whale 흰긴수염고래
   ocean 바다
   diamond 다이아몬드
   lively 활발한

52 다양한 최상급 표현

· 원급이나 비교급을 이용하여 최상급의 의미를 갖는 다양한 문장으로 표현할 수 있다.

the+최상급 ~	가장 ~한(하게)
= 부정주어+so[as]+원급+as ~	어떤 것도 ~만큼 ~하지 않은(않게)
= 부정주어+비교급+than ~	어떤 것도 ~보다 더 ~하지 않은(않게)
= 비교급+than any other+단수명사	다른 어떤 ~보다 더 ~한(하게)
= 비교급+than all the other+복수명사	다른 어떤 ~들보다 더 ~한(하게)

Sally is **the prettiest** girl in this town.
= **No other girl** in this town is **so(as) pretty as** Sally.
= **No other girl** in this town is **prettier than** Sally.
= Sally is **prettier than any other girl** in this town.
= Sally is **prettier than all the other girls** in this town.

Practice

A. 다음 문장의 뜻이 모두 같도록 빈칸에 알맞은 말을 쓰시오.

1. Jupiter is the largest planet in the solar system.
   = _____ _____ in the solar system is _____ _____ _____ Jupiter.
   = _____ _____ in the solar system is _____ _____ Jupiter.
   = Jupiter is _____ _____ _____ other planet in the solar system.
   = Jupiter is _____ _____ all the other _____ in the solar system.

2. Trust is the most important thing of all.
   = Nothing of all is _____ _____ _____ trust.
   = _____ of all is _____ _____ _____ trust.
   = Trust is _____ _____ _____ any other thing of all.
   = Trust is _____ _____ _____ all the other things of all.

B. 다음 우리말과 같도록 괄호 안의 말을 이용하여 문장을 완성하시오.

1. 사랑은 인생에서 가장 중요한 것이다. (important)
   → Nothing is _____ _____ as love in life.
   → _____ is _____ _____ than love in life.
   → Love is _____ _____ _____ all the other things in life.

2. 빅벤은 세계에서 가장 큰 시계이다. (large)
   → Big Ben is _____ _____ _____ in the world.
   → Big Ben is _____ than all _____ _____ _____ in the world.
   → _____ _____ clock in the world is _____ _____ Big Ben.

Grammar Tip

any other 다음에는 단수명사가 오고 all the other 다음에는 복수명사가 온다.

A. planet 행성
   solar system 태양계
   trust 믿음

B. clock 시계
   life 인생, 삶

A. 다음 문장의 빈칸에 알맞은 것을 고르시오.

1. She looks even _____ than usual.
   ① happy ② happier ③ more happy ④ the most happy

2. Summer is _____ season of the year.
   ① the hot ② the hotter ③ the hottest ④ the most not

3. Come as _____ as you can!
   ① quick ② quicker ③ the quickest ④ the most quick

4. Who is _____ singer in your country?
   ① famous ② more famous ③ most famous ④ the most famous

B. 다음 표를 보고, 빈칸에 알맞은 말을 쓰시오.

	사과	바나나	멜론
Siena	3	4	6
Julian	3	8	2

1. Siena has _____ many apples as Julian.
2. Julian has _____ _____ many bananas as Siena.
3. Siena has _____ _____ _____ melons than Julian.

C. 다음 두 문장이 같은 뜻이 되도록 빈칸에 알맞은 말을 쓰시오.

1. This bag is heavier than that backpack.
   = That backpack is _____ _____ this bag.

2. Seoul is larger than any other city in Korea.
   = Seoul is _____ _____ _____ in Korea.

3. The jeans are not as expensive as the suit.
   = The jeans are _____ _____ _____ the suit.

4. Judy came back home as soon as possible.
   = Judy came back home as soon _____ _____ _____.

D. 다음 우리말과 같도록 괄호 안의 말을 이용하여 문장을 완성하시오.

1. 이것은 이 가게에서 제일 싼 셔츠이다. (cheap)
   → This is _____ _____ _____ in this shop.

2. 축구가 야구보다 덜 재미있다. (interesting)
   → Soccer is _____ _____ _____ baseball.

3. 그녀는 이 팀에서 최고의 선수 중 한 명이다. (good, player)
   → She is _____ _____ _____ _____ _____ on this
   team.

4. 네가 오래 머물수록, 떠나기 더욱더 어려워진다. (long, hard)
   → _____ _____ you stay, _____ _____ it is to leave.

Grammar Tip

비교급을 강조할 때는 much, even, still, a lot 등을 사용하여 나타낸다.

A. season 계절
   wet 젖은

「배수+as+원급+as」는 「배수+ 비교급+than」으로 바꾸어 나타낼 수 있다.

B. melon 멜론

「less+원급+than」 = 「not as(so) +원급+as」와 같으며 not은 동사 와 주어의 인칭에 주의하여 부정문 을 만든다.

C. light 가벼운
   suit 정장

less는 little의 비교급이므로 다음 에는 항상 원급이 와야 한다.

D. player 운동선수
   hard 힘든, 어려운

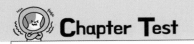 

[1-2] 다음 빈칸에 알맞은 것을 고르시오.

1.

> Jamie is not as _____ as Brian.

① youth   ② young
③ younger   ④ youngest
⑤ the youngest

2.

> The cheetah is _____ animal on land.

① fast   ② faster
③ the faster   ④ the fastest
⑤ fastest

3. 다음 빈칸에 알맞지 <u>않은</u> 것은?

> This restaurant is _____ busier than before.

① much   ② even
③ still   ④ a lot
⑤ very

4. 다음 밑줄 친 부분이 어법상 <u>어색한</u> 것은?
① My sister is <u>smarter</u> than I.
② Jenny is the <u>famousest</u> of all.
③ This book is as <u>thick</u> as that one.
④ I can swim as <u>good</u> as my uncle.
⑤ The <u>lighter</u> it is, the cheaper it is.

5. 다음 두 문장의 뜻이 같도록 빈칸에 알맞은 말을 쓰시오.

> The problem is not so easy as that one.
> = The problem is _____ _____ than that one.

→ _____

6. 다음 주어진 문장과 의미가 같은 것은?

> Sam is not so diligent as his brother.

① His brother is very diligent.
② Sam is as diligent as his brother.
③ His brother is more diligent than Sam.
④ Sam is more diligent than his brother.
⑤ His brother is not so diligent as Sam.

[7-8] 다음 우리말과 같도록 빈칸에 알맞은 것을 고르시오.

7.

> 날씨가 점점 더 더워지고 있다.
> → It is getting _____.

① hot   ② hot and hot
③ hot and hotter   ④ hotter and hot
⑤ hotter and hotter

8.

> Anna는 그녀의 자매들보다 훨씬 더 우아하다.
> → Anna is _____ graceful than her sisters.

① much more   ② much very
③ very much   ④ more much
⑤ very more

9. 다음 중 의미가 나머지와 <u>다른</u> 것은?
① Tom is the tallest boy in my class.
② Tom is as tall as any other boy in my class.
③ No other boy in my class is taller than Tom.
④ Tom is taller than all the other boys in my class.
⑤ No other boy in my class is not as tall as Tom.

10. 다음 우리말과 같도록 괄호 안의 말을 이용하여 빈칸에 쓰시오.

> 그는 세상에서 가장 위대한 발명가 중 한 명이다.
> → He is _____ inventors in the world. (great)

→ _____

11. 다음 중 어법상 어색한 것은?
   ① Jason studied as hard as Jack.
   ② I came back early than my dad.
   ③ They should be more careful.
   ④ Korean is as important as English.
   ⑤ That box is much heavier than that one.

12. 다음 두 문장의 뜻이 같지 않은 것은?
   ① She ran as fast as possible.
      = She ran as fast as she could.
   ② The man is not taller than Kate.
      = Kate is taller than the man.
   ③ No other thing is as precious as time.
      = Time is the most precious thing.
   ④ Nothing is more important than health.
      = Nothing is as important as health.
   ⑤ Sue is the cleverest girl in her class.
      = Sue is even clever girl in her class.

13. 다음 중 빈칸에 공통으로 알맞은 말을?

> · I have as _____ money as you.
> · The sun is _____ bigger than the earth.

   ① much   ② very
   ③ more   ④ less
   ⑤ even

14. 다음 중 표의 내용과 일치하는 것은?

	Jane	Emma	Kevin
신장(cm)	155	180	175
몸무게(kg)	42	58	84

   ① Jane is as tall as Emma.
   ② Emma is heavier than Kevin.
   ③ Kevin is twice as heavy as Jane.
   ④ Kevin is the tallest of the three.
   ⑤ Emma is not so tall as Jane.

15. 다음 중 올바른 문장은?
   ① Her voice is louder than you.
   ② His car is biger than mine.
   ③ Busan is very hotter than Seoul.
   ④ I got a better score than I did before.
   ⑤ Can you exchange this shirt for a largest one?

16. 다음 문장의 빈칸에 공통으로 알맞은 말을 쓰시오.

> · The _____ I learn, the _____ I want to know.
> · She is _____ beautiful than cute.

→ _____

17. 다음 우리말을 바르게 영작한 것은?

> 이 연필은 저것보다 두 배 더 길다.

   ① This pencil is twice long that one.
   ② This pencil is twice long than that one.
   ③ This pencil is twice as long as that one.
   ④ This pencil is twice as longer as that one.
   ⑤ This pencil is twice longer as that one.

18. 다음 중 밑줄 친 부분이 올바른 것은?

① It's getting <u>warm and warm</u> in spring.
② He is one of <u>the richest man</u> in town.
③ He looks <u>happiest</u> when he eats something.
④ He is the <u>most famous</u> boy of the six.
⑤ This shirt is <u>very larger</u> than that one.

19. 다음 두 문장의 의미가 같도록 빈칸에 들어갈 말이 바르게 짝지어진 것은?

> As it got dark, it became cold.
> = The _____ it got, the _____ it became.

① dark - cold
② dark - colder
③ darker - cold
④ darker - colder
⑤ darkest - coldest

20. 다음 대화의 밑줄 친 부분에서 어법상 어색한 것은?

> Mother : What a beautiful day!
> James : Yes. Today is ①the best day in this week.
> Mother : Great. Look at ②the big tree.
> James : The tree is ③still taller than I. Now It is ④the tallest tree ⑤of our garden.
> Mother : Right. Three years ago, it was as tall as you.

〈서술형 문제〉

21. 다음 괄호 안의 말을 이용하여 우리말을 영작하시오.

> 그녀의 학교는 나의 학교보다 두 배 더 크다.
> (twice, as, big)

→ _____

22. 다음 두 문장이 같은 뜻이 되도록 바꿀 때, <u>잘못된</u> 부분을 고쳐 문장을 다시 쓰시오.

> If he leaves earlier, he will arrive sooner.
> = The early he leaves, the soon he will arrive.

→ _____

23. 다음 문장을 참고하여 문장의 빈칸에 알맞은 말을 쓰시오.

> Kate is 155cm tall. Nancy is 155cm.
> Lucy is 165cm tall.

(1) Kate is _____ Nancy.
(2) Nancy is _____ as Lucy.
(3) Kate is _____ than Lucy.

24. 다음 표의 가격을 보고, 괄호 안의 단어를 이용하여 각 문장을 완성하시오.

drinks	coffee	Latte	soda
price	$4	$5	$3

(1) Soda is _____ coffee. (than)
(2) Soda is _____ of all the drinks. (cheap)
(3) Latte is _____ coffee. (than)

25. 다음 밑줄 친 부분 중 어법상 <u>어색한</u> 것을 찾아 바르게 고쳐 쓰시오.

> The <u>largest</u> State in the US is Alaska. Most of it is forests and mountains. However it is a <u>very important</u> state to the US. The <u>second largest</u> State is Texas. Texas is three times <u>larger as</u> Korea. It is also <u>as important as</u> Alaska. It gives lots of oil to the US.

_____ → _____

관계사란 무엇인가?

관계사에는 관계대명사와 관계부사가 있으며, 관계대명사는 접속사와 대명사 역할을 하고, 관계부사는 접속사와 부사의 역할을 한다. 관계사는 앞에 있는 (대)명사를 수식하는 형용사절을 이끈다. 관계대명사와 관계부사에 -ever를 붙이면 복합관계대명사와 복합관계부사가 된다.

This is the purse **which** I am looking for. (관계대명사)

I remember the day **when** I first met you. (관계부사)

Whoever wins the game, I will be happy. (복합관계대명사)

관계대명사와 관계부사는 어떻게 쓰이는가?

선행사가 사람, 사물, 동물 등일 경우에는 관계대명사를 쓰고, 선행사가 시간, 장소, 이유, 방법일 때는 관계부사를 쓴다. 관계부사는 「전치사＋관계대명사」로 바꿔 쓸 수 있다.

I remember the day **when[= on which]** I first met you.

Chapter 8. 관계사

53 주격 관계대명사

- 관계대명사는 접속사와 대명사의 역할을 하며 관계대명사가 이끄는 절은 앞에 있는 명사(선행사)를 꾸며주는 역할을 한다. 관계대명사는 역할에 따라 주격, 소유격, 목적격으로 나뉜다.
- 관계대명사가 이끄는 절에서 관계대명사가 주어 역할을 하고 선행사가 사람일 때는 who, 선행사가 사물이나 동물일 때는 which를 쓴다.

선행사	주격 관계대명사	예문
사람	who/that	This is the girl. + She speaks English well. → This is the girl **who**[that] speaks English well.
사물, 동물	which/that	That is a machine. + It makes ice cream. → That is a machine **which**[that] makes ice cream.

* 주격 관계대명사 뒤에는 동사가 오며 동사는 선행사의 인칭과 수에 일치한다.
* 주격 관계대명사 who나 which는 관계대명사 that과 바꿔 쓸 수 있다.

 Practice

A. 다음 괄호 안에 알맞은 것을 고르시오.

1. We saw the man (who, which) rode a unicycle.

2. The oranges (who, that) are in the basket are fresh.

3. She is a teacher (that, which) teaches them science.

4. That's the dog (who, which) saved its owner from the fire.

B. 다음 우리말과 같도록 괄호 안의 말을 이용하여 문장을 완성하시오.

1. 너는 안경 쓴 그 소녀를 아니? (who)
   → Do you know the girl _____ _____ glasses?

2. 어린이들은 유익한 책들을 보고 있다. (which)
   → Children are reading books _____ _____ instructive.

3. 두더지는 땅 속에 사는 동물이다. (that)
   → A mole is an animal _____ _____ under the ground.

C. 다음 두 문장을 관계대명사를 이용하여 한 문장으로 쓰시오.

1. This is the woman. + She is a famous pianist.
   → _____

2. The bag belongs to Emma. + It was stolen.
   → _____

3. The people have just arrived there. + They are tourists.
   → _____

Grammar Tip

주격 관계대명사가 이끄는 절에서 주어는 선행사이기 때문에 동사는 선행사의 인칭과 수에 일치한다.

A. unicycle 외발자전거
owner 주인

B. instructive 유익한
mole 두더지

문장에서 선행사와 공통되는 부분을 찾아 관계대명사로 연결한다.

C. pianist 피아니스트
belong 속하다

Unit

54 | 소유격 관계대명사

- 선행사가 관계대명사절에서 관계대명사 뒤의 명사와 소유 관계일 때 whose를 사용하며 「소유격 관계대명사+명사
+동사」의 어순이다.

선행사	소유격 관계대명사	예문
사람, 사물, 동물	whose	I know the boy. + His mother is an actress. → I know the boy **whose mother** is an actress.

*소유격 관계대명사 뒤에는 명사가 온다.

- 선행사가 사물일 때 문어적 표현으로 of which를 이용하여 나타내기도 한다.

The people look at the house. The wall of it is white.

→ The people look at the house **of which the wall** is white.

= The people look at the house **whose wall** is white.

Practice

A. 다음 괄호 안에 알맞은 것을 고르시오.

1. Look at the roof (which, whose) top is covered with snow.

2. He is the student (who, whose) play baseball well.

3. Tom has a car (which, whose) engine is silent.

4. Alice has a brother (who, whose) dream is to be a pilot.

5. I lost a pen (of which, which) the case is silver.

B. 다음 우리말과 같도록 괄호 안의 말을 이용하여 문장을 완성하시오.

1. 표지가 초록색인 책은 John의 것이다. (cover)

→ The book _____ _____ is green is Jone's.

2. 나는 취미가 그리기인 소년을 알고 있다. (hobby)

→ I know the boy _____ _____ is drawing.

3. 나는 머리가 허리까지 내려오는 여자를 보았다. (hair)

→ I saw a woman _____ _____ came down to her waist.

C. 다음 두 문장을 관계대명사를 이용하여 한 문장으로 쓰시오.

1. Alex has a friend. + Her name is Kelly.

→ _____

2. This is the hat. + The price of the hat is very high.

→ _____

3. He is the man. + His birthday is today.

→ _____

4. I have a neighbor. + His brother lives in Germany.

→ _____

Grammar Tip

주격 관계대명사 뒤에는 동사가 오고 소유격 관계대명사 뒤에는 명사가 온다.

A. engine 엔진
case 케이스, 용기

선행사가 관계대명사 뒤의 명사와 소유 관계일 때는 whose를 쓴다.

B. cover 표지
hobby 취미
waist 허리

C. price 가격
neighbor 이웃
Germany 독일

unit 55 목적격 관계대명사

· 관계대명사가 관계사절에서 목적어로 쓰일 때 선행사가 사람이면 whom(who), 선행사가 사물이면 which를 쓴다. 관계대명사가 이끄는 절에서 목적어 역할을 관계대명사가 한다.

선행사	목적격 관계대명사	예문
사람	whom/who/that	She is the woman. + I met her at the meeting. → She is the woman **who(m)** I met at the meeting. = She is the woman **that** I met at the meeting.
사물, 동물	which/that	This is a smartphone. + I bought it yesterday. → This is a smartphone **which** I bought yesterday. = This is a smartphone **that** I bought yesterday.

＊ 관계대명사가 목적격으로 쓰인 경우에는 생략이 가능하다.
＊ 목적격 관계대명사 whom(who)나 which는 관계대명사 that과 바꿔 쓸 수 있다.

Practice

A. 다음 괄호 안에 알맞은 것을 고르시오.

1. Is this the ring (whom, which) he gave to you?

2. She is the girl (who, which) Karen introduced to me.

3. The movie (who, that) I saw last night was interesting.

4. That's the man (whom, which) we invited to the party.

5. I bought the backpack (who, that) you mentioned then.

B. 다음 우리말과 같도록 괄호 안의 말을 이용하여 문장을 완성하시오.

1. 이것은 내가 갖고 싶었던 손목시계이다. (want)
   → This is the watch _____ _____ _____ to buy.

2. 나는 그녀가 대화하고 있는 그 여자를 안다. (be)
   → I know the woman _____ _____ _____ talking with.

3. 우리가 지난달에 방문했던 미술관은 닫았다. (visit)
   → The gallery _____ _____ _____ last month is closed.

C. 다음 두 문장을 관계대명사를 이용하여 한 문장으로 쓰시오.

1. This is the music. + He likes it the most.
   → _____

2. The songs are so sweet. + He composed them for her.
   → _____

3. The man is my nephew. + They saw him in my house.
   → _____

4. What is the title of the novel? + You read it recently.
   → _____

Grammar Tip

목적격 관계대명사가 이끄는 절은 「목적격 관계대명사＋주어＋동사」의 어순이며 관계대명사가 목적어 역할을 한다.

A. introduce 소개하다
   mention 언급하다

B. watch 손목시계
   gallery 미술관

관계대명사절은 선행사를 수식하는 역할을 하기 때문에 주어와 동사의 관계를 잘 파악해야 한다.

C. compose 작곡하다
   nephew (남자) 조카
   title 제목
   recently 최근에

56 | 관계대명사 what

· 관계대명사 what은 선행사를 포함하는 관계대명사로 what(= the thing(s) which[that])이 이끄는 관계대명사절은 문장에서 주어, 목적어, 보어 역할을 하며 '~하는 것(들)'로 해석한다.

관계대명사	예문
선행사를 포함하는 관계대명사 what = the thing(s) which[that]	What[The thing which] I said is true. 〈주어〉 I know what[the thing that] she wants. 〈목적어〉 This is what I have been looking for. 〈보어〉

＊관계대명사 what은 선행사를 포함하는 관계대명사로 형용사절이 아닌 명사절을 이끈다.

· 관계대명사 what은 선행사가 없다는 점에서 접속사 that과 혼동을 할 수 있는데, 접속사 that은 지칭하는 것과 뜻이 없지만, what은 명사의 역할을 한다.

I didn't know what you wanted. 〈관계사절에서 목적어를 포함하고 있다.〉

I didn't know that you wanted the bike. 〈that을 빼도 완전한 문장이 된다.〉

A. 다음 괄호 안에서 알맞은 것을 고르시오.

1. (What, That) is important is to do your best.
2. That is the house (what, which) he built himself.
3. Please show me (what, which) is in your pocket.
4. This is the thing (what, that) the singer gave to me.
5. (What, Which) I want from you is a sincere apology.

B. 다음 문장에서 <u>틀린</u> 부분을 찾아 바르게 고쳐 쓰시오.

1. The thing what we really need is time. _____
2. We will remember that you have done for us. _____
3. That he told me turned out to be true. _____
4. We found what the man would come here. _____
5. I understand that he is talking about now. _____

C. 다음 밑줄 친 부분에 유의하여 문장을 우리말로 해석하시오.

1. <u>What</u> did he buy yesterday? _____
2. This is <u>what</u> he bought yesterday. _____

D. 다음 우리말과 같도록 괄호 안의 말을 이용하여 문장을 완성하시오.

1. 그들은 내가 충고한 것을 듣지 않았다. (advise)
   → They didn't listen to _____ _____ _____.
2. 그가 말하는 것과 그가 행동하는 것이 다르다. (say, do)
   → _____ _____ _____ is different from _____ _____ _____.

Grammar Tip

관계대명사 what은 선행사를 포함하고 있으며 the thing(s) which[that]으로 바꾸어 쓸 수 있다.

A. pocket 주머니
sincere 진정한, 진심 어린
apology 사과

B. turn out 증명하다
understand 이해하다

의문대명사 what은 의문문을 만들고, 관계대명사 what은 두 문장을 연결하는 연결사로 선행사를 포함하고 있다.

D. advise 충고하다
different 다른

A. 다음 문장의 괄호 안에서 알맞은 것을 고르시오.

1. The movie (who, which) I saw last week was impressive.
2. Who is the student (whom, whose) nickname is 'Angel'?
3. This is (that, what) they wanted yesterday.
4. I know the girl (who, whom) is sitting on the chair.

B. 다음 문장의 밑줄 친 부분을 바르게 고쳐 쓰시오.

1. Show me <u>that</u> you bought at the shop. _____
2. You can see the man <u>whom</u> is standing at the gate.

_____
3. He knows the person <u>whose</u> stole the car. _____
4. <u>Which</u> I need now is a good night's sleep. _____

C. 다음 문장의 빈칸에 알맞은 관계대명사를 쓰시오.

1. He lent a book _____ cover was blue.
2. This is the picture _____ I like the most.
3. They cannot believe _____ she said.
4. This is the woman _____ Susan saw at the party.

D. 다음 두 문장을 관계대명사를 이용하여 한 문장으로 쓰시오.

1. He wants a new car. + The roof of the car can be open.

→ _____

2. I read a magazine. + It was full of exciting stories.

→ _____

3. We are looking for the man. + He was called Jackson.

→ _____

E. 다음 우리말과 같도록 괄호 안의 말을 이용하여 문장을 완성하시오.

1. 우울증을 앓는 많은 사람들이 있다. (suffer)

→ There are many people _____ _____ from depression.

2. 당신 손에 갖고 있는 것을 줄 수 있나요? (have)

→ Can you give me _____ _____ _____ in your hand?

3. 이 책은 모국어가 영어가 아닌 학생들을 위한 것이다. (mother tongue)

→ This book is for students _____ _____ _____ is not English.

Grammar Tip

관계대명사로 선행사가 사람이면 who를, 사물이나 동물이면 which를 쓰며 who와 which는 that으로 쓸 수 있다.

A. impressive 인상적인
   nickname 별명

관계대명사 what은 선행사를 포함하고 있으면 '~하는 것'으로 해석한다.

B. gate 대문, 정문

C. lend 빌리다
   believe 믿다

D. open 열린
   look for ~을 찾다

주격 관계대명사 뒤에는 동사가 오고, 소유 관계를 나타내는 소유격 관계대명사 뒤에는 명사가 온다.

E. suffer 고생하다, 앓다
   depression 우울증
   mother tongue 모국어

57 관계대명사 that을 쓰는 경우

- 관계대명사 that은 주격, 목적격의 모든 관계대명사와 바꾸어 쓸 수 있다.
  She is the girl **that(= who)** plays the piano well.

- 선행사에 따라 관계대명사 that을 써야 하는 경우가 있다.

선행사가 '사람+동물[사물]'일 때	Look at the boy and his dog **that** are running in the park.
선행사 앞에 최상급, 서수, the only, the very, the same, all, no, every, any, -thing 등이 올 때	It was the best pizza **that** I have ever eaten. Brian is the only person **that** she likes.
의문문에서 의문사가 사용된 경우	Who stole the bike **that** Sam bought yesterday?

- 관계대명사 that은 소유격이나 전치사의 목적어, 계속적 용법으로 쓰일 수도 없다. (Unit 58, 59)
  That is the house **in that** he was born. (×) → **in which** (○)

 Practice

A. 다음 괄호 안에 알맞은 것을 모두 고르시오.

1. This is the best restaurant (who, which, that) I know.
2. The problem (who, which, that) we have is money.
3. Who is the woman (who, which, that) has blonde hair?
4. I know the old man (who, which, that) won the race.
5. This is the same watch (what, which, that) she gave me.
6. He didn't say anything (who, which, that) we want to know.

B. 다음 우리말과 같도록 괄호 안의 주어진 단어를 이용하여 완성하시오.

1. 그는 내가 믿는 유일한 사람이다. (only)
   → He is _____ _____ _____ _____ I trust.

2. Jane은 내가 본 가장 키가 큰 여자이다. (tall)
   → Jane is _____ _____ _____ _____ I've ever seen.

3. 그들은 그들이 필요한 모든 것을 가지고 있다. (everything)
   → They _____ _____ _____ they need.

C. 다음 두 문장을 관계대명사 that을 이용하여 한 문장으로 쓰시오.

1. He is the first man. + He invented the phone.
   → _____

2. She is the smartest girl. + She goes to this school.
   → _____

3. You may borrow any book. + You want it.
   → _____

Grammar Tip

의문문에서 의문사로 who나 which가 사용된 경우에는 관계대명사 that을 쓴다.

A. problem 문제
blonde 금발의
race 경주

선행사 앞에 최상급, 서수, the only, the very, the same, all, no, every, any, -thing 등이 올 때 관계대명사 that을 쓴다.

B. trust 신뢰하다

C. invent 발명하다
borrow 빌리다

58 관계대명사의 용법

· 관계대명사는 제한적 용법과 계속적 용법이 있다.

제한적 용법	관계대명사절이 선행사를 수식하여 그 의미를 한정할 때 쓴다.
	I know the man **who** is a good doctor. (그 남자를 한정해 줌.)
계속적 용법	관계대명사절이 선행사의 의미를 보충 설명할 때 쓴다. 선행사 뒤에 콤마(,)를 쓰고 「접속사+대명사」로 바꿀 수 있다.
	I know the man, **who** is a good doctor. (그 남자에 대해 정보 제공함.)

* 관계대명사 that과 what은 계속적 용법으로 쓸 수 없다.

· 계속적 용법에서 앞에 나온 구나 절이 선행사가 되는 경우에는 관계대명사 which를 쓴다.

The girls wanted to come here, **which** was impossible.

Practice

A. 다음 문장의 빈칸에 알맞은 관계대명사를 쓰시오.

1. My sister, _____ is a teacher, lives in New Zealand.
2. I don't like the man, _____ is very lazy.
3. The barn, _____ my father built, needs repairing.
4. I know the boy, _____ sister is studying medical science.
5. She tried to persuade her parents, _____ was useless.

B. 다음 두 문장이 같은 뜻이 되도록 〈보기〉의 접속사를 이용하여 문장을 완성하시오.

〈보기〉 and	but	for

1. We like Mark, who is kind and smart.
   → We like Mark, _____ _____ is kind and smart.
2. He tried to open the door, which he found impossible.
   → He tried to open the door, _____ he found _____ impossible.
3. She bought a new car, which was very expensive.
   → She bought a new car, _____ _____ was very expensive.

C. 다음 우리말과 같도록 괄호 안의 말을 이용하여 문장을 완성하시오.

1. Amy는 시험에 합격했고, 그것은 우리를 놀라게 했다. (surprise)
   → Amy passed the exam, _____ _____ us.
2. Cathy는 나의 직장 동료인데, 병원에 입원해 있다. (be)
   → Cathy, _____ _____ my colleague, is in the hospital.
3. Joe는 늦게 집에 왔고, 그것이 그의 엄마를 화나게 했다. (make)
   → Joe came home late, _____ _____ his mom angry.

Grammar Tip

제한적 용법은 관계대명사절이 선행사를 수식하는 구조로 해석하고, 계속적 용법일 때에는 앞에서부터 차례로 해석한다.

A. lazy 게으른
repairing 보수, 수선
medical 의학의
persuade 설득하다

관계대명사 계속적 용법은 「접속사+대명사」로 바꾸어 쓸 수 있다.

B. impossible 불가능한

C. surprise 놀라게 하다
colleague 직장 동료
in the hospital 입원하여

Unit 59 전치사+관계대명사

· 관계대명사가 전치사의 목적어일 때, 전치사는 관계대명사 앞이나 관계대명사절 끝에 온다.

관계대명사가 전치사의 목적어일 때		
전치사가 관계대명사절 끝에 오는 경우	who/whom/that/which	The girl **who(m)** I talked **to** is her sister. = The girl **that** I talked **to** is her sister.
전치사가 관계대명사 앞에 오는 경우	「전치사+whom(사람)」 또는 「전치사+which(사물)」 *「전치사+who[that]」는 쓸 수 없다.	= The girl **to whom** I talked is her sister. The girl **to who[that]** I talked is her sister. (×)
관계대명사가 목적격으로 쓰여 생략 가능한 경우	관계대명사를 생략할 경우 전치사는 관계대명사절 뒤에 둔다.	= The girl I talked **to** is her sister. The girl **to** I talked is her sister. (×)

Practice

A. 다음 괄호 안에 알맞은 것을 고르시오.

1. This is the bank (which, at which) my brother works.

2. This is the problem (in which, in that) we are interested.

3. Kate is the girl (with, with whom) I share a dorm room.

4. The bed (in, for) which we slept was too hard.

5. That's a subject (from, about) which I have never thought.

B. 다음 우리말과 같도록 전치사를 이용하여 문장을 완성하시오.

1. 그들이 사는 마을은 매우 조용하다.
   → The town _____ _____ they live is very quiet.

2. 그는 Ann과 함께 파티에 온 남자이다.
   → He is the man _____ _____ Ann came to the party.

3. 그는 내가 찾고 있었던 그 소년이다.
   → He is the boy _____ _____ I was looking.

C. 다음 두 문장을 「전치사+관계대명사」 형태의 한 문장으로 쓰시오.

1. The music was very good. + We listened to it.
   → _____

2. I have found the data. + I was looking for it.
   → _____

3. The colored pencil is red. + John is writing with it.
   → _____

Grammar Tip

관계대명사가 전치사의 목적어일 경우에는 전치사의 위치에 따른 관계대명사의 사용에 주의한다.

A. share 나누다
dorm 기숙사

관계대명사절에서 동사와 함께 쓰는 전치사를 생략하지 않도록 주의한다.
listen to ~을 듣다
wait for ~를 기다리다
write with ~을 가지고 쓰다
look for ~을 찾다

B. quiet 조용한

C. data 자료, 데이터
colored pencil 색연필

Unit 60 관계대명사의 생략

· 문장에서 목적격 관계대명사는 생략할 수 있어 생략한 형태로 쓰는 경우가 많다.

생략이 가능한 경우	제한적 용법의 목적격 관계대명사	London is the city (**which**) he was born in.
	「주격 관계대명사+be동사」	The woman (**who is**) wearing a pink hat is my sister.
생략이 불가능한 경우	계속적 용법의 목적격 관계대명사	London is the city, **which** he was born in.
	제한적 용법의 목적격 관계대명사 앞에 전치사가 있는 경우	London is the city **in which** he was born.

* 「주격 관계대명사+be동사」가 생략된 경우 남은 분사구가 명사를 뒤에서 수식한다.
This is the book (**which was**) written by Hemingway.

Practice

A. 다음 문장에서 생략할 수 있는 부분에 밑줄 그으시오.

1. The chair which Harry is sitting on is broken.

2. Look at the player who is jogging at the playground.

3. Do you know the woman who is talking to Paul?

4. He fell in love with Alice whom he met yesterday.

B. 다음 우리말과 같도록 빈칸에 알맞은 말을 쓰시오.

1. 영어로 쓰여진 많은 책들을 읽어라.
   → Read many _____ _____ in English.

2. 기타를 연주하는 저 소년은 나의 친척이다.
   → That boy, _____ _____ _____ is my relative.

3. 이것은 내가 우울할 때 듣는 음악이다.
   → This is the song _____ _____ I listen when I am depressed.

C. 다음 두 문장을 관계대명사를 이용하여 한 문장으로 쓰시오.
(관계대명사가 생략된 형태로 쓸 것)

1. Look at the bright stars. + They are shining in the sky.
   → _____

2. The bread is delicious. + He bought it yesterday.
   → _____

3. I have a watch. + It was made in Switzerland.
   → _____

4. The girl is my cousin. + She is surprised at the news.
   → _____

Grammar Tip

제한적 용법의 목적격 관계대명사는 생략하여 쓸 수 있다.

A. broken 고장 난
playground 운동장
fall in love with
~와 사랑에 빠지다

목적격 관계대명사 앞에 전치사가 있는 경우에는 관계대명사를 생략할 수 없다.

B. relative 친척
depressed 우울한

C. bright 밝은
shine 빛나다
Switzerland 스위스

A. 다음 괄호 안에 알맞은 것을 고르시오.

1. This is the only camera (that, which) she has.
2. She is the prettiest girl (that, who) I've ever seen.
3. We have two daughters, (that, who) became doctors.
4. The club (to which, which) he belongs is famous.
5. I can't remember the hotel (at that, at which) we stayed.

B. 다음 두 문장이 같도록 <보기>의 접속사를 이용하여 문장을 완성하시오.

<보기> and	but	for

1. This is a new bike, which was made in Germany.
   → This is a new bike, _____ _____ was made in Germany.
2. We like the show, which is very fun and exciting.
   → We like the show, _____ _____ is very fun and exciting.
3. Leo is my classmate, who I don't like.
   → Leo is my classmate, _____ I don't like _____.

C. 다음 두 문장을 관계대명사를 이용하여 한 문장으로 쓰시오.
(관계대명사가 생략된 형태로 쓸 것)

1. Look at the children. + They are holding balloons.
   → _____
2. I will meet Jake. + We talked about him yesterday.
   → _____
3. Is this a drama? + It was written by Shakespeare.
   → _____
4. Wastes pollute water. + They are carried from land to sea.
   → _____

D. 다음 우리말과 같도록 괄호 안의 말을 이용하여 문장을 완성하시오.

1. Jason은 그것을 할 수 있는 유일한 사람이다. (person)
   → Jason is the _____ _____ _____ can do it.
2. 그녀는 내가 알고 싶은 것을 아무것도 말해 주지 않는다. (anything)
   → She doesn't say _____ _____ I want to know.
3. 나는 그 열쇠를 찾으려고 노력했지만, 불가능했다. (impossible)
   → I tried to find the key, _____ was _____.
4. 그들은 눈 덮인 산 위로 오르고 있었다. (cover)
   → They climbed up the mountain _____ _____ snow.

Grammar Tip

전치사가 관계대명사 앞에 쓰인 경우 관계대명사 that이나 who는 쓸 수 없다.

A. belong to ~에 속하다
   stay 머무르다

관계대명사의 계속적 용법은 관계대명사절이 선행사에 대해 부가적인 설명을 할 때 사용한다.

B. Germany 독일
   classmate 반 친구, 급우

목적격 관계대명사와 「주격 관계대명사+be동사」는 문장에서 생략할 수 있다.

C. hold 잡다
   balloon 풍선
   drama 연극
   pollute 오염시키다

D. anything 아무것
   impossible 불가능한
   climb 오르다

Unit 61 관계부사 when, where

- 관계부사는 접속사와 부사 역할을 하면서 관계부사가 이끄는 절 안에서 선행사를 대신하여 부사 역할을 한다. 「전치사＋관계대명사」를 관계부사로 바꿀 수 있다.

선행사	관계부사	전치사＋관계대명사	예문
시간 (the time)	when	in[at] which	I remember the day. + I met you on the day. → I remember the day **when** I met you. = I remember the day **on which** I met you. = I remember the day **which** I met you **on**.
장소 (the place)	where	in[at, on] which	This is the house. + I live in the house. → This is the house **where** I live. = This is the house **in which** I live. = This is the house **which** I live **in**.

＊ when, where의 관계부사절도 콤마(,)를 이용하여 계속적 용법으로 쓸 수 있다.

- 관계대명사와 관계부사의 차이 : 관계대명사절은 불완전한 문장이고 관계부사절은 완전한 문장이다.

This is the town **which** I visited two years ago. (목적어가 빠짐 / 관계대명사)

This is the town **where** my parents got married. (빠진 문장 성문 없음 / 관계부사)

Practice

A. 다음 괄호 안에서 알맞은 것을 고르시오.

1. This is the place (which, where) they can play.

2. I can't forget the day (when, where) Tom was born.

3. July is the month (which, when) people go on vacation.

4. I remember the summer (which, in which) I went camping.

B. 다음 밑줄 친 부분을 알맞게 고쳐 쓰시오.

1. This is the place <u>when</u> I park my bike. _____

2. This is the city <u>where</u> we visited last year. _____

3. Tell me the <u>place</u> when the next train will leave. _____

4. Is there any store in <u>where</u> I can buy some stamps? _____

C. 다음 두 문장을 관계부사를 이용하여 한 문장으로 쓰시오.

1. The room was uncomfortable. + We slept in the room.
→ _____

2. Friday was the day. + They heard the news on the day.
→ _____

3. Winter is a season. + We go skiing in this season.
→ _____

4. This is the river. + The man often goes fishing in the river.
→ _____

Grammar Tip

관계부사는 접속사와 부사 역할을 하며 「전치사＋관계대명사」로 바꿀 수 있다.

A. vacation 휴가
camping 캠핑

B. park 주차하다
stamp 우표

관계부사절에서 관계부사는 문장 구성 요소가 아니기 때문에 관계부사를 빼고 해석해도 완전한 문장이 된다.

C. uncomfortable 불편한
hear 듣다
season 계절

62 관계부사 why, how

- 관계부사에는 when과 where 외에도 why와 how가 있는데, 관계부사를 결정할 때는 앞에 선행사로 어떤 것이 쓰였는지에 따라 달라진다. 관계부사를 「전치사+관계대명사」로 바꿀 수 있다.
- 선행사가 the way일 때는 선행사(the way)와 관계부사 how 중 하나만 쓴다.

선행사	관계부사	전치사+관계대명사	예문
이유 (the reason)	why	for which	I know the reason. + He left her for the reason. → I know the reason **why** he left her. = I know the reason **for which** he left her.
방법 (the way)	how	in which	Tell me the way. + You won the race in the way. → Tell me the way **in which** you won the race. = Tell me **how** you won the race. = Tell me the way you won the race. ＊ Tell me **the way how** you won the race. (×)

＊관계부사 why의 경우에도 the reason why를 쓰기 보다는 the reason이나 why 중 하나를 생략하고 쓰는 경우가 많다.

 Practice

A. 다음 괄호 안에서 알맞은 것을 고르시오.

1. Nobody knows the reason (in, for) which she quit her job.
2. I will show him (why, how) I memorize English words.
3. Do you know (the reason, the way) why he is angry?
4. That was the way (how, in which) I solved the problem.
5. I don't know the reason (how, why) she isn't talking to me.

B. 다음 우리말과 같도록 빈칸에 알맞은 말을 쓰시오.

1. 이것이 내가 나의 옷장을 정리하는 방법이다.
   → This is _____ _____ I organize the stuff in my closet.

2. 당신이 오지 않았던 이유를 설명해 보세요.
   → Please explain the _____ _____ you didn't come.

3. Nick은 컴퓨터로 작성하는 방법을 알고 있다.
   → Nick knows the _____ _____ _____ computers work.

C. 다음 두 문장을 관계부사를 이용하여 한 문장으로 쓰시오.

1. Tell me the way. + You made this robot in the way.
   → _____

2. We knows the reason. + He refuses to eat for the reason.
   → _____

3. He shows me the way. + Airbags work in the way.
   → _____

Grammar Tip

선행사가 the way일 경우 선행사 the way와 관계부사 how 중 하나만 써야 한다.

A. quit 그만두다, 멈추다
memorize 암기하다
solve 풀다

B. organize 정리하다
stuff 물건, 것(들)
closet 벽장, 수납실
work 작동하다

C. refuse 거절하다, 거부하다
airbag 에어백

Unit 63 관계부사와 선행사의 생략

- 관계부사 where를 제외한 나머지 관계부사는 관계부사절에서 관계부사를 생략할 수 있다.
  I don't know the reason (**why**) she left me.

- 관계부사 앞에 the place, the time, the reason 같은 일반적인 의미의 선행사가 오는 경우 선행사를 생략하여 관계부사만 두는 경우가 많다. → 이 경우 관계부사절은 명사절이 된다.

선행사+관계부사 형용사절	관계부사절은 앞에 있는 선행사를 수식하는 형용사절 This is **the place where** I usually park my car. 　　　　　　선행사　　　　관계부사절(= 형용사절)
(선행사 생략) 관계부사 명사절	관계부사절은 선행사 대신 명사절이 되어 주어, 목적어, 보어 역할 This is **where** I usually park my car. 　　　관계부사절(= 보어 역할을 하는 명사절)

＊관계부사 how는 선행사 the way와 how 중 하나를 반드시 생략해야 한다.

Practice

A. 다음 밑줄 친 부분을 알맞게 고쳐 쓰시오.

1. Can you show me <u>the way how</u> you dance?　＿＿＿＿＿＿

2. He knows the reason <u>when</u> you should apologize to her.
   ＿＿＿＿＿＿

3. I know the <u>day</u> where the accident happened.　＿＿＿＿＿＿

B. 다음 우리말과 같도록 빈칸에 알맞은 말을 쓰시오.

1. 이곳이 내가 손수건을 잃어버린 곳이다.
   → This is ＿＿＿＿＿ I lost my handkerchief.

2. 그는 어제 화가 난 이유를 말하지 않았다.
   → He didn't say ＿＿＿＿ ＿＿＿＿ he was upset yesterday.

3. 너는 다음 기차가 도착할 시간을 알고 있니?
   → Do you know ＿＿＿＿ ＿＿＿＿ the next train will arrive?

4. 불타는 차에서 탈출했던 방법을 말해 주세요.
   → Tell me ＿＿＿＿ ＿＿＿＿ you escaped from the burning car.

C. 다음 문장을 생략된 관계부사나 선행사를 넣어 다시 쓰시오.

1. August 27th is the day the second semester starts.
   → ＿＿＿＿＿＿＿＿＿＿＿＿＿＿＿＿＿＿＿＿＿＿

2. Tony wants to know where Julia lives.
   → ＿＿＿＿＿＿＿＿＿＿＿＿＿＿＿＿＿＿＿＿＿＿

3. She tells me the reason Jay made such a decision.
   → ＿＿＿＿＿＿＿＿＿＿＿＿＿＿＿＿＿＿＿＿＿＿

Grammar Tip

A. accident 사건, 사고
apologize 사과하다

where를 제외하고 나머지 관계부사는 선행사와 관계부사 중 하나를 생략할 수 있다.

B. handkerchief 손수건
escape 탈출하다
burning 불타는

C. second semester 2학기
decision 결정

Unit 64 복합관계대명사

• 복합관계대명사는 관계대명사에 -ever를 붙인 형태로 '어떤 ~라도(= any)'라는 뜻의 선행사를 포함하며 명사절이나 양보의 부사절을 이끈다.

복합관계대명사	명사절	양보의 부사절
who(m)ever	anyone who(m) (~하는 사람은 누구든지)	no matter who(m) (누가 ~하든지)
whichever	any one that (~하는 것은 어느 것이든지)	no matter which (어느 것이 ~하더라도)
whatever	anything that (~하는 것은 무엇이든지)	no matter what (무엇을 ~하든지)

〈명사절〉 **Whoever** comes will be welcome. (= **Anyone who**)

　　　　Choose **whichever** you like. (= **any one that**)

　　　　Take **whatever** you want. (= **anything that**)

〈부사절〉 **Whatever** you say, I'll not listen to you. (= **No matter what**)

* 복합관계대명사가 이끄는 양보를 나타내는 부사절은 콤마(,)에 의해 주절과 분리된다.

Practice

A. 다음 괄호 안에서 알맞은 것을 고르시오.

1. Give the bag to (who, whoever) wants it.

2. You can invite (whomever, whichever) you like.

3. (Whoever, Whatever) comes first will be served first.

4. (Whatever, Whichever) happens, come back by ten o'clock.

B. 다음 두 문장이 같은 뜻이 되도록 빈칸에 알맞은 말을 쓰시오.

1. No matter what you do, you need courage.
   → _____ you do, you need courage.

2. Choose any one that you want to have.
   → Choose _____ you want to have.

3. Whatever they call me, I don't care.
   → _____ _____ _____ they call me, I don't care.

C. 다음 우리말과 같도록 빈칸에 알맞은 말을 쓰시오.

1. 누가 그 경기를 이기더라도, 나는 행복할 것이다.
   → _____ wins the game, I will be happy.

2. 우리가 뭐라고 말을 해도, 그녀는 마음을 바꾸지 않을 것이다.
   → _____ _____ _____ we say, she won't change her mind.

3. 나와 같이 가기를 원하는 사람은 누구든지 데려갈 것이다.
   → I'll take _____ _____ wants to go with me.

Grammar Tip

복합관계대명사는 관계대명사에 -ever를 붙인 형태로 선행사를 포함하고 있다.

A. serve 제공하다

복합관계대명사는 명사절이나 양보의 부사절을 이끄는데 복합관계대명사절 뒤에 콤마(,)가 오면 양보를 나타낸다.

B. courage 용기
　 care 신경 쓰다

C. change 바꾸다
　 mind 마음

113

Unit 65 복합관계부사

• 복합관계부사는 관계부사에 -ever를 붙인 형태로 선행사를 포함하며 시간이나 장소의 부사절과 양보의 부사절을 이끈다.

복합관계대명사	시간, 장소의 부사절	양보의 부사절
whenever	at any time when / every time (~할 때는 언제든지 / ~할 때마다)	no matter when (언제 ~하든지)
wherever	at any place where / every place (~하는 곳은 어디든지 / ~하는 곳마다)	no matter where (어디서 ~하든지)
however	–	no matter how (아무리 ~해도)

Come to see me **whenever** you like. (= **at any time that**)
You will be welcome **whenever** you come. (= **no matter when**)
Whenever she comes, she brings a friend. (= **every time**)
You may go **wherever** you want. (= **at any place that**)
However humble it may be, there is no place like home. (= **No matter how**)
* however는 「however+형용사[부사]+주어+동사」의 형태로 '아무리 ~해도'라는 뜻이다.

Practice

A. 다음 괄호 안에서 알맞은 것을 고르시오.
1. (Where, Wherever) you are, they will find you.
2. I'll be there for you (wherever, whenever) you need me.
3. (However, How) rich they are, they can't buy the building.
4. Call me at any time (when, whenever) you are free.

B. 다음 문장을 복합관계부사를 이용하여 문장을 다시 쓰시오.
1. No matter where you go, you must exercise every day.
   → _____
2. No matter how fast he ran, he couldn't catch the thief.
   → _____
3. Every time the kid sees me, she bursts into tears.
   → _____

C. 다음 우리말과 같도록 빈칸에 알맞은 말을 쓰시오.
1. 그녀는 아무리 많이 먹더라도, 결코 살이 찌지 않는다.
   → _____ much she eats, she never gets fat.
2. 그 배우는 방문하는 곳마다 많은 사람들을 만난다.
   → _____ the actor visits, he meets many people.
3. 네가 아무리 열심히 해도, 결과는 같을 것이다.
   → _____ _____ _____ _____ you do, the effect
   will be the same.

Grammar Tip

복합관계부사 however는 문장에서 「however+형용사+주어+동사」의 형태로 양보의 부사절을 이끈다.

A. building 빌딩
   free 한가한

B. thief 도둑
   burst into 갑자기 ~하다
   tear 눈물

복합관계부사는 선행사를 포함하고 있기 때문에 문장에서 선행사가 없다.

C. actor 배우
   effect 결과

A. 다음 문장의 괄호 안에서 알맞은 것을 고르시오.

1. The place (where, which) we spent the beach was nice.
2. Do you know the reason for (why, which) she is sad?
3. Please tell me (how, what) we handle the machine.
4. I don't know the time (when, where) the train left.

B. 다음 문장의 밑줄 친 부분을 바르게 고쳐 쓰시오.

1. I don't like the way in <u>how</u> she talks. _____
2. He was born in the year <u>which</u> the war ended. _____
3. This is the house <u>where</u> James lives in. _____
4. I wonder the reason <u>how</u> he did't do his homework.
   _____

C. 다음 <보기>에서 알맞은 것을 골라 빈칸에 쓰시오.

<보기> whenever   whoever   wherever   whatever   however

1. I will give you _____ you need.
2. _____ tired she is, she always smiles.
3. Take your cell phone with you _____ you go.
4. We will welcome you _____ you come here.
5. _____ wishes to join the club should fill out the form.

D. 다음 두 문장이 같은 뜻이 되도록 빈칸에 알맞은 말을 쓰시오.

1. I remember the time in which you broke your arm.
   = I remember the time _____ you broke your arm.

2. I'll do anything that is good for you.
   = I'll do _____ is good for you.

3. However much it costs, she'll buy the clothes.
   = _____ _____ _____ much it costs, she'll buy the clothes.

E. 다음 우리말과 같도록 괄호 안의 단어를 이용하여 문장을 완성하시오.

1. 당신이 그 퍼즐을 풀었던 방법을 나에게 알려 주세요. (tell)
   → _____ _____ _____ you solved the puzzle.

2. 이 게임을 이기는 사람이 누구든 챔피언이 될 것이다. (win)
   → _____ _____ this game will be the champion.

3. 당신이 나의 도움이 필요할 때마다, 당신과 있을 것이다. (need)
   → _____ _____ you _____ my help, I'll be with you.

Grammar Tip

관계부사는 「전치사＋관계대명사」를 대신하는 말로 접속사와 부사 역할을 한다.

A. handle 다루다
   machine 기계

B. end 끝나다
   wonder 궁금하다

복합관계사의 형태는 「관계사＋ -ever」로 선행사를 포함하며 명사절이나 부사절을 이끈다.

C. cell phone 핸드폰
   welcome 환영하다
   fill out 작성하다
   form 양식

D. arm 팔
   cost (비용이) 들다

선행사가 the way일 때는 선행사 the way와 관계부사 how 중 하나만 쓴다.

C. puzzle 퍼즐
   champion 챔피언

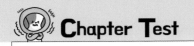 

[1~2] 다음 빈칸에 알맞은 것을 고르시오.

1.
> I know the boy _____ dad is disabled.

① who   ② which
③ whose   ④ that
⑤ what

2.
> It doesn't matter why she did that. Show me _____ she did that.

① what   ② who
③ when   ④ why
⑤ how

3. 다음 밑줄 친 부분의 쓰임이 나머지와 다른 것은?
① She has a son <u>who</u> is a soldier.
② I don't know a girl <u>who</u> plays the piano.
③ <u>Which</u> do you like better, tea or coffee?
④ The car <u>which</u> is made in Germany is very expensive.
⑤ Look at the people <u>who</u> are waiting for the taxi.

4. 다음 빈칸에 공통으로 알맞은 것은?
> · This is _____ I want to eat.
> · I wonder _____ he bought for Sally.

① who   ② what
③ that   ④ which
⑤ where

5. 다음 밑줄 친 부분을 한 단어로 바꾸어 쓰시오.
> I'll do <u>anything that</u> is good for you.

→ _____

6. 다음 빈칸에 **that**을 쓸 수 없는 것은?
① I know the man _____ lives in Busan.
② She is the woman _____ I met yesterday.
③ I like Sam, _____ is smart and kind.
④ The only problem _____ they have is money.
⑤ Look at the boy and his dog _____ are running in the park.

7. 다음 빈칸에 공통으로 알맞은 말을 쓰시오.
> · This is the book _____ my mom borrowed from the library.
> · He is tallest boy _____ I've ever seen.

→ _____

8. 다음 우리말을 바르게 영작한 것은?
> 나는 영화를 보았는데, 아주 재미있었다.

① I watched a movie, which I found it interesting.
② I watched a movie, which I found interesting.
③ I watched a movie, who I found it interesting.
④ I watched a movie, who I found interesting.
⑤ I watched a movie, what I found it interesting.

9. 다음 빈칸에 들어갈 말이 바르게 짝지어진 것은?
> · Saturday is the day _____ I am free.
> · This is the place _____ the accident happened.

① where – how   ② where – when
③ when – when   ④ when – where
⑤ how – where

10. 다음 두 문장의 뜻이 같도록 빈칸에 알맞은 것은?

> Whatever you may say, I can't believe it.
> = _____ you may say, I can't believe it.

① Anyone who　　② Any one that
③ No matter what　④ No matter who
⑤ Every time that

11. 다음 중 어법상 옳은 문장은?

① Show me that is in your pocket.
② This is the place in where we study.
③ Look at the horse which color is white.
④ He is the first man which reached the North Pole.
⑤ I live in Seoul, which is the biggest in Korea.

12. 다음 중 <보기>의 밑줄 친 what과 쓰임이 다른 것은?

> <보기>
> What is important is to follow the rules.

① This is what I want to tell you.
② He asked me what I wanted to have?
③ What I want to buy is a smartphone.
④ I don't understand what you're saying.
⑤ That is what I have been looking for.

13. 다음 두 문장을 한 문장으로 바르게 고친 것은?

> I didn't like the way.
> + She treated me in the way.

① I didn't like the way he treated me in.
② I didn't like he treated me in the way.
③ I didn't like how he treated me.
④ I didn't like the way how he treated me.
⑤ I didn't like the way that he treated me.

14. 다음 중 밑줄 친 부분을 생략할 수 없는 것은?

① She is the woman whom I talked about.
② This is the picture that I took last week.
③ The bench which they are sitting on is broke.
④ This is the subject in which we are interested.
⑤ They look at the boys who are playing baseball there.

[15-16] 다음 우리말과 같도록 빈칸에 알맞은 것을 고르시오.

15.
> 나는 내가 너를 처음으로 만났던 날을 결코 잊지 않을 것이다.
> → I'll never forget the day _____ I first met you.

① who　　　　② why
③ where　　　④ what
⑤ when

16.
> 내가 어디에 가든지, 나는 항상 네 생각을 할 것이다.
> → _____ I'll always think of you.

① Wherever I go　② Where I go
③ Whenever I go　④ When I go
⑤ whatever I go

17. 다음 밑줄 친 부분 중 어색한 것은?

① I like the bag that she bought for me.
② This is the house in that Bill was born.
③ This is the best hotel that I know.
④ They gave their daughter everything that they had.
⑤ The car and the driver that fell down the cliff were not found.

18. 다음 빈칸에 알맞지 <u>않은</u> 것은?

> This is the place _____.

① is baking bread

② in which my uncle works

③ which the old man lives in

④ where children can play

⑤ that I can rest

[19-20] 다음 중 어법상 <u>어색한</u> 문장을 고르시오.

19. ① London is the city where Jill lives.

② This is the reason why he was happy.

③ Is there any store in which we can buy some vegetables.

④ This is the town where I visited two years ago.

⑤ She knows somebody who works in the general hospital.

20. ① Choose whichever you want.

② Come and see whenever you like.

③ No matter what busy you are, you shouldn't skip meals.

④ Whoever comes now, the people won't open the door.

⑤ Wherever you go, you must exercise every day.

〈서술형 문제〉

21. 다음 두 문장을 관계대명사를 이용하여 한 문장으로 완성하시오.

> Cathy is writing a book.
> + The topic of the book is about peace.

→ _____

[22-23] 우리말과 뜻이 같도록 주어진 단어를 바르게 배열하여 문장을 완성하시오.

22.
> 축구는 많은 사람들이 관심 있는 스포츠이다.
> (many, interested, people, which, are, in)

→ Soccer is the sport _____
_____.

23.
> 네가 아무리 열심히 노력해도, 너는 그 일을 오늘 끝낼 수 없다. (hard, may, however, you, try)

→ _____, you
can't finish the work today.

24. 다음 표를 보고, 관계대명사 what을 이용하여 문장을 완성하시오.

(1) 먹고 싶은 것	피자와 파스타
(2) 사고 싶은 것	분홍색 스카프

Today I will meet my friend Bella. This is what I want for my friend.

(1) _____ for lunch is pizza and pasta.

(2) _____ for my friend is a pink scarf.

25. 다음 구입한 목록을 보고, 관계부사를 이용하여 문장을 완성하시오.

(1) 구입한 곳	HS몰에 있는 Good Sense
(2) 구입한 이유	예전 지갑이 낡아서

I bought a new purse last Sunday.

(1) Good Sense in the HS Mall is the store _____ the purse.

(2) The reason _____ is that my old purse was worn out.

접속사란 무엇인가?
접속사는 단어나 구, 절을 서로 연결하는 말이다.

접속사에는 어떤 것이 있는가?
접속사에는 등위접속사와 종속접속사 그리고 상관접속사가 있다.
종속접속사는 종속절을 주절에 연결해 주는 역할을 하고, 상관접
속사는 두 개의 요소가 짝을 이루어 하나의 접속사 역할을 한다.
The key point is **whether** he will accept our offer.
You need to buy **both** a tent **and** a sleeping bag.

Chapter 9. 접속사

Unit 66 명사절을 이끄는 접속사

- 접속사가 명사처럼 주어, 목적어, 보어 역할을 하는 종속절을 이끄는 경우 이를 명사절이라고 한다.
- that: '~하는 것, ~라는 것'이라는 뜻으로 문장에서 주어, 목적어, 보어 역할을 하는 명사절을 이끈다. 목적어절이나 보어절에서는 that을 생략할 수 있다.

주어 : ~하는 것은	That he is a good student is certain. = It is ceratin **that** he is a good student. *It: 가주어 / that절: 진주어
목적어 : ~하는 것을	I can't believe **(that)** he is a professor.
보어 : ~라는 것이다	The problem is **(that)** she was absent from the class.
동격 : ~라는	The fact **that** she got married was surprising. *fact, news, idea, rumor 등의 뒤에서 명사와 동격의 의미

- whether(if): '~인지 아닌지'의 뜻으로 명사절을 이끌며, whether가 쓰인 경우에는 뒤에 or not이 오기도 한다.
  I wonder **whether** she will pass the exam (or not).
  He asked **if** he could help.

Practice

A. 다음 괄호 안에 알맞은 것을 고르시오.

1. It was not true (if, that) she was a thief.
2. I hope (that, whether) she will get better soon.
3. I don't know (that, whether) the news is true or not.
4. (It, That) the earth is round is true.
5. I don't know (that, if) she will go there.

B. 다음 빈칸에 알맞은 접속사를 쓰시오.

1. The novel reminds me _____ love is important.
2. I wonder _____ she will come tonight.
3. _____ she can speak French is true.
4. _____ is certain _____ he will not return.
5. They don't care _____ he takes a picture or not.

C. 다음 문장에서 틀린 곳을 찾아 바르게 고쳐 쓰시오.

1. He asked me if it would snow or not. _____
2. I'm clear that he is stupid. _____
3. I thought if the man was guilty. _____
4. It is certain whether his new song will be a big hit.
   _____

Grammar Tip

that은 주어, 목적어, 보어의 종속절을 이끄는 접속사이다.

A. thief 도둑
  round 둥근

B. novel 소설
  remind 상기시키다
  care 관심을 가지다

whether는 대부분 if로 바꾸어 쓸 수 있지만 명사절이 주어나 보어로 쓰인 경우에는 바꾸어 쓸 수 없으며 if는 목적어절에만 쓴다.

C. stupid 어리석은
  guilty 유죄의

67 조건의 접속사

if: (만약) ~라면	조건의 부사절에서는 현재시제가 미래를 대신한다. '~해라, 그러면 ~'의 뜻인 「명령문+and」로 바꾸어 쓸 수 있다. If we <u>hurry</u> now, we'll catch the train. = **Hurry** now, **and** we'll catch the train.
unless: (만약) ~하지 않는다면	「if ~ not」 혹은 '~해라, 그렇지 않으면 ~'의 뜻인 「명령문+or」로 바꾸어 쓸 수 있다. **Unless** you <u>get up</u> early, you will be late for school. = If you **don't** get up early, you will be late for school. = **Get** up early, **or** you will be late for school.

Practice

A. 다음 괄호 안에서 알맞은 것을 고르시오.

1. (If, Unless) you need money, I will lend you some.

2. I'll help you (if, unless) I am busy.

3. If you (don't, won't) join us, we will not go on a picnic.

4. (If, Unless) there are seats on the bus, I'll go on foot.

5. (If, Unless) you don't study hard, you will fail the exam.

B. 다음 두 문장이 같은 뜻이 되도록 빈칸에 알맞은 말을 쓰시오.

1. If you don't pass the test, what will you do?
   = _____ you pass the test, what will you do?

2. Unless you stop drinking, your health will get worse.
   = _____ you _____ stop drinking, your health
   will get worse.

3. You will miss the train if you don't wake up early.
   = You will miss the train _____ you wake up early.

4. She will never come back unless he changes his mind.
   = She will never come back _____ he _____ change
   his mind.

C. 다음 우리말과 같도록 괄호 안의 주어진 말을 이용하여 문장을 완성하시오.

1. 조심하지 않으면, 너는 넘어질 것이다. (fall)
   → _____ you are careful, you _____ _____ down.

2. 만약 내일 눈이 온다면, 우리는 눈사람을 만들 것이다. (snow)
   → _____ it _____ tomorrow, we will make a snowman.

Grammar Tip

조건의 부사절에서는 현재시제가 미래를 대신한다. 또한 부사절은 문장에서 앞뒤에 모두 올 수 있는데, 앞에 올 때는 콤마(,)를 넣는다.

A. lend 빌려주다
   picnic 소풍
   seat 좌석

B. health 건강
   change one's mind
   마음을 바꾸다

C. careful 주의 깊은
   fall down 넘어지다
   snowman 눈사람

Unit 68 | 시간의 접속사 1

• 접속사가 시간, 이유, 조건, 목적 등을 나타내는 종속절을 이끄는 경우 이를 부사절이라고 한다. 시간의 부사절에서는 현재시제로 미래를 표현한다.

when: ~할 때	한 시점에 발생한 것을 나타내는 시간의 접속사이다. **When** he came home, dinner was ready.
while: ~하는 동안	어떤 일이 발생하는 기간을 말할 때 사용한다. **While** you were studying hard, your mom came back.
as: ~하면서, ~할 때, 　　~하자마자	동시적으로 일이 발행한 경우에 사용하는 시간의 접속사이다. **As** he was dancing, he came up to me. Amy listened to the music **as** she studied. **As** the thief entered the store, the alarm started ringing.

Practice

A. 다음 두 문장을 괄호 안의 접속사를 이용하여 한 문장으로 완성하시오.

1. You seemed very happy. You played the guitar. (when)
   → You seemed very happy _____ you played the guitar.

2. Mom made some cookies. I was taking care of Jamie. (while)
   → Mom made some cookies _____ I was taking care of Jamie.

3. Billy got a lot of experience. Time passed. (as)
   → Billy got a lot of experience _____ time passed.

B. 다음 괄호 안에서 알맞은 것을 고르시오.

1. I will call her when I (finish, will finish) my homework.

2. (Whether, While) I was walking home, I met a strange man.

3. (As, Unless) the man saw the police officer, he ran away.

4. I did the dishes (when, that) my wife fell asleep.

C. 다음 우리말과 뜻이 같도록 빈칸에 알맞은 말을 쓰시오.

1. 집을 나설 때에는 문 잠그는 것을 잊지 말아라.
   → _____ you leave your house, don't forget to lock the door.

2. 내가 책을 읽는 동안 누군가 문을 노크했다.
   → Someone knocked the door _____ I was reading books.

3. 나는 버스를 기다리면서 음악을 들었다.
   → _____ I was waiting for a bus, I listened to music.

4. 내가 없는 동안 나의 딸들이 집을 청소했다.
   → _____ I was away, my daughters cleaned the house.

Grammar Tip

while은 '~하는 동안'이라는 뜻 외에도 '반면에, ~이지만'의 의미도 갖고 있다.
Some people are rich, **while** others are poor.

A. seem ~인 것처럼 보이다
take care of 돌보다
experience 경험
pass (시간이) 흐르다

B. run away 도망가다
fall asleep 잠들다

C. lock 잠그다
knock 노크하다
clean 청소하다

Unit 69 시간의 접속사 2

- 시간의 접속사에는 before, after, until, since, as soon as 등 다양한 접속사가 있다.

before: ~전에	I had to finish my work **before** I had dinner. = I had to finish my work **before** having dinner.
after: ~후에	What will you do **after** you solve the problem? = What will you do **after** solving the problem?
until[till]: ~할 때까지	You can't watch TV **until** you've done your homework.
since: ~ 이후로, ~이래로	I have lived in New York **since** I was born. * since는 주로 과거시제의 절을 이끌어 완료시제와 쓰인다.
as soon as: ~하자마자	**As soon as** the boy saw the girl, he ran away.

Practice

A. 다음 괄호 안에서 알맞은 것을 고르시오.

1. They fell asleep (since, before) the film ended.

2. It's been ten years (since, after) we graduated from school.

3. Foreigners waited at the door (until, before) the shop opened.

4. Five years have passed (before, since) I left home.

B. 다음 우리말과 같도록 괄호 안의 말을 이용하여 문장을 완성하시오.

1. 나는 저녁을 먹은 후 숙제를 먼저 할 것이다. (eat)
   → _____ _____ _____ dinner, I'll do my homework first.

2. 나는 런던으로 떠나기 전에 나의 반 친구들을 만났다. (leave)
   → I met my classmates _____ _____ _____ for London.

3. 그녀는 대학 졸업한 이후로 여기서 일하고 있다. (finish)
   → She has worked here _____ _____ _____ university.

4. 그는 미국으로 돌아갈 때까지 나와 함께 지낼 것이다. (go)
   → He will stay with me _____ _____ _____ back to America.

5. 그 어린이는 그의 엄마를 보자마자 울기 시작했다. (see)
   → _____ _____ _____ the child _____ his mom, he started crying.

C. 다음 문장에서 틀린 부분을 찾아 바르게 고쳐 쓰시오.

1. 나는 Sally가 그곳으로 올 때까지 한 시간을 기다렸다.
   I waited for an hour since Sally got there. _____

2. 지난번에 그녀를 만난 이래로 오랜 시간이 지났다.
   A long time passed since I last saw her. _____

Grammar Tip

before와 after가 접속사로 쓰이면 뒤에 「주어+동사」가 오는데, 뒤에 명사구나 동명사가 오는 전치사로 쓰이기도 한다.

A. film 영화
   graduate from ~를 졸업하다
   foreigner 외국인

B. classmate 반 친구
   university 대학교
   stay 머무르다

since는 주로 과거시제의 절을 이끌어 현재완료와 쓰인다.

C. last 지난번에
   beach 해변

123

A. 다음 문장의 괄호 안에서 알맞은 것을 고르시오.

1. The fact (that, since) Nick couldn't drive surprises them.

2. I don't know (while, whether) she will come or not.

3. (Unless, As) it rains, we will take a trip.

4. You can catch the train (if, that) you hurry up.

5. We had to come back home (before, unless) he came.

B. 다음 괄호 안의 접속사를 이용하여 한 문장으로 완성하시오.

1. I'm not sure. + The rumor is true. (whether)

   → _____

2. We don't know. + He will invite us to his party. (if)

   → _____

3. I'll tell her the truth. + She comes this evening. (when)

   → _____

4. They haven't seen him. + He went to Paris. (since)

   → _____

C. 다음 두 문장이 같은 뜻이 되도록 빈칸에 알맞은 말을 쓰시오.

1. If you don't pass the test, what will you do?

   = _____ you pass the test, what will you do?

2. Wash your hands before you eat a snack.

   = Eat a snack _____ you wash your hands.

3. That the earth is round is true.

   = _____ is true _____ the earth is round.

D. 다음 우리말과 같도록 괄호 안의 말을 이용하여 문장을 완성하시오.

1. 내일 날이 맑다면, 나는 낚시를 갈 것이다. (be)

   → _____ _____ _____ sunny tomorrow, I will go fishing.

2. 비가 그칠 때까지 우리는 여기서 기다릴 것이다. (stop)

   → We will wait here _____ _____ _____ _____ .

3. 그들이 나를 보자마자 나에게 달려왔다. (see)

   → As _____ _____ _____ _____ me, they ran to me.

4. 그가 집에 왔을 때 저녁은 준비되어 있었다. (come)

   → _____ _____ _____ home, the dinner was ready.

Grammar Tip

that은 문장에서 주어, 목적어, 보어 역할을 하는 명사절을 이끄는데, 앞에 나온 명사를 설명하는 동격절을 이끌기도 한다.

A. surprise 놀라게 하다
   trip 여행

since는 주로 과거시제의 절을 이끌어 현재완료와 쓰인다.

B. rumor 소문
   invite 초대하다
   truth 진실

unless는 '(만약) ~하지 않는다면'의 뜻으로 if~not으로 바꾸어 쓸 수 있다.

C. snack 간식

D. ready 준비된
   go fishing 낚시 가다

Unit 70 이유의 접속사

· 어떤 결과에 대한 이유나 원인을 말할 때 because, as, since를 이용하여 나타낸다.

because: ~ 때문에	직접적인 이유를 말할 때 쓴다. **Because** it snowed heavily, I couldn't attend there.
since: ~이니까	이미 알고 있는 이유를 말할 때 쓰인다. **Since** today is a holiday, the markets are closed.
as: ~이므로	보충적인 이유를 설명할 때 쓰인다. **As** it was raining, we couldn't play soccer.

· because와 같은 의미의 because of는 전치사구로 뒤에 동명사나 명사구가 온다.

Because of snowing heavily[heavy snow], I couldn't attend the meeting.

Practice

A. 다음 괄호 안에서 알맞은 것을 고르시오.

1. I had to stay at home (until, because) I didn't feel well.

2. We didn't eat out (before, as) it was very cold outside.

3. He wants to be a doctor (if, since) he likes to help people.

4. They are hungry (because, because of) skipping breakfast.

B. 다음 괄호 안의 접속사를 이용하여 한 문장으로 완성하시오.

1. She was not happy. + She didn't enjoy her work. (since)
   → _____

2. Tom didn't go out. + It was very hot. (because)
   → _____

3. My father grew older. + He became less talkative. (as)
   → _____

C. 다음 우리말과 같도록 괄호 안의 말을 이용하여 문장을 완성하시오.

1. 그는 지갑을 잃어버렸기 때문에 빵을 살 수 없었다. (because)
   → He couldn't buy bread _____ _____ _____ his wallet.

2. 그는 종종 거짓말을 하기 때문에 나는 그를 좋아하지 않는다. (as)
   → _____ _____ _____ _____, I don't like him.

3. 너도 알다시피 그녀는 천재이다. (as)
   → _____ _____ _____, she is a genius.

4. 당신이 그 꽃병을 깼기 때문에 10달러를 지불해야 한다. (since)
   → _____ _____ _____ the vase, you have to pay 10 dollars.

Grammar Tip

because 뒤에는 「주어+동사」 형태의 절이 오고 because of 뒤에는 명사구나 동명사가 온다.

A. well 건강한, 몸이 좋은
　　 skip 거르다

B. talkative 수다스러운

C. wallet 지갑
　　 lie 거짓말하다
　　 genius 천재
　　 vase 꽃병

71 양보의 접속사

- 양보의 접속사에는 thought, although, even if, even though가 있다.

though, although: ～에도 불구하고, ～이지만	**Though** he is poor, he is happy.
	Although she doesn't love me, I love her.
even if, even though: 비록 ～일지라도	**Even if** he becomes a millionaire, I don't want to get married to him.
	Even though you don't like it, I recommend it.

- despite, in spite of는 양보의 의미를 갖는 전치사(구)로 뒤에는 명사구나 동명사가 온다.
  He went to school **in spite of[despite]** the heavy storm.

Practice

A. 다음 괄호 안에서 알맞은 것을 고르시오.

1. (Though, Because) it rained, the match was not cancelled.

2. They are sad (as, even though) they have everything.

3. (Though, Despite) the exam, Joe played computer games.

4. (Even though, Since) she had a cold, she went to work.

5. (As, Even if) you don't like him, you have to help him.

B. 다음 괄호 안의 접속사를 이용하여 한 문장으로 완성하시오.

1. We practiced hard. We lost the game. (although)
   → _____

2. The bag was light. She couldn't lift it. (even if)
   → _____

3. I couldn't sleep. I was very tired. (though)
   → _____

4. The man is old. He can do the project. (even though)
   → _____

C. 다음 우리말과 같도록 빈칸에 알맞은 접속사를 쓰시오.

1. Sam은 키는 작지만, 훌륭한 요리사이다.
   → _____ Sam is short, he is a great chef.

2. 비록 그녀는 늦게 일어났지만, 학교에 늦지 않았다.
   → _____ _____ she got up late, she wasn't late for school.

3. 비록 그는 실패했더라도, 다시 그 일을 시작했다.
   → _____ _____ _____ _____, he started doing the
   work again.

Grammar Tip

despite, in spite of는 양보의 의미를 갖고 있는 전치사(구)로 뒤에는 명사구나 동명사가 온다.

A. cancel 취소하다
   everything 모든 것

B. lose 지다, 분실하다
   lift 들어 올리다
   project 과제, 프로젝트

C. chef 요리사
   fail 실패하다

Unit 72 | 상관접속사

· 두 개의 요소가 짝을 이루어 하나의 접속사 역할을 하는 것을 상관접속사라고 한다.

both A and B: A와 B 둘 다 → 복수 취급	**Both** Amy **and** Jim are in the classroom.
not only A but also B: A 뿐만 아니라 B도 = B as well as A → B에 인칭과 수 일치	**Not only** the toys **but also** the books are for sale. = The books **as well as** the toys are for sale.
either A or B: A 또는 B 둘 중 하나 → B에 인칭과 수 일치	**Either** he **or** his brother is a famous singer.
neither A nor B: A도 B도 둘 다 아닌 → B에 인칭과 수 일치	She is **neither** a painter **nor** a dancer.

＊ not A but B : 'A가 아니라 B'라는 뜻이다.

The woman is **not** a nurse **but** a doctor.

Practice

A. 다음 빈칸에 알맞은 말을 쓰시오.

1. Both Judy _____ Ben will attend the meeting.

2. The backpack is not mine _____ Billy's.

3. She is _____ _____ a good student _____ also a good player.

4. This album is popular in the US as _____ _____ in Korea.

B. 다음 괄호 안에 알맞은 것을 고르시오.

1. (Either, Neither) he or she knows the fact.

2. She has neither friends (or, nor) relatives to call.

3. He can speak not only French (but also, and) Spanish.

4. My brother as well as I (is, am) not in the room.

C. 다음 우리말과 같도록 빈칸에 알맞은 말을 쓰시오.

1. 그녀와 그녀의 여동생은 쿠키를 굽고 있다.

   → _____ she _____ her sister are baking cookies.

2. 그와 나 중에 하나는 오늘밤 진실을 말해야 한다.

   → _____ he _____ I have to tell the truth tonight.

3. 너 뿐만 아니라 나도 그 결과에 만족한다.

   → _____ _____ you but I _____ satisfied with the result.

   = I _____ _____ _____ you am satisfied with the result.

4. 당신은 집에 있을 수도 나와 함께 갈 수도 없다.

   → _____ you can stay at home _____ you can go with me.

Grammar Tip

not olny A but also B에서 also 는 일반적으로 생략하고 쓰는 경우도 많다.

A. attend 참석하다
album 앨범
popular 인기 있는

not only A but also B, either A or B, neither A nor B에서 동사의 수는 B에 일치시킨다.

B. relative 친척
Spanish 스페인어

C. bake 굽다
satisfied 만족한
result 결과, 성적

Unit 73 접속부사

· 부사(구)이면서 접속사처럼 문장과 문장을 연결하는 역할을 하는 것을 접속부사라고 한다.

결과	therefore(그러므로), as a result(그 결과), accordingly(따라서), thus(그래서)	They studied hard. **Therefore**, they passed the exam.
대조	however(그러나), on the other hand(반면에), nevertheless(그럼에도 불구하고)	She is beautiful. **However**, she is not kind.
첨가	in addition(덧붙여 말하면), besides(게다가, 이외에도), moreover(게다가, 더욱이), furthermore(더욱이)	His son behaves well in school. **In addition**, he studies hard.
예시	for example(예를 들면), for instance(예를 들면)	I like spicy vegetables. **For example**, I like onions.

Practice

A. 다음 빈칸에 알맞은 말을 〈보기〉에서 골라 쓰시오.

〈보기〉 however   therefore   besides   nevertheless

1. It rained. _____, we went on a picnic.

2. He looked for everywhere. _____, he couldn't find his wallet.

3. I couldn't get the tickets. _____, I delayed our departure.

4. This food is very good. _____, it's not difficult to cook.

B. 다음 괄호 안에서 알맞은 것을 고르시오.

1. Put the food in the refrigerator. (Besides, Otherwise), the food will go bad.

2. My father went jogging every morning. (As a result, For instance), he lost weight.

3. I don't want to see the movies. (Nevertheless, Besides), I don't have money.

4. David is very tall (Moreover, For example), he is handsome.

C. 다음 우리말과 같도록 빈칸에 알맞은 말을 쓰시오.

1. 강한 폭풍우가 있었다. 그 결과, 그는 방향을 잃었다.
   → There was a strong storm. _____, he lost his way.

2. 나는 축구하기를 원한다. 그러나 그는 농구하기를 원한다.
   → I want to play soccer. _____, he wants to play basketball.

3. James는 아파 보였다. 그럼에도 불구하고 그는 학교에 갔다.
   → James looked sick. _____, he went to school.

Grammar Tip

접속부사는 대부분 두 번째 문장의 맨 앞에 위치하는데, 경우에 따라서는 중간이나 마지막에 오기도 한다.

A. everywhere 모든 곳
   delay 연기하다
   departure 출발

B. refrigerator 냉장고
   weight 무게
   handsome 잘생긴

C. fail 실패하다, 망치다
   basketball 농구

Review Test

A. 다음 괄호 안에 알맞은 것을 고르시오.

1. (Even though, Because) it rains, I have to go to the mountain.
2. She was upset (although, because) I didn't call her then.
3. This book is (not only, as well as) funny but sad.
4. Neither my wife (nor, or) I will be there.
5. He got a serious flu. (Besides, Thus), he was absent from work.

B. 다음 우리말과 같도록 괄호 안의 말을 알맞게 배열하시오.

1. 너나 네 동생 중 하나는 가야 한다. (or, either, you, your brother)
   → _____ has to go.
2. 그 시간에는 버스가 없기 때문에 우리는 택시를 타야 했다.
   (no, because, was, bus, there)
   → We had to take a taxi _____
   at that time.
3. 그녀는 아름답다. 게다가 그녀는 현명하다. (she, wise, in addition, is)
   → She is beautiful. _____.

C. 다음 두 문장이 같은 뜻이 되도록 빈칸에 알맞은 말을 쓰시오.

1. The man was lazy. So he didn't succeed in business.
   = The man didn't succeed in business _____ he was lazy.
2. Joseph didn't eat all day. Also, he didn't drink all day.
   = Joseph _____ ate _____ drank all day.
3. The movie was interesting. The movie was instructive, too.
   = The movie was instructive _____ _____ _____
   interesting.
4. Not only Peter but also Julia likes the magazine.
   = Peter likes the magazine. _____ Julia likes the magazine.

D. 다음 우리말과 같도록 괄호 안의 말을 이용하여 문장을 완성하시오.

1. 그는 아마 군인 아니면 경찰관일 것이다. (soldier, either)
   → He is probably _____.
2. 샘의 남동생과 샘은 지금 파리를 여행 중이다. (travel, both)
   → _____ in Paris now.
3. 비록 내가 A를 받지 못했지만 나는 열심히 공부했다. (even if, an A)
   → I studied hard _____.
4. 지진이 발생했다. 그 결과 많은 사람들이 죽었다. (as a result, many)
   → The earthquake happened. _____.
5. 어제는 공휴일이므로 나는 집에서 영화를 보았다. (a holiday, since)
   → _____, I watched a movie at home.

Grammar Tip

not olny A but also B에서 also 는 일반적으로 생략하고 쓰는 경우 도 많다.

A. serious 심각한
   absent 결근(결석)한

either A or B에서 동사의 수는 B 에 일치시킨다.

B. take a taxi 택시를 타다
   wise 현명한

C. lazy 게으른
   business 사업
   instructive 교육적인
   magazine 잡지

D. probably 아마도
   travel 여행하다
   earthquake 지진
   holiday 공휴일, 휴가

129

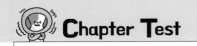 

[1-2] 다음 빈칸에 알맞은 것을 고르시오.

1.

Joe finished the work _____ he was very tired.

① if   ② but
③ though   ④ or
⑤ because

2.

Either she and you _____ always early for the party.

① am   ② are
③ is   ④ will be
⑤ will not

3. 다음 밑줄 친 that의 쓰임이 나머지와 다른 것은?
① I heard that he has won the race.
② That the man is guilty is not certain.
③ It's true that Judith was late for school.
④ She will do anything that I ask her to.
⑤ He realized that he had made a mistake then.

4. 다음 우리말과 같도록 빈칸에 알맞은 것은?

네가 좋든 싫든 그들은 내일 올 것이다.
→ They will come tomorrow, _____ you like it or not.

① either   ② though
③ that   ④ if
⑤ whether

5. 다음 밑줄 친 부분 중 쓰임이 잘못된 것은?
If ①the weather ②will be sunny ③this afternoon, we ④will go ⑤to the beach.

6. 다음 빈칸에 because를 쓸 수 없는 것은?
① He often tells lies _____ we can't trust him.
② The boy was hungry _____ he didn't have breakfast.
③ They didn't swim here _____ the lake was deep.
④ I couldn't go to the meeting _____ I caught a cold.
⑤ They couldn't get into the office _____ they didn't have the key.

7. 다음 우리말을 바르게 영작한 것은?

Lucy는 소설도 만화책도 읽지 않는다.

① Lucy doesn't read both novels and comic books.
② Lucy reads either novels or comic books.
③ Lucy reads not only novels but also comic books.
④ Lucy reads neither novels nor comic books.
⑤ Lucy reads comic books as well as novels.

8. 다음 빈칸에 공통으로 알맞은 말을 쓰시오.

· I saw Ann, _____ she didn't see me.
· Bill is not a Canadian _____ an American.

→ _____

9. 다음 빈칸에 들어갈 말이 바르게 짝지어진 것은?

· I'm sure _____ he'll pass the exam.
· The bell rang _____ they were watching a TV show.

① that – while   ② that – if
③ while – after   ④ while – until
⑤ since – while

10. 다음 밑줄 친 말 대신 쓸 수 있는 것은?

> We wonder <u>whether</u> he is going to join us next week.

① that   ② if
③ when   ④ and
⑤ even if

11. 다음 중 어법상 옳은 문장은?

① He neither smokes or drinks.
② As soon as he saw her, he ran away.
③ Take this medicine, or you'll get better.
④ The question is if I want this.
⑤ She will call you when she will arrive at the airport.

12. 다음의 문장과 뜻이 같은 것은?

> Tom had breakfast without washing his face.

① Tom washed his face and had breakfast.
② Tom didn't wash his face, but had breakfast.
③ Tom had breakfast after he washed his face.
④ Tom washed his face before he had breakfast.
⑤ Tom washed his face, but didn't have breakfast.

13. 다음 빈칸에 공통으로 알맞은 것은?

> · You will get fat _____ you eat too much fast food.
> · I don't know _____ tomorrow will snow a lot.

① while   ② since
③ until   ④ if
⑤ though

14. 다음 중 밑줄 친 since의 쓰임이 나머지와 <u>다른</u> 것은?

① I could fix the bike <u>since</u> you helped me.
② <u>Since</u> she was not busy, she could get away from the office.
③ He wanted to be a doctor <u>since</u> he liked to help sick people.
④ Mary has taught history <u>since</u> last year.
⑤ He was happy <u>since</u> he enjoyed his project.

[15~16] 다음 두 문장의 뜻이 같도록 빈칸에 알맞은 것을 고르시오.

15.

> She can remember his face, but she can't remember his name.
> = She can remember his face. _____ she can't remember his name.

① Besides   ② However
③ Therefore   ④ In addition
⑤ For example

16.

> John is very tall. But his brother is short.
> = John is very tall, _____ his brother is short.

① if   ② as
③ when   ④ because
⑤ though

17. 다음 우리말과 같도록 빈칸에 들어갈 말이 바르게 짝지어진 것은?

> 그와 나 둘 중 하나가 잘못한 것이다.
> → _____ he _____ I am to blame.

① Not, but   ② Both, and
③ Either, or   ④ Neither, nor
⑤ Not only, but also

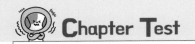 

18. 다음 밑줄 친 부분 중 어색한 것은?

① The clock struck ten <u>as</u> I got home.

② He can solve the question <u>even if</u> he is young.

③ They couldn't go to school <u>because</u> raining heavily.

④ The people visited Italy <u>as well as</u> France.

⑤ <u>As soon as</u> the child saw his mom, he started to cry.

19. 다음 밑줄 친 that의 쓰임이 어색한 것은?

① <u>That</u> she failed in the exam was true.

② They knew <u>that</u> English was very fun.

③ The rumor is <u>that</u> the cute girl is a liar.

④ We want to know <u>that</u> he will succeed or not.

⑤ At first he didn't know the fact <u>that</u> she was married.

20. 다음 중 어법상 어색한 문장은?

① I hope that we will meet again soon.

② The farmer is happy though he is poor.

③ We'll go on a picnic if it is sunny next weekend.

④ Sarah was happy while she was staying in the town.

⑤ Jack has played baseball until he was young.

〈서술형 문제〉

21. 다음 우리말과 같도록 괄호 안의 단어들을 바르게 배열하여 문장을 완성하시오.

그 아기가 깨어나자마자 내게 알려 주세요.
(the baby, up, as, wakes, as, soon)

= Please let me know _____
_____.

22. 다음 도서 대출 규정을 보고 주어진 접속사를 이용하여 문장을 완성하시오.

〈도서 대출 규정〉
1. 도서 대출 권수 : 1인 대출 권수는 3권
2. 도서 연체 시 : 권당 1일에 벌금 200원
3. 도서 분실 시 : 동일한 책 구입

(1) _____ your books on time, you have to pay a fine. (unless)

(2) _____ your books, you need to buy the same books. (if)

23. 다음 두 문장이 같은 뜻이 되도록 빈칸에 알맞은 말을 쓰시오.

Martin can speak French as well as Spanish.

= Martin can speak _____ _____ _____
_____ _____ French.

24. 다음 두 문장을 괄호 안의 말을 이용하여 한 문장으로 완성하시오.

Jim will not go to the party. + Hellen will not go to the party, either. (neither)

→ _____

25. 다음 표를 보고 문장을 완성하시오.

	can swim	have a cat	have a dog
James	○	×	×
Kate	○	×	○
Eric	×	○	○

(1) Both James _____ _____ _____ swim.

(2) Eric _____ _____ _____. Besides, he has a dog.

(3) Kate doesn't have a cat but she _____
_____ _____.

가정법이란 무엇인가?

가정법은 현재나 과거에 대한 사실이나 상황을 반대로 말하거나 상상하여 말하는 것이다. 가정법 과거는 현재의 사실을 가정, 상상하는 표현이고, 과거완료는 과거의 사실을 가정, 상상하는 표현이다.

If I **were** a bird, I **could fly** to you. (가정법 과거)

If he **had studied** hard, he **could have passed** the exam. (가정법 과거완료)

가정법은 어떻게 표현하는가?

상황이나 사실이 언제 일어났는지에 따라 동사의 시제를 바꾸어 표현하며 If, I wish, as if[though] 등을 이용하여 나타낸다.

I **wish** my daughter were a doctor.

Jamie acts **as if** she were my teacher.

Chapter 10. 가정법

Unit 74 if 가정법 과거

- 가정법 과거는 현재의 사실을 반대로 가정, 상상하여 현재나 미래에 실현 가능성이 희박한 일을 가정, 상상해 보는 것이다.
- 「If+주어+동사의 과거형 ~, 주어+조동사의 과거형(would/could)+동사원형 ~.」의 형태로 '만약 ~라면, ~일텐데'의 의미이다. if절에서 be동사는 인칭과 수에 상관없이 were를 쓴다.

  If he **knew** her phone number, he **could call** her.
  → As he doesn't know her phone number, he can't call her. (직설법 전환)
  If I **were** young again, I **could do** anything.
- 가정법 과거에서 if를 생략하면 주어와 동사의 위치가 바뀐다. (「동사+주어」로 시작)

  Knew he her phone number, he **would call** her.
  Were I young again, I **could do** anything.

Practice

A. 다음 괄호 안에서 알맞은 것을 고르시오.

1. If I (were, am) you, I would get a job.
2. If the car broke down, I (will, would) not know what to do.
3. If I (had, have) a lot of money, I could buy such a house.
4. If she (does, did) more exercise, she would be healthier.
5. If he (helped, helps) me, I could make a success.

B. 다음 두 문장이 같은 뜻이 되도록 빈칸에 알맞은 말을 쓰시오.

1. As I am so sick, I can't go to the movies.
   = If I _____ so sick, I _____ go to the movies.
2. As he is not here now, I can't help him.
   = If he _____ here now, I _____ help him.
3. If I had an extra pencil, I could lend you one.
   = As I _____ _____ an extra pencil, I _____ lend you one.
4. If I knew his address, I could send him a letter.
   = As I _____ _____ his address, I can't send him a letter.

C. 다음 우리말과 같도록 빈칸에 알맞은 말을 쓰시오.

1. 만약 그녀가 더 열심히 공부한다면, 시험에 통과할 텐데.
   → If she _____ harder, she _____ _____ the test.
2. 만약 그녀가 차를 가져온다면, 나는 사무실에 갈 수 있을 텐데.
   → _____ she brought the car, I _____ _____ to the office.
3. 만약 내가 부자였다면, 거대한 배를 살 수 있을 텐데.
   → _____ I _____ rich, I _____ _____ a huge ship.

Grammar Tip

가정법 과거에서 if절의 be동사는 인칭과 수에 상관없이 항상 were를 쓴다.

A. break down 고장나다
exercise 운동
success 성공

가정법 과거를 직설법의 현재형으로 바꿀 때 긍정은 부정, 부정은 긍정으로 바뀐다.

B. extra 여분의
lend 빌려주다
address 주소

C. huge 거대한

Unit 75 | if 가정법 과거완료

- 가정법 과거완료는 과거의 사실을 반대로 가정, 상상하여 과거에 실현 가능성이 희박한 일을 가정, 상상해 보는 것이다.

- 「If+주어+had+p.p. ~, 주어+조동사의 과거형(would/could)+have+p.p. ~.」의 형태로 '만약 ~했다면, ~했을 텐데'의 의미이다.

  If we **had taken** a taxi, we **wouldn't have missed** the train.

  → As we didn't take a taxi, we missed the train. (직설법 전환)

- 가정법 과거에서 if를 생략하면 주어와 동사의 위치가 바뀐다. (「동사+주어」로 시작)

  Had we taken a taxi, we **wouldn't have missed** the train.

Practice

A. 다음 빈칸에 괄호 안의 동사를 알맞게 바꾸어 쓰시오.

1. If I _____ wise, I wouldn't have bought clothes. (be)

2. If he _____ to me, he wouldn't make a mistake. (listen)

3. We _____ on a hike if it had been fine yesterday. (go)

4. If I _____ you, I would have said hello. (meet)

B. 다음 두 문장이 뜻이 같도록 빈칸에 알맞은 말을 쓰시오.

1. If Amy had seen you, she would have returned the books.
   = As Amy _____ _____ you, she _____ _____ the books.

2. As Judy was busy, she couldn't talk with Harry.
   = If Judy _____ _____ busy, she _____ _____ _____ with Harry.

3. If he had taken the medicine, he could have recovered quickly.
   = As he _____ _____ the medicine, he _____ _____ quickly.

4. If I had not believed in myself, I could not have succeeded.
   = As I _____ in myself, I _____ _____.

C. 다음 우리말과 같도록 괄호 안의 말을 이용하여 문장을 완성하시오.

1. 그가 열심히 연습했다면, 경주에서 우승했을 텐데. (practice, won)
   → If he _____ hard, he _____ the race.

2. 내가 키가 컸다면, 농구를 잘했을 텐데. (be, play)
   → If I _____ tall, I _____ basketball well.

3. 눈이 오지 않았더라면, 우리는 산에 올라갈 수 있었을 텐데. (snow, climb)
   → If it _____, we _____ the mountain.

Grammar Tip

A. wise 현명한
   mistake 실수
   contact 연락하다

가정법 과거완료를 직설법의 과거형으로 바꿀 때 과거완료는 과거로 바뀌게 되며 긍정은 부정, 부정은 긍정으로 바뀐다.

B. return 돌려주다
   medicine 약
   recover 회복하다

if를 이용하여 실현 가능성이 희박할 때는 가정법으로 쓰고, 실현 가능성이 있을 때는 단순 조건문으로 쓴다.
If John helps me, I can do the work. (단순 조건문)

C. race 경주
   climb 오르다

76 | I wish+가정법 과거/과거완료

- I wish 가정법 문장은 실현 불가능한 소망이나 현재 또는 과거 사실과 반대되는 소망을 말할 때 사용된다. 주어로 I가 많이 쓰이지만 다른 주어가 오기도 한다.

	I wish+가정법 과거 → 현재 사실과 반대, 실현 불가능한 소망	I wish+가정법 과거완료 → 과거 사실과 반대, 실현 불가능한 소망
형태	I wish+주어+동사의 과거형	I wish+주어+동사의 과거완료형
의미	'~라면 좋을 텐데'	'~라면 좋았을 텐데'
예문	I wish I were tall. = I am sorry I am not tall.	I wish I had tried my best. = I am sorry I didn't try my best.

*I wish 가정법 과거의 경우도 be동사는 인칭과 수에 관계없이 were를 쓴다.

Practice

A. 다음 두 문장이 뜻이 같도록 빈칸에 알맞은 말을 쓰시오.

1. I wish I were as rich as he.
   = I am sorry I _____ _____ as rich as he.

2. Sally is sorry she didn't go to the concert yesterday.
   = Sally wishes she _____ _____ to the concert yesterday.

3. He wishes he had studied harder at that time.
   = He is sorry he _____ _____ harder at that time.

4. I wish I heard the happy news.
   = I am sorry I _____ _____ the happy news.

B. 다음 괄호 안의 말을 이용하여 가정법 문장을 완성하시오.

1. He wishes he _____ his new neighbors. (know)

2. I wish I _____ to the theater last night. (go)

3. Thomas wishes his son _____ an architect. (be)

C. 다음 우리말과 같도록 괄호 안의 말을 이용하여 문장을 완성하시오.

1. 내가 수영하는 방법을 배우면 좋을 텐데. (learn)
   → I wish I _____ how to swim.

2. 네가 항구에 더 일찍 도착했으면 좋았을 텐데. (arrive)
   → I wish you _____ _____ the port earlier.

3. 그가 런던에서 더 많은 시간을 가졌으면 좋았을 텐데. (have)
   → I wish he _____ _____ more time in London.

4. 그녀는 그 팔찌를 잃어버리지 않았다면 좋을 텐데. (lose)
   → I wish she _____ _____ the bracelet.

Grammar Tip

「I wish+가정법 과거」는 「I am sorry+현재」로 바꾸어 쓸 수 있고, 「I wish+가정법 과거완료」는 「I am sorry+과거」로 바꾸어 쓸 수 있다.

A. concert 콘서트
   hear 듣다

I wish 가정법 문장에서 과거의 부사(구)가 있으면 가정법 과거완료이다.

B. neighbor 이웃
   architect 건축가

C. port 항구
   bracelet 팔찌

Unit 77 | as if(though)+가정법 과거/과거완료

- If로 시작하지 않지만 가정의 의미를 나타내는 관용적 표현으로는 I wish와 as if[though]가 있다.
- 「as if[though]+가정법」 구문은 현재 또는 과거의 사실과 반대되거나 실현 가능성이 적은 것을 가정할 때 사용한다.

	as if[though]+가정법 과거	as if[though]+가정법 과거완료
형태	~ as if[though]+주어+동사의 과거형	~ as if[though]+주어+동사의 과거완료형
의미	'마치 ~인 것처럼'	'마치 ~였던 것처럼'
예문	He acts **as if** he **were** a pilot. = In fact, he is not a pilot.	He acts **as if** he **had been** a genius. = In fact, he was not a genius.

* as if(though) 가정법 과거의 경우도 be동사는 인칭과 수에 관계없이 were를 쓴다.

Practice

A. 다음 두 문장이 같은 뜻이 되도록 빈칸에 알맞은 말을 쓰시오.

1. She talks as if she were a nurse.
   = In fact, she _____ _____ a nurse.

2. You look as if you had been sick.
   = In fact, you _____ _____ sick.

3. In fact, he doesn't read all the books on the shelf.
   = He talks _____ _____ he _____ all the books on the shelf.

4. You look as if you had been friendly with him.
   = In fact, you _____ _____ friendly with him.

B. 다음 문장에서 틀린 부분을 찾아 바르게 고쳐 쓰시오.

1. Alice acts as if she was a queen.
   _____

2. He looks as if he saw a ghost last night.
   _____

3. She talks as if she were in London for a long time.
   _____

C. 다음 우리말과 같도록 괄호 안의 말을 이용하여 문장을 완성하시오.

1. 그녀는 마치 전에 파리를 방문했던 것처럼 말한다. (visit)
   → She talks as if she _____ _____ Paris before.

2. 그는 마치 그 소식을 들은 것처럼 보인다. (hear)
   → He looks as if he _____ the news.

3. 그는 마치 시험에 합격했던 것처럼 행동한다. 사실 그는 시험에 합격하지 못했다. (pass)
   → He acts _____ _____ he _____ _____ the exam.
   In fact, he _____ _____ the exam.

Grammar Tip

「as if+가정법 과거」는 주절의 동사와 같은 시제의 반대되는 일을 가정한다. 또한 「as if+가정법 과거완료」는 주절의 동사보다 한 시제 전의 반대되는 일을 가정한다.

A. shelf 선반, 책장
   friendly 친절한

B. queen 왕비, 여왕
   ghost 유령

as if 가정법 과거 문장에서 be동사는 인칭과 수에 상관없이 were를 쓴다.

Unit 78 without(but for), 혼합가정법

- If절이 아닌 without, but for를 이용하여 가정법을 나타낼 수 있는데, 주절의 형태로 가정법 과거인지, 가정법 과거완료인지 구분한다.

	Without[But for] ~, 가정법 과거	Without[But for] ~, 가정법 과거완료
의미	'~이 없다면'	'~이 없었다면'
동의어	If it were not for ~, 가정법 과거	If it had not been for ~, 가정법 과거완료
도치	Were it not for ~, 가정법 과거	Had it not been for ~, 가정법 과거

Without[But for] you, I couldn't do it. ← 현재 있는 것을 없다고 가정
= If it were not for you[Were it not for you], I couldn't do it.
Without[But for] you, I couldn't have done it. ← 과거에 있었던 것을 없다고 가정
= If it had not been for you[Had it not been for you], I couldn't have done it.

- 혼합가정법은 과거의 사실이 현재까지 영향을 미칠 때 사용하며 '(과거에) ~라면, (현재에) ~ 텐데.'라는 의미이며 시간을 나타내는 부사(구)에 유의한다.
[If+주어+had+pp, 주어+조동사의 과거형(would, could 등)+동사원형]
If I had practiced harder, I would pass the test now.

Practice

A. 다음 두 문장이 뜻이 같도록 빈칸에 알맞은 말을 쓰시오.

1. Without your help, they would be very lonely.
= _____ _____ _____ _____ _____ your help, they would be very lonely.

2. If it had not been for his wisdom, we would had been lost.
= _____ _____ his wisdom, we would had been lost.

3. Without money, I could not have bought anything.
= _____ _____ _____ _____ _____ _____ money, I could not have bought anything.

4. If it had not been for the coat, he would have been cold.
= _____ _____ _____ _____ _____ the coat, he would have been cold.

B. 다음 우리말과 같도록 빈칸에 알맞은 말을 쓰시오.

1. 너의 지지가 없다면, 그녀는 실패할 것이다.
→ Without your support, she _____ _____.

2. 음악이 없다면, 나의 삶은 매우 지루했을 것이다.
→ _____ _____ music, my life _____ _____ very boring.

3. 내가 열심히 공부했었다면, 지금 교수가 되어 있을 텐데.
→ _____ I _____ _____ hard, I _____ _____ a professor now.

Grammar Tip

without 가정법 구문은 주절의 형태로 가정법 과거인지, 가정법 과거완료인지 구분하다.

A. lonely 외로운
wisdom 지혜
be lost 길을 잃다

B. support 지지
boring 지루한
professor 교수

A. 다음을 서로 관계있는 것끼리 연결하시오.

1. If he were here, • • I could live in a fairyland.
2. If you had come, • • we would have been happy.
3. I wish • • she knew everything about it.
4. She looks as if • • I could meet him.

B. 다음 밑줄 친 부분을 바르게 고쳐 쓰시오.

1. If I was you, I would be satisfied with myself. _____
2. With his help, I couldn't have passed the exam. _____
3. She talks as if she was in hospital at that time. _____
4. If you took my advice, you would have been happier now.

_____

5. If I have knew your phone number, I would have called you.

_____

C. 다음 두 문장이 같은 뜻이 되도록 빈칸에 알맞은 말을 쓰시오.

1. As I am not rich, I cannot buy a new car.
   = If I _____ rich, I _____ _____ a new car.

2. I wish I knew the secret of her success.
   = I'm sorry I _____ _____ the secret of her success.

3. She talks as if she had seen the movie.
   = In _____, she _____ _____ the movie.

4. If it had not been for the accident, he would have arrived earlier.
   = _____ _____ the accident, I would have arrived earlier.

5. Without your support, I wouldn't finish the project.
   = _____ _____ _____ _____ _____ your support,
   I wouldn't finish the project.

D. 다음 우리말과 같도록 괄호 안의 말을 이용하여 문장을 완성하시오.

1. 내가 너라면, 그가 말하는 것을 믿지 않을 텐데. (believe)
   → If I _____ you, I _____ _____ _____ what he says.

2. 공기와 물이 없다면, 우리는 살 수 없을 텐데. (live)
   → _____ air and water, we _____ _____.

3. 그는 마치 그 소문에 대해 모든 것을 알고 있는 것처럼 말한다. (know)
   → He talks _____ _____ you _____ everything about the
   rumor.

4. 만약 그가 죽지 않았다면, 그는 지금 스무 살이 되었을 것이다. (be)
   → If he _____ _____ _____, he _____ _____
   twenty now.

Grammar Tip

가정법 과거 문장에서는 if절의 be 동사는 반드시 were를 사용한다.

A. fairyland 동화의 나라

B. be satisfied with ~에 만족하다
   advice 충고

without 가정법 구문은 주절의 형태로 가정법 과거인지, 가정법 과거 완료인지 구분하다.

C. secret 비밀
   success 성공
   accident 사고

D. believe 믿다
   rumor 소문
   die 죽다

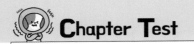 

[1–2] 다음 빈칸에 알맞은 것을 고르시오.

1.
> If Sally had been taller, she _____ very popular.

① will be   ② would be
③ would have been   ④ would had been
⑤ would have being

2.
> I wish we _____ there last night.

① are   ② was
③ were   ④ have been
⑤ had been

3. 다음 두 문장이 같은 뜻이 되도록 빈칸에 알맞은 것은?
> You look as if you had been sleepy.
> = In fact, you _____ sleepy.

① are   ② aren't
③ were   ④ weren't
⑤ had been

4. 다음 빈칸에 공통으로 알맞은 것은?
> · We couldn't live _____ water and air.
> · I couldn't do the work _____ your help.

① but   ② that
③ with   ④ for
⑤ without

5. 다음 중 의미상 빈칸에 알맞은 것은?
> I would take a walk, _____.
> But it is raining heavily.

① if it rains   ② if it rained
③ if it isn't raining   ④ if it doesn't rain
⑤ if it were not raining

6. 다음 우리말을 바르게 영작한 것은?
> 내가 지금보다 더 부지런하면 좋았을 텐데.

① I wish I were more diligent than now.
② I wish I am more diligent than now.
③ I wish I was more diligent than now.
④ I wish I have been more diligent than now.
⑤ I wish I had been more diligent than now.

[7–8] 다음 문장과 뜻이 같은 것을 고르시오.

7.
> If I hadn't been busy, I could have played with them.

① As I am busy, I can't play with them.
② As I am busy, I could play with them.
③ As I was busy, I could play with them.
④ As I was busy, I couldn't play with them.
⑤ As I had been busy, I couldn't play with them.

8.
> I am sorry I did not send him a card.

① I wish I don't send him a card.
② I wish I had sent him a card.
③ I wish I could send him a card.
④ I wish I had not sent him a card.
⑤ I wish I have not sent him a card.

9. 다음 문장의 내용과 일치하는 것은?
> If I had got up late yesterday, I would have missed the bus.

① I missed the bus yesterday.
② I didn't get up late yesterday.
③ I didn't get up early yesterday.
④ I will not miss the bus today.
⑤ I don't want to miss the bus today.

10. 다음 빈칸에 들어갈 말이 바르게 짝지어진 것은?

> · _____ your kindness, I would be lonely.
> · If I _____ thirsty, I would have drunk something.

① If – was
② As – were
③ But – were
④ Without – had been
⑤ As – had been

[11-12] 다음 밑줄 친 부분과 바꿔 쓸 수 있는 것을 고르시오.

11.
> But for your wake-up call, I couldn't have gone to school early.

① If there isn't your wake-up call
② If it is not for your wake-up call
③ If it were not for your wake-up call
④ If there hadn't been your wake-up call
⑤ If it had not been for your wake-up call

12.
> Hadn't you advised me, I would have finished it.

① As you advise me, I don't finish it.
② As you advise me, I won't finish it.
③ As you advised me, I didn't finish it.
④ As you advised me, I finished it.
⑤ As you hadn't advised me, I didn't finished it.

13. 다음 두 문장의 의미가 서로 다른 것은?

① I am not rich.
  = I wish I were rich.
② I am sorry he doesn't agree with her.
  = I wish he agreed with her.
③ As she is so tired, she can't do it.
  = If she weren't so tired, she could do it.
④ In fact, he isn't crazy.
  = He acts as if he had been crazy.
⑤ As he is not here, I can't help him.
  = If he were here, I could help him.

14. 다음 중 문장의 뜻이 나머지와 다른 것은?

① As there was a heater, I didn't catch a cold.
② Without a heater, I would have caught a cold.
③ But for a heater, I would have caught a cold.
④ If it were not for a heater, I would have caught a cold.
⑤ Had it not been for a heater, I would have caught a cold.

15. 다음 대화의 빈칸에 알맞은 것은?

> A: What a nice car! Is this yours?
> B: Yes, it's mine.
> A: _____, I would buy a nice car.

① As I am not rich
② If I had a nice car
③ If I had a lot of money
④ If I hadn't lots of money
⑤ Though I was very rich

16. 다음 두 문장이 같은 뜻이 되도록 빈칸에 알맞은 말을 쓰시오.

> As I didn't know your birthday, I couldn't buy your present.

= _____ I _____ your birthday, I _____ _____ _____ your present.

17. 다음 중 어법상 옳은 문장은?

① I wish I am a famous singer now.
② I wish they haven't come to the party.
③ If he had studied hard, he wouldn't have failed the exam.
④ If I had seen the movie, I would be satisfied with it.
⑤ You talk as if something special is happening to you.

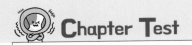 

18. 다음 우리말과 같도록 빈칸에 알맞은 것은?

> 그는 마치 그 소식에 대해 모든 것을 알고 있는 것처럼 말한다.
> → He talks _____ everything about the news.

① if he knows
② as if he knows
③ if he knew
④ as if he knew
⑤ if he had known

[19-20] 다음 문장에서 어법상 어색한 것을 고르시오.

19. ① If I had had time, I could visit Jane.
② If you see her, tell her to come back.
③ If he had known your address, he would have sent you a letter.
④ If I were a composer, I could compose nice songs.
⑤ If you had not driven carefully, you would have had the accident.

20. ① Were I you, I would try my best.
② My brother acts as if he were an adult.
③ Without the moon, the night will be dark.
④ But for his advice, I wouldn't have made it.
⑤ If it were not for electricity, we would have to use candles.

〈서술형 문제〉

21. 다음 문장을 if 가정법 문장으로 바꿔 쓰시오.

> As he isn't rich, he can't build schools in poor countries.

= _____

_____

22. 다음 표를 보고, I wish로 시작하는 문장을 완성하세요.

	(1) 현재의 소망	(2) 과거의 아쉬움
Billy	playing the piano well	taking piano lessons

(1) "I wish _____."
(2) "I wish _____
when I was young."

23. 다음 문장을 if를 생략한 문장으로 바꿔 쓰세요.

(1) If he were your true friend, he would be here now.
→ _____
_____

(2) If I had practiced more, I would have won the game.
→ _____
_____

24. 다음 우리말과 같도록 빈칸에 알맞은 말을 쓰시오.

> 그의 도움이 없었다면 우리는 실패했을 것이다.

→ _____ his help, we could have failed.
→ _____ _____ his help, we could have failed.

25. 다음 대화의 빈칸에 주어진 단어를 알맞은 형태로 바꿔 쓰시오.

> A: Congratulations! I heard you passed the final exam.
> B: Thank you. If I _____ (study) harder, I _____ (can won) a scholarship. I will study harder to win it.

일치란 무엇인가?

문장 내에서 밀접한 관계가 있는 어구끼리는 수, 인칭, 시제 등을 일치시키는데, 주로 주어와 동사의 일치와 시제의 일치가 있다.

The boy **sings** a song.
The boys **sing** a song.
She **thinks** that he **tells** the truth.

화법이란 무엇인가?

화법이란 어떤 사람이 말한 것을 내용 그대로 표현하는 방식인 직접화법과, 말한 내용을 전달하는 사람의 입장에서 적절히 바꾸는 방식인 간접화법이 있다.

He **said to** me, "You looked beautiful yesterday." (직접화법)
= He **told** me (that) I had looked beautiful the day before. (간접화법)

Chapter 11. 일치와 화법

Unit 79 수의 일치(단수)

- 주어의 수와 인칭에 따라 주어와 동사를 일치시키는 것을 수의 일치라고 한다. 주어가 단수 취급하는 것은 단수형 동사를 쓴다.

  (1) 시간, 거리, 금액, 산술적 계산과 학문 이름, 동일인 등은 단수 취급한다.

    Two hours **is** too long to wait. (시간)　　　　Twenty dollars **is** expensive for a meal. (금액)

    Bread and butter **is** my usual lunch. (전체가 하나)　　Physics **is** my favorite subject. (학문)

    The poet and teacher **is** dead. (동일인)

  (2) 'each, every, -body, -thing, -one'은 단수동사를 사용한다.

    Every child **has** a different dream.　　Nobody **knows** the answer.

  (3) '분수, some[most, half, the rest] of the+단수명사', 'the number of+복수명사'는 단수동사를 사용한다.

    Two thirds of the apple **is** bad.　　Most of the book **is** written.

    The number of students **has** been increasing.

Practice

A. 다음 괄호 안의 동사를 알맞게 변환하여 쓰시오. (현재시제)

1. Three fourths of the apple _____ rotten. (be)
2. Curry and rice _____ my favorite food. (be)
3. Dozen _____ the number twelve. (mean)
4. Every dog _____ playing balls. (like)
5. The number of cars _____ about ten in the yard. (be)
6. Three kilometers _____ a long way to walk. (be)
7. Economics _____ a difficult subject. (be)
8. Half of my income _____ spent on food. (be)

B. 다음 문장에서 틀린 부분을 찾아 바르게 고쳐 쓰시오.

1. Each student have a gift for Christmas. _____
2. The number of members were increasing. _____
3. Some of the news in the reports are good. _____
4. Five months are too long to me. _____
5. Romeo and Juliet are a tragedy. _____

C. 다음 우리말과 같도록 괄호 안의 말을 이용하여 문장을 완성하시오.

1. 수학은 내가 가장 좋아하는 과목이 아니다. (mathematics)

   → _____ _____ not my favorite subject.

2. 각각의 학생이 문제를 풀어야만 한다. (have to)

   → _____ _____ _____ _____ solve the problem.

3. 1주일에 50달러는 나에게는 거금이다. (be)

   → _____ _____ a week _____ a big sum to me.

Grammar Tip

시간, 거리, 금액, 산술적 계산과 학문 이름, 동일인 그리고 'each, every, -body, -thing, -one'은 단수동사를 사용한다.

A. rotten 썩은
　 dozen 12개짜리 한 묶음
　 income 수입

physics, economics, politics, mathematics 등의 학문명은 복수이지만 단수 취급한다.

B. increase 증가하다
　 report 보고서
　 tragedy 비극

C. solve 풀다
　 big sum 거금

unit 80 수의 일치(복수)

- 주어에 따라서 동사가 결정되는데, 복수 취급하는 주어는 복수형 동사와 일치시킨다.

  (1) shoes, pants, glasses, scissors 등 짝을 이루는 복수명사 등은 복수동사를 사용한다.

  <u>Your scissors</u> **are** very sharp.   <u>The shoes</u> **are** small on me.

  (2) '분수, some[most, half, the rest] of the+복수명사', 'a number of+복수명사', 'both A and B'는 복수 동사를 사용한다.

  <u>Two thirds of the apples</u> **are** green.   <u>A number of</u> workers **are** fired.

  <u>Both he and his brother</u> **like** basketball.

  (3) 「the+형용사」가 복수명사로 쓰이거나 and로 연결된 복수의 사물은 복수동사를 사용한다.

  <u>The rich</u> **walk** to the house.   <u>The black and the white dog</u> **were** hers. (두 마리의 개)

  *<u>The black and white dog</u> **was** hers. (한 마리의 개/바둑이)

- 「There+동사+주어」에서는 주어가 복수이면 복수동사, 단수이면 단수동사를 사용한다.

  There **is** <u>an apple</u> in the basket.   There **are** <u>three boys</u> in the classroom.

Practice

A. 다음 괄호 안의 동사를 알맞게 변환하여 쓰시오. (현재시제)

1. A number of patients _____ dying. (be)
2. Most of the audiences _____ teenagers. (be)
3. Your new sneakers _____ over there. (be)
4. Half of the students _____ glasses. (wear)
5. Both Jim and Amy _____ baseball. (like)
6. The rest of the windows _____ broken. (be)
7. My pants _____ very nice. (be)
8. The old _____ talking each other. (be)

B. 다음 우리말과 같도록 괄호 안의 말을 이용하여 문장을 완성하시오.

1. 많은 사람들이 무대에서 노래한다. (sing)
   → A _____ of people _____ on the stage.
2. 그 나무의 잎들이 떨어지기 시작한다. (begin)
   → _____ _____ the tree _____ to fall. (begin)
3. 학생들 대부분은 그를 알고 있다. (know)
   → _____ _____ the students _____ him.
4. 그 수박들의 반은 씨가 없다. (be)
   → _____ _____ the watermelons _____ seedless.
5. 지하철 안에 10명의 남자가 있다. (be)
   → _____ _____ _____ _____ in the subway.

Grammar Tip

shoes, boots, glasses, pants, scissors, sneakers, mittens 등 짝을 이루는 것은 복수 취급한다.

A. patient 환자
audience 청중
broken 깨진

of 뒤에 수식어가 따르더라도 주어가 복수이면 동사는 주어의 수에 일치시킨다.
one of my friends (단수)
apples of the tree (복수)

B. stage 무대
watermelon 수박
seedless 씨가 없는

unit 81 | 시제 일치

· 문장이 두 개 이상의 절로 구성될 때, 주절과 종속절의 동사는 시제를 일치시켜야 한다.

주절의 시제가 현재이면, 종속절의 시제는 어떤 시제라도 올 수 있다.	They **know** that he **lives** in China. (현재) They **know** that he **will go** to China. (미래) They **know** that he **lived** in China. (과거) They **know** that he **has gone** to China. (현재완료)
주절의 동사가 과거인 경우에는 종속절의 시제는 과거 또는 과거완료가 와야 한다.	They **knew** that he **lived** in China. (과거) They **knew** that he **had gone** to China. (과거완료)

Practice

A. 다음 우리말과 뜻이 같도록 괄호 안에서 알맞은 것을 고르시오.

1. 나는 내가 실수를 했다는 것을 안다.
   → I know that I (make / made) a mistake.

2. 그는 상품 값을 지불했다고 말했다.
   → He said that he (has paid / pays) for the goods.

3. 나는 그가 그 시합을 이길 수 있다고 생각했다.
   → I thought that he (can win / could win) the game.

4. 그녀는 나를 봐서 행복했다고 말했다.
   → She told me that she (is / was) happy to see me.

B. 다음 밑줄 친 부분이 어법상 맞으면 ○표, 틀리면 바르게 고치시오.

1. He said that he <u>had been</u> to Japan. _____

2. It was so windy that they <u>can't</u> go on a picnic. _____

3. We know that you <u>will have</u> a good time. _____

4. Tom told her that she <u>has had</u> a cold. _____

C. 다음 문장을 바꾸어 쓸 때 빈칸에 알맞은 말을 쓰시오.

1. He thinks that he can do anything.
   → He thought that he _____ _____ _____.

2. They know that he is a carpenter.
   → They knew that he _____ _____ _____.

3. I believe that she will pass the exam.
   → I believed that she _____ _____ _____ _____.

4. She says that he wanted to go abroad.
   → She said that he _____ _____ to go abroad.

Grammar Tip

주절의 시제가 현재이면, 종속절의 시제는 어떤 시제도 올 수 있고, 주절의 동사가 과거인 경우에는 종속절의 시제는 과거 또는 과거완료가 와야 한다.

A. mistake 실수
   pay 지불하다
   goods 상품

B. picnic 소풍
   cold 감기

C. anything 무엇이든
   carpenter 목수
   abroad 해외에, 해외로

Unit 82 시제 일치의 예외

• 주절의 시제가 현재에서 과거로 바뀔지라도 종속적의 시제가 변하지 않는 경우가 있는데, 이러한 것을 시제의 예외라고 한다.

(1) 항상 현재를 쓰는 경우

현재의 습관, 보편적인 사실, 속담, 격언, 불변의 진리 등	He said that he **goes** to church on Sundays. (습관) She told me that two and two **makes** four. (진리) I told her that all that glitters **is** not gold. (속담)

(2) 항상 과거를 쓰는 경우

종속절이 역사적인 사실인 경우	He said that the French Revolution **broke out** in 1789.
종속절이 가정법으로 표현된 경우	He wishes he **were** young again. → He wished he **were** young again.

Practice

A. 다음 괄호 안에서 알맞은 것을 고르시오.

1. Jim told me that his school (begin / begins) at nine.
2. We know that Columbus (discovers / discovered) America.
3. They knew that the sun (rise / rises) in the east.
4. Amy said that she (get / gets) up at six every morning.
5. He learns that Korean War (breaks / broke) out in 1950.

B. 다음 밑줄 친 부분을 과거시제로 고쳐 문장을 다시 쓰시오.

1. He <u>teaches</u> me that light travels faster than sound.
   → _____

2. The man <u>says</u> that Shakespeare was born in 1564.
   → _____

3. We <u>know</u> that water boils at 100 degrees celsius.
   → _____

C. 다음 우리말과 같도록 괄호 안의 주어진 말을 이용하여 문장을 완성하시오.

1. 그는 정직이 최선이라고 말했다. (say, be)
   → He _____ that honesty _____ the best policy.

2. 나는 세종대왕이 한글을 발명했다는 것을 안다. (know, invent)
   → I _____ that King Sejong _____ Hangul.

3. 그녀는 지구가 둥글다고 배웠다. (learn, be)
   → She _____ that the earth _____ round.

Grammar Tip

주절이 과거일지라도 종속절이 현재의 습관, 보편적인 사실, 속담, 격언, 불변의 진리 등을 나타내면 현재시제를 사용하며 역사적 사실은 과거시제를 사용한다.

A. discover 발견하다

B. light 빛
   sound 소리, 음성
   celsius 섭씨

C. honesty 정직
   policy 정책, 방침
   round 둥근

A. 다음 괄호 안의 동사를 알맞게 변환하여 쓰시오. (현재시제)

1. Half of the oranges _____ fresh. (be)

2. Most of the necklaces _____ mine. (be)

3. Ten miles _____ not a long way to drive. (be)

4. A number of the students in our class _____ tired. (be)

5. Every person here _____ to the community. (belong)

6. Physics _____ his favorite subject. (be)

7. Two thirds of work _____ finished. (be)

8. Ten years _____ a long time to wait. (be)

B. 다음 밑줄 친 부분을 바르게 고치시오.

1. The professor and the student <u>agrees</u> on that point.

   _____

2. Every man and woman <u>need</u> love. _____

3. Neil Armstrong <u>landes</u> on the moon in 1969. _____

4. He thought that he <u>will</u> become famous. _____

5. The teacher taught us that the sun <u>set</u> in the west.

   _____

C. 다음 우리말과 뜻이 같도록 괄호 안의 말을 바르게 배열하시오.

1. 나는 그가 부지런했다고 생각했다. (was, thought, that, I, he, diligent)

   → _____

2. 10분은 이 시험을 끝내기에 충분한 시간이다. (enough, minutes, Ten, is)

   → _____ to complete this test.

3. 잼을 바른 빵은 내가 가장 좋아하는 아침 식사이다.

   (is, bread, my, with, jam)

   → _____ favorite breakfast.

4. 그 노인은 시간은 화살처럼 간다고 말했다. (time, flies, an arrow, like)

   → The old man said that _____

D. 다음 우리말과 같도록 괄호 안의 말을 이용하여 문장을 완성하시오.

1. 나는 내 팔찌를 잃어버렸다는 것을 알았다. (find, lost)

   → I _____ that I _____ _____ my bracelet.

2. 그 가구들의 대부분이 매우 값이 싸다. (most, be)

   → _____ _____ the furniture _____ very cheap.

3. Bill은 3 더하기 4는 7이 된다고 말했다. (say, make)

   → Bill _____ that three and four _____ seven.

 **Grammar Tip**

시간이나 거리가 하나의 형태를 나타낼 때는 단수 취급하지만 합쳐진 시간이나 거리는 복수 취급한다.
Ten years have passed since he died.

A. necklace 목걸이
　　community 공동체
　　physics 물리학

every, each, 거리, 시간 등은 단수 취급한다.

B. agree 동의하다
　　land 착륙하다

C. diligent 부지런한
　　complete 완료하다
　　arrow 화살

most of 뒤에 단수명사가 오면 단수 취급하고 복수명사가 오면 복수 취급한다.

D. bracelet 팔찌
　　furniture 가구

Unit 83 평서문의 간접화법

· 평서문의 직접화법을 간접화법으로 전환할 때, 전달동사를 바꾸고 시제나 대명사, 부사(구)도 알맞게 바꾼다.

전달동사	say → say, say to → tell
주절과의 연결어	인용 부호 삭제 → that
인칭대명사 변경	직접화법의 1인칭은 주절의 주어와, 2인칭은 주절의 목적어와 일치, 3인칭은 변화 없음 * 격변화에 맞게 변경
시제 일치	피전달문의 시제는 전달동사의 시제와 일치

부사구 변경

here → there
this(these) → that(those)
today → that day
tomorrow → the next day
tonight → that night
now → then
yesterday → the day before (the previous day)
ago → before
last night → the previous night

I **said**, "I **have** a beautiful ring." (직접화법)

→ I **said** that I **had** a beautiful ring. (간접화법)

She **said to** him, "**You will** go to the market **tomorrow**."

→ She **told** him that **he would** go to the market **the next day**.

Practice

A. 다음 문장을 간접화법으로 바꿀 때 빈칸에 알맞은 말을 쓰시오.

1. He said, "I am hungry now."
   → He _____ that he _____ hungry _____.

2. She said to me, "You are afraid of these snakes."
   → She _____ me that _____ _____ afraid of _____ snakes.

3. He said to me, "I won't go to school tomorrow."
   → He _____ me that _____ _____ go to school the next day.

B. 다음 문장을 직접화법으로 바꿀 때 빈칸에 알맞은 말을 쓰시오.

1. She told me that I had to study then.
   → She said to me, "_____"

2. Joe said that he had seen the circus the day before.
   → Joe said, "_____"

3. He told her that he would watch the movie.
   → He said to her, "_____"

C. 다음 우리말과 같도록 괄호 안의 말을 이용하여 문장을 완성하시오.

1. 그는 "나는 여기에 어제 도착했어."라고 말했다. (arrive)
   → He said "I _____ yesterday."
   → He _____ that _____ there _____.

2. 그녀는 "나는 그 박물관을 내일 방문할 거야."라고 말했다. (visit)
   → She said, "I _____ the museum tomorrow."
   → She said that _____ the museum _____.

Grammar Tip

직접화법을 간접화법으로 바꿀 때 시제도 일치시킨다.

A. afraid 두려운

간접화법의 시제가 과거완료이면 직접화법은 과거로 바꾼다.

B. circus 서커스

C. arrive 도착하다
museum 박물관

unit 84 의문사가 없는 의문문의 간접화법

• 의문사가 없는 의문문의 간접화법은 if나 whether를 이용하는데, 전달동사를 ask로 바꾸고 「if[whether]+주어+동사」의 순서로 바꾸며 시제나 대명사, 부사(구)도 알맞게 바꾼다.

전달동사	say (to) → ask
주절과의 연결어	인용 부호 삭제 → if[whether] 이용 / 피전달문은 「주어+동사」 어순
인칭대명사 변경	직접화법의 1인칭은 주절의 주어와, 2인칭은 주절의 목적어와 일치, 3인칭은 변화 없음 * 격변화에 맞게 변경
시제 일치	피전달문의 시제는 전달동사의 시제와 일치

He **said to** her, "Do you love me?" → He **asked** her if[whether] she loved him.
She **said to** me, "Is this your car?" → She **asked** me if[whether] that was my car.

Practice

A. 다음 문장을 간접화법으로 바꿀 때 빈칸에 알맞은 말을 쓰시오.

1. He said to me, "Are you busy?"
   → He _____ me whether _____ _____ busy.

2. She said to me, "Did you go to the theater last night?
   → She _____ me if _____ _____ _____ to the theater the previous night.

3. I said to her, "Will you be at the conference?"
   → I _____ her _____ _____ _____ _____ at the conference.

B. 다음 문장을 직접화법으로 바꿀 때 빈칸에 알맞은 말을 쓰시오.

1. I asked the doctor If I had to take the medicine.
   → I said to the doctor, "_____"

2. Kate asked me If I was listening to her.
   → Kate said to me, "_____"

3. She asked him if he could swim in the lake.
   → She said to him, "_____"

C. 다음 우리말과 같도록 괄호 안의 말을 이용하여 문장을 완성하시오.

1. 그녀는 내게 "내가 과자를 좀 먹어도 되니?"라도 물었다. (have, can)
   → She _____ me _____ some cookies.

2. Amy는 우리에게 "너는 그 소년의 이름을 아니?"라고 물었다. (know)
   → Amy _____ us _____ the boy's name.

Grammar Tip

직접화법에서 주절의 시제가 과거이고 전달문의 시제가 현재 완료나 과거인 경우, 간접화법에서 종속절의 시제를 과거완료로 바꾼다.

A. theater 극장
   conference 학회, 회의

B. medicine 약

직접화법에서 1인칭은 주절의 주어와 2인칭은 주절의 목적어와 인칭을 맞게 변경하고 문장의 위치에 맞게 격변화를 시켜준다.

C. cookie 쿠키

85 | 의문사가 있는 의문문의 간접화법

- 의문사가 있는 의문문의 간접화법은 의문사를 이용하는데, 전달동사를 ask로 바꾸고 「의문사＋주어＋동사」의 순서로 바꾸며 시제나 대명사, 부사(구)도 알맞게 바꾼다.

전달동사	say (to) → ask
주절과의 연결어	인용 부호 삭제 → 의문사 이용 / 피전달문은 「주어＋동사」 어순
인칭대명사 변경	직접화법의 1인칭은 주절의 주어와, 2인칭은 주절의 목적어와 일치, 3인칭은 변화 없음 ＊ 격변화에 맞게 변경
시제 일치	피전달문의 시제는 전달동사의 시제와 일치

She **said to** him, "When is your birthday?" → She **asked** him **when his birthday was**.

I **said to** her, "What did you eat for lunch?" → I **asked** her **what she had eaten** for lunch.

Practice

A. 다음 문장을 간접화법으로 바꿀 때 빈칸에 알맞은 말을 쓰시오.

1. He says to me, "Who will be your coach?"
   → He _____ me _____ will be _____ _____.

2. She said to me, "What time is it?"
   → She _____ me _____ _____ _____ _____.

3. He said to her, "Why did you shout at me?"
   → He _____ her _____ _____ _____ _____ at him.

B. 다음 괄호 안의 말을 바르게 배열하여 문장을 완성하시오.

1. (was, what, address, her)
   → I asked him _____.

2. (sent, who, him, had, the present)
   → He asked me _____.

3. (cap, bought, he, had, where, the)
   → My mother asked him _____.

C. 다음 우리말과 같도록 괄호 안의 말을 이용하여 문장을 완성하시오.

1. 그녀는 그에게 "너는 어디 가고 싶어?"라고 물었다. (want)
   → She _____ him _____ to go.

2. 그녀는 그들에게 "누가 그 꽃병을 깨뜨렸니?"라고 물었다. (break)
   → She _____ them _____ the vase.

3. 그녀는 그녀의 딸에게 "오늘 왜 화가 났니?"라고 물었다. (be)
   → She _____ her daughter _____ that day.

Grammar Tip

what time, how long, how old 등은 서로 분리할 수 없는 한 덩어리로 같이 나타내며 의문사가 주어일 경우에는 「의문사＋동사」 순서로 쓴다.

A. coach 코치, 감독
shout 소리치다

B. address 주소
present 선물

C. vase 꽃병

unit

86 명령문의 간접화법

- 명령문의 간접화법은 명령문의 동사를 to부정사로 바꾸고 부정명령문은 not to부정사의 형태로 바꾸어서 전환한다. 또한 전달동사는 문맥에 따라 tell, order, ask, advise 등으로 바꾼다.

전달동사	say (to) → tell(지시), order(명령), ask(요청), advise(충고)
주절과의 연결어	인용 부호 삭제 → to부정사(긍정명령문), not to부정사(부정명령문)
인칭대명사 변경	직접화법의 1인칭은 주절의 주어와, 2인칭은 주절의 목적어와 일치, 3인칭은 변화 없음 * 격변화에 맞게 변경
시제 일치	피전달문의 시제는 전달동사의 시제와 일치

I **said to** the boys, "Be quiet." → I **told** the boys **to be** quiet.
She **said to** him, "Clean the room." → She **ordered** him **to clean** the room.
You **said to** me, "Help her." → You **asked** me **to help** her.
He **said to** me, "Don't go there." → He **advised** me **not to go** there.

Practice

A. 다음 괄호 안의 말을 이용하여 빈칸에 알맞은 말을 쓰시오.

1. She said to them, "Don't fight each other." (order)
 → She _____ them _____ _____ _____ each other.

2. My mom said to me, "Walk your dog." (told)
 → My mom _____ me _____ _____ _____ dog.

3. He said to me, "Take care of yourself." (advise)
 → He _____ me _____ _____ care of _____.

4. She said to me, "Give me some candies." (ask)
 → She _____ me _____ _____ _____ some candies.

B. 다음 괄호 안의 말을 바르게 배열하여 문장을 완성하시오.

1. (her, to, ten dollars, lend)
 → She asked him _____.

2. (open, the door, me, asked, to)
 → He _____.

3. (to, smoking, advised, him, stop)
 → The doctor _____.

C. 다음 간접화법을 직접화법으로 바꿀 때 알맞은 말을 쓰시오.

1. Mother ordered me not to play with the ball inside.
 → Mother said to me, "_____"

2. The doctor advised me to get plenty of rest.
 → The doctor said to me, "_____"

3. The boy asked me not to tell them the truth.
 → The boy said to me, "_____"

Grammar Tip

문맥에 따라 명령일 경우에는 tell, order를 사용하고 부탁이나 요청일 경우에는 ask, 충고일 경우에는 advise를 쓴다.

A. each other 서로서로
walk 산책시키다

B. lend 빌려주다
stop 끊다

C. inside 안에서
plenty of 충분한
truth 진실, 사실

A. 다음 괄호 안에서 알맞은 것을 고르시오.

1. Mike asked me (if / that) I had an extra pen.
2. He told me that I (was / am) very honest.
3. Mother told us (not to touch / don't touch) it.

B. 다음 밑줄 친 부분을 바르게 고치시오.

1. He told me that he had come there <u>ago</u>. _____
2. Tom told me that he <u>will</u> help me. _____
3. She asked me <u>who was he</u>. _____
4. My father asked me <u>study</u> hard. _____

C. 다음 문장을 간접화법으로 바꿀 때 빈칸에 알맞은 말을 쓰시오.

1. I said to her, "I can play the piano."
   → I _____ her that I _____ _____ the piano.
2. He said to me, "Can you mail the letter for me?"
   → He _____ me _____ _____ _____ mail the letter for him.
3. She said to me, "Why are you crying?"
   → She _____ me _____ _____ _____ crying.
4. She said to me, "Brush your teeth three times a day."
   → She _____ me _____ _____ my teeth three times a day.

D. 다음 우리말과 같도록 괄호 안의 말을 이용하여 문장을 완성하시오.

1. 그는 그녀에게 "너는 아주 행복해 보여."라고 말했다. (look)
   → He _____ her that _____ _____ so happy.
2. 나는 James에게 "너는 어디에 사니?"라고 물었다. (live)
   → I _____ James _____ _____ _____.
3. Tom은 나에게 "너는 그 음악을 좋아하니?"라고 물었다. (like)
   → Tom _____ me _____ _____ _____ the music.

E. 다음 직접화법을 간접화법으로 바꾸시오.

1. He said to Judy, "Are you leaving today?"
   → _____
2. He said to me, "Do you know her address?"
   → _____
3. He said to me, "When did you buy your watch?"
   → _____
4. Mom said to me, "Don't be late for school."
   → _____

 **Grammar Tip**

부정명령문을 간접화법으로 전환할 때는 「not+to부정사」의 형태로 바꾸어 나타낸다.

A. extra 추가의, 여분의
   honest 정직한

ago는 과거시제에 쓰고 before는 현재완료나 과거완료시제에 쓴다.

C. mail 보내다, 부치다
   noise 소음

D. look ~처럼 보이다

의문사가 없는 의문문을 간접화법으로 바꿀 때, 「if[whether]+주어+동사」의 형태로 쓴다. 의문사가 있는 의문문은 「의문사+주어+동사」로 쓴다.

E. leave 떠나다
   watch 손목시계

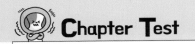 

[1-2] 다음 빈칸에 알맞은 것을 고르시오.

1.
> Everything _____ ready for the meal.

① is   ② are
③ have   ④ has
⑤ been

2.
> She told me that she usually _____ to bed early.

① is   ② are
③ go   ④ goes
⑤ went

3. 다음 밑줄 친 부분의 쓰임이 잘못된 것은?
① Ten miles <u>are</u> a long distance.
② Each woman <u>has</u> her own hat.
③ Economics <u>is</u> my favorite subject.
④ Some of my friends <u>wear</u> glasses.
⑤ Leaves of the tree <u>go</u> red and yellow.

4. 다음 빈칸에 알맞지 않은 것은?
> Curry and rice _____ delicious.

① is   ② are
③ was   ④ looks
⑤ looked

5. 다음 빈칸에 공통으로 알맞은 것은?
> · I _____ him if he could swim.
> · My mom _____ me not to go out.

① said   ② told
③ ordered   ④ asked
⑤ advised

6. 다음 우리말과 같도록 빈칸에 알맞은 것은?
> 그녀는 나에게 무엇을 하고 있었는지 물었다.
> → She asked me _____.

① what you were doing
② what was she doing
③ what she was doing
④ what was I doingh
⑤ what I was doing

[7-8] 다음 문장을 간접화법으로 바꿀 때 빈칸에 알맞은 것을 고르시오.

7.
> He said to us, "Open your books."
> → He told us _____.

① to open our books
② to open your books
③ if we open our books
④ if you open your books
⑤ whether we open our books

8.
> Maria said to me, "Do you love me?"
> → Maria asked me _____.

① that I love her
② that I loved her
③ if you love me
④ whether I love her
⑤ whether I loved her

9. 다음 빈칸에 들어갈 말이 바르게 짝지어진 것은?
> · Two-thirds of the basket _____ full.
> · Both brothers _____ alive now.

① is – is   ② is – are
③ were – is   ④ were – are
⑤ were – were

10. 다음 주어진 문장과 의미가 같은 것은?

> Mom said to us, "Don't make noises."

① Mom said that we didn't make noises.
② Mom told us that she didn't make noises.
③ Mom told us to not make noises.
④ Mom told us not to make noises.
⑤ Mom asked us if we didn't make noises.

[11-12] 다음 밑줄 친 부분이 어법상 어색한 것을 고르시오.

11. ① The news about her <u>is</u> good.
② The black and white dog <u>sleep</u> now.
③ Bread with butter <u>is</u> my breakfast.
④ Hide and seek <u>is</u> an interesting game.
⑤ Every boy in the library <u>studies</u> hard.

12. ① They learned that the sun <u>rises</u> in the east.
② He said that he usually <u>goes</u> to school at eight.
③ The girl said to her that water <u>boils</u> at 100℃.
④ He knows that World War Ⅱ <u>breaks</u> out in 1939.
⑤ The teacher said to us that honesty <u>is</u> the best policy.

13. 다음 중 화법 전환이 <u>잘못된</u> 것은?

① He said to me, "Who is she?"
 → He asked me who she was.
② Ann said to them, "Don't eat snacks."
 → Ann ordered them not eat snacks.
③ He said to her, "You can stay here"
 → He told her that she could stay there.
④ I said to him, "Can you play the piano?"
 → I told him if he could play the piano.
⑤ She said to him, "Go home at once."
 → She told him to go home at once.

14. 다음 직접화법을 간접화법으로 바꿀 때 밑줄 친 단어를 바르게 고친 것은?

> He said, "She left for Paris yesterday."
> → He said that she had left for Paris <u>yesterday</u>.

① today
② before
③ then
④ the next day
⑤ the day before

15. 다음 대화의 빈칸에 알맞은 것은?

> A: I have finished my homework.
> B: Sorry. What did you say?
> A: I said that I _____.

① finished my homework
② finishes my homework
③ have finished my homework
④ had finished my homework
⑤ had not finished my homework

16. 다음 문장의 빈칸에 알맞은 것은? (2개)

> I heard that he _____ America.

① visits
② visited
③ lives in
④ has been to
⑤ had gone to

17. 다음 중 어법상 <u>어색한</u> 것은?

① I asked her whether she knew him.
② We realized that there were someone in the dark.
③ She told me that she would watch the movie.
④ *Rome and Juliet* was written by Shakespeare.
⑤ A writer and teacher was invited to the conference.

18. 다음 두 문장이 같은 뜻이 되도록 빈칸에 알맞은 말을 쓰시오.

> The man said to her, "Where do you want to buy the gift?"

= The man _____ her _____ _____
_____ to buy the gift.

[19 – 20] 다음 문장을 간접화법으로 바르게 바꾼 것을 고르시오.

19.
> He said to me, "I'm a math teacher."

① He said that he is a math teacher.
② He said that he was a math teacher.
③ He told me that he is a math teacher.
④ He told me that he was a math teacher.
⑤ He said to me that he was a math teacher.

20.
> I said to her, "Is he coming back tonight?"

① I asked her if he is coming back tonight.
② I asked her if he was coming back tonight.
③ I asked her if he was coming back that night.
④ I told her that he was coming back tonight.
⑤ I told her that he was coming back that night.

<서술형 문제>

21. 다음 주어진 말로 문장을 전환할 때 빈칸에 알맞은 말을 쓰시오.

> She thinks that he is diligent.

→ She thought that _____ _____ _____
when he was young.

22. 다음 <보기>에서 알맞은 말을 골라 빈칸에 쓰시오.

> <보기>
> the number of   a number of   most

· _____ people are at the airport.
· _____ of the people are foreign
tourists.
· _____ tourists coming to Korea
is increasing these days.

23. 다음 우리말과 같도록 주어진 단어를 바르게 배열하시오.

> 그녀는 나에게 내일 어디에서 공부할 것인지 물었다. (she, would, where, I, me, the next day, asked, study)

→ _____

24. 다음 우리말과 같도록 빈칸에 알맞은 말을 쓰시오.

> 나는 그녀에게 "그가 언제 죽었나요?"라고 물었다. 그녀는 그가 죽은 이후로 10년이 흘렸다고 말했다. 그녀는 나에게 "10년은 긴 시간이죠."라고 말했다.

→ I _____ her "_____ did he die?" She
said that ten years had _____ _____ he
died. She _____ to me "_____ _____ is
a long time."

25. 다음 대화를 읽고, 문장을 완성하시오.

> *Doctor*: What's the matter?
> *Joseph*: I have a fever and a runny nose.
> *Doctor*: You have a cold. Take some
> medicine and get some rest.

(1) The doctor asked Joseph _____.
(2) The doctor advised him _____
_____.

특수구문이란 무엇인가?

문장 속에서 특별히 강조하고 싶은 말에 새로운 말을 추가하거나, 강조하고 싶은 말을 먼저 말하거나, 반복되는 말을 생략할 수 있는데 이럴 경우 문장의 어순이나 형태가 달라지는 것을 특수구문이라 한다. 이런 특수구문에는 강조, 도치, 생략이 있다.

My mother **does like** singing with family. (강조)

Here he comes. (도치)

I do **not** like **all** of them. (부분부정)

I can't ski well, but my sister **can**. (생략)

Chapter 12. 특수구문

87 강조(동사, 명사, 부정어)

· 강조는 어떤 사실이나 대상에 대해 강조하거나 관심을 유도하기 위해 새로운 말을 넣거나 형식을 변형하는 것이다.

강조	형식	의미	예문
동사 강조	do(does, did)+동사원형 ＊주어의 인칭, 수, 시제에 맞게 조동사 do 이용	'정말로', '꼭'	I **do** take a walk every morning. She **does** know everything about you. He **did** come here.
명사 강조	the very+명사 / 재귀대명사	'직접', '바로'	He is **the very** man I am looking for. I will do it **myself**.
부정어 강조	not ~ at all[in the least]	'도무지', '전혀'	He is **not** honest **at all**. I am **not** happy **in the least**.

Practice

A. 다음 강조하는 표현이 되도록 알맞은 것을 고르시오.

1. She (does / do) pass the exam.

2. He did not do his homework (in the least / himself).

3. They did the project (itself / themselves).

4. This is (the very / a very) wallet I want to have.

B. 다음 밑줄 친 부분을 강조하는 표현이 되도록 빈칸에 알맞은 말을 쓰시오.

1. Ellen made this spaghetti.
   → Ellen made this spaghetti _____.

2. They like playing basketball in the park.
   → They _____ _____ playing basketball in the park.

3. I spent time with my family yesterday.
   → I _____ _____ time with my family yesterday.

4. The machine did not help them do the work.
   → The machine did not help them do the work _____
   _____.

C. 다음 우리말과 같은 뜻이 되도록 빈칸에 알맞은 말을 쓰시오.

1. 이것은 내가 편안함을 느끼는 바로 그 의자이다.
   → This is _____ _____ _____ I feel comfortable.

2. 그 남자는 한달에 두 번 그가 직접 잔디를 깎는다.
   → He _____ cuts the grass twice a month.

3. 나는 그의 음악을 전혀 좋아하지 않는다.
   → I did _____ like his music _____ _____.

Grammar Tip

일반동사를 강조할 때는 조동사 do
를 시제에 맞게 쓴다.

A. project 프로젝트, 과제
wallet 지갑

B. spend 보내다
machine 기계

명사의 강조는 명사 앞에 the very
를 넣거나 문장 끝이나 주어 뒤에 재
귀대명사를 넣는다.

C. comfortable 편안한
grass 잔디, 풀

Unit 88 강조(It ~ that)

- 문장 속에서 주어나 목적어, 부사(구, 절) 등을 강조하기 위해 It ~ that 강조구문을 사용하며, It is[was]와 that 사이에 강조할 말을 넣는다.

I met Amy at the museum this morning.

→ **It was** I **that(who)** met Amy at the museum this morning. (주어 강조)

→ **It was** Amy **that(whom)** I met at the museum this morning. (목적어 강조)

→ **It was** at the park **that(where)** I met Amy this morning. (장소 강조)

→ **It was** this morning **that(when)** I met Amy at the museum. (시간 강조)

* '~인 것은 바로 ~이다[였다]'로 해석하며 강조 대상에 따라 that 대신에 who(m)(사람), which(사물), when(시간), where(장소) 등이 올 수 있다.

Practice

A. 다음 밑줄 친 부분을 〈It ~ that〉 구문을 사용하여 강조하시오.

1. Carol met <u>his client</u> at the station.
   → _____

2. Billy played soccer <u>after school</u>.
   → _____

3. I broke <u>the window</u> at that time.
   → _____

4. Susan wrote the report <u>in the library</u>.
   → _____

B. 다음 문장의 밑줄 친 부분을 바르게 고쳐 쓰시오.

1. It <u>is</u> Johns that she saw at the corner yesterday. _____

2. It was the product <u>who</u> I advertised on the Internet. _____

3. It is at this restaurant that the young man <u>worked</u>. _____

C. 다음 우리말과 같도록 괄호 안의 말을 이용하여 문장을 완성하시오.

1. 진정한 재산은 바로 건강이다.
   → _____ is _____ _____ is real wealth. (health)

2. 내가 여기에 도착한 것은 바로 지난 일요일이었다. (last)
   → _____ was _____ _____ _____ I arrived here.

3. 공항에서 그녀를 만난 사람은 바로 Eric이었다. (Eric)
   → _____ was _____ _____ met in the airport at that time.

4. 그녀가 지난 주말에 산 것은 바로 이 드레스였다. (dress)
   → _____ was _____ _____ she bought last weekend.

Grammar Tip

It ~ that 강조구문에서 강조되는 어구가 사람일 경우에는 who, 장소일 경우에는 where, 시간일 경우에는 when, 사물일 경우에는 which를 쓸 수 있다.

A. client 고객
   station 역
   report 보고서

It ~ that 강조구문에서 시제가 과거이면 It was ~ that을, 현재이면 It is ~ that을 사용한다.

B. corner 모퉁이
   advertise 광고하다

C. wealth 부, 재산
   airport 공항
   weekend 주말

Unit 89 | 도치(장소 부사(구), 부정어)

- 문장은 보통 「주어+동사」의 어순인데, 장소의 부사(구)를 문장의 맨 앞에 놓아 강조할 경우 「장소의 부사(구)+동사+주어」의 어순이 된다. 하지만 주어가 대명사일 경우에는 「주어+동사」의 어순을 유지한다.

  On the beach sat the woman. (부사구+동사+주어)   **Here** we are. (부사+대명사주어+동사)

- 부정어 never, little, hardly, seldom 등이 동사를 부정하여 의미를 강조할 경우할 경우 「부정어+조동사+주어+본동사」의 형태가 된다.

  I never dreamed that I would be a doctor.

  → **Never did** I dream that I would be a doctor.

  I have seldom read a report that was so full of lies.

  → **Seldom have** I **read** a report that was so full of lies.

Practice

A. 다음 문장을 주어진 단어로 시작하여 다시 쓰시오.

1. The balls are under the table.
   → Under _____.

2. It hardly rains in the desert.
   → Hardly _____.

3. The vase is next to the window.
   → Next to _____.

4. We never saw him again.
   → Never _____.

B. 다음 우리말과 같도록 괄호 안의 말을 이용하여 문장을 완성하시오.

1. 얼마나 많은 일이 남았는지 그는 거의 알지 못했다. (know)
   → Little _____ _____ _____ how much work was left.

2. 좀처럼 나는 그렇게 아름다운 여자를 보지 못했다. (see)
   → Seldom _____ _____ _____ such a beautiful woman.

3. 그 의자 뒤에 그의 아버지가 서 있다. (stand)
   → Behind the chair _____ _____ _____.

C. 다음 우리말과 뜻이 같도록 괄호 안의 말을 알맞게 배열하시오.

1. 여기 그 택시가 온다. (the, comes, taxi)
   → Here _____.

2. 내 머리 위로 무당벌레가 날아갔다. (head, the, flew, ladybug, my)
   → Over _____.

3. 거의 그는 학교에 늦지 않는다. (late, school, was, for, he)
   → Rarely _____.

Grammar Tip

부정어 도치에서 일반동사가 아닌 be동사가 있는 경우에는 「부정어+be동사+주어」의 어순으로 쓴다.

A. desert 사막

hardly, little, seldom 등의 부정어는 부정의 의미를 내포하고 있으므로 not과 함께 쓰이지 않는다.

B. be left 남다
behind ~ 뒤에

C. over ~ 위에
ladybug 무당벌레

Unit 90 도치(so, neither+동사+주어)

- 상대방의 의견에 동의할 때 긍정문에서는 「so+동사+주어」, 부정문에서는 「neither+동사+주어」의 형태로 나타 낸다. 동사는 앞에 쓰인 동사의 종류에 맞춘다.

so+동사+주어	'~도 또한 그렇다'	A: She was a teacher. B: **So was** he. (=He was a teacher, too.)
neither+동사+주어	'~도 또한 아니다'	A: He cannot swim. B: **Neither can** I. (=I cannot swim, either.)

- 조동사나 be동사가 없을 때는 조동사 do를 이용하며 앞 문장의 시제와 일치시킨다.
  A: She likes to play tennis.　　B: **So do** I.

Practice

A. 다음 빈칸에 so나 neither를 포함하여 알맞은 말을 쓰시오.

1. He likes swimming.　　　　　　　– ＿＿＿＿ ＿＿＿＿ she.
2. She was not a movie star.　　　　– ＿＿＿＿ ＿＿＿＿ he.
3. He would like to succeed.　　　　– ＿＿＿＿ ＿＿＿＿ I.
4. I am proud of my father.　　　　　– ＿＿＿＿ ＿＿＿＿ I.
5. Ben doesn't want to raise a dog. – ＿＿＿＿ ＿＿＿＿ I.

B. 다음 우리말과 같도록 괄호 안의 말을 알맞게 배열하시오.

1. 나는 미국에 가고 싶고, 그녀 또한 그렇다.
   (America, to, and, she, would, go, so)
   → I would like to ＿＿＿＿＿＿＿＿＿＿＿＿＿＿＿＿＿.

2. 나는 다음 일요일 거기에 안 갈 것이고, Jane 또한 그렇다.
   (neither, will, next, there, Sunday, Jane, and)
   → I won't go ＿＿＿＿＿＿＿＿＿＿＿＿＿＿＿＿＿.

3. Linda는 좋은 변호사이고, Jimmy 또한 그렇다.
   (so, lawyer, good, Jimmy, is, and, a)
   → Linda is ＿＿＿＿＿＿＿＿＿＿＿＿＿＿＿＿＿.

C. 다음 우리말과 같도록 빈칸에 알맞은 말을 쓰시오.

1. Jessy는 어젯밤 TV를 보지 않았어. – Mark도 또한 그랬어.
   → Jessy didn't watch TV last night. – ＿＿＿＿ ＿＿＿＿ ＿＿＿＿.

2. 나는 영어 공부를 하고 있어. – 그도 또한 그래.
   → I am studying English. – ＿＿＿＿ ＿＿＿＿ ＿＿＿＿.

3. 그는 독일에 가 본 적이 없어. – 나도 또한 그래.
   → He has never been to Germany. – ＿＿＿＿ ＿＿＿＿ ＿＿＿＿.

4. Bill은 내일 늦을 거야. – 나도 또한 그래.
   → Bill will be late tomorrow. – ＿＿＿＿ ＿＿＿＿ ＿＿＿＿.

Grammar Tip

조동사나 be동사가 없을 때에는 조동사 do를 이용하며 앞 문장의 시제와 일치시킨다.

A. movie star 영화배우
   proud 자랑스러운
   raise 기르다

B. would like to ~하고 싶다
   lawyer 변호사

완료시제처럼 조동사 have가 있는 경우에는 have를 so 뒤에 쓰며, 앞 문장의 시제와 일치시킨다.

C. Germany 독일

Unit 91 부분부정과 전체부정

- 부분부정과 전체부정은 의미에 유의해야 하는데, 부분부정은 전체 중에 일부만 아니라는 것을 표현할 때 사용한다.

- 부분부정은 every, all, both, always 등의 부사가 not과 함께 쓰여 '모두(항상) ~인 것은 아니다'의 의미로 전체가 아닌 일부를 부정한다.

  I do **not** know **both** of them. (부분부정)　　　She did **not** invite **all** of them. (부분부정)

  → I do **not** know **either** of them. (전체부정)　　→ She did **not** invite **any** of them. (전체부정)

- 전체부정은 any, any-, either이 not과 결합하여 none, nothing, neither, nobody, never 등의 표현으로 쓰이면 '아무도 ~하지 않다'라는 뜻으로 전체부정을 나타낸다.

  I have **none** of these.(=I **don't** have **any** of these.)　　**Nobody** likes her.

Practice

A. 다음 부분부정은 전체부정이, 전체부정은 부분부정이 되도록 빈칸에 알맞은 말을 쓰시오.

1. Not everybody likes her.

   → _____ likes her.

2. I haven't met either of the teachers.

   → I haven't met _____ of the teachers.

3. Both of my mom and dad are not chubby.

   → _____ of my mom and dad are chubby.

B. 다음 우리말과 같도록 빈칸에 알맞은 말을 쓰시오.

1. 그 영화 둘 다 무섭지 않다.

   → _____ of movies is scary.

2. 모든 학생이 여기에 온 것은 아니다.

   → _____ _____ the students came here.

3. 그가 항상 그 회의에 가는 것은 아니다.

   → He _____ _____ go to the meeting.

4. 나는 그들 중 아무도 사랑하지 않는다.

   → I _____ love _____ of them.

5. 그 방문객들 중 아무도 일찍 떠나지 않았다.

   → _____ of the tourists left early.

6. 모든 세균이 인간에게 해로운 것은 아니다.

   → _____ _____ the germs are harmful to humans.

7. 아무도 그 일을 하루에 끝낼 수 없다.

   → _____ _____ can finish the work in a day.

Grammar Tip

부정어 not과 every, all, both, always 등과 함께 쓰이면 부분부정의 의미를 갖는다.

A. chubby 통통한

both, neither, either은 대상이 둘일 때 쓰며, all, any는 대상이 셋 이상일 때 쓴다. 또한 every, neither, either 등이 주어로 쓰일 때는 단수동사를 쓴다.

B. scary 무서운
tourist 방문객
germ 세균
harmful 해로운

92 | 생략(공통부분, 주어+be동사)

· 영어에서는 불필요한 말이나 반복을 피하기 위해 반복되는 말을 생략하기도 한다.

1. 접속사로 연결되어 반복되는 어구는 생략할 수 있다.	Jane went to Paris and Amy (went) to Rome.
2. 질문의 응답에서 동사가 반복될 때 조동사만 사용한다.	*A*: Will you be back soon? *B*: Yes, I will (be back soon).
3. 비교급 구문에서 뒤의 말이 중복되면 생략할 수 있다.	Brian is as tall as Jim (is).
4. to부정사가 반복되는 경우 to만 사용하고 동사원형은 생략한다.	I want to go on a trip to China, but my dad doesn't want to (go on a trip to China).
5. 때, 조건, 양보의 부사절에서 부사절 속의 주어와 주절의 주어와 같을 때 「주어+be동사」의 생략이 가능하다.	When (she was) young, she was very smart.
6. if 부사절에서 주어가 주절의 주어와 다르더라도 「주어+be동사」를 생략해 관용적 표현으로 if necessary [possible, any] 등으로 쓰기도 한다.	I'll go with you if (it is) necessary.
7. 감탄문에서 「주어(주로 대명사)+be동사」를 생략할 수 있다.	What a wonderful day (it is)!

*1~4번은 공통부분의 생략이고, 5~7번은 「주어+be동사」의 생략이다.

Practice

A. 다음 밑줄 친 부분을 생략된 어구를 넣어 다시 쓰시오.

1. Tom loves mountains and Jane lakes. _____

2. I can run faster than you. _____

3. You may go if you want to. _____

4. *A*: Can you dance? *B*: Yes, I can. _____

5. If at work, I can't answer your questions. _____

6. Call me again, if possible. _____

B. 다음 우리말과 같도록 빈칸에 알맞은 말을 쓰시오.

1. 그는 비록 가난했지만 행복했다.
   → _____ _____, he was happy.

2. 어떤 사람들은 공원에 가고 다른 사람들은 극장에 간다.
   → Some people go to the park, and others to _____ _____.

3. 그녀는 내가 Ann을 만나기를 바랐지만, 나는 그러고 싶지 않았다.
   → She wanted me to meet Ann, but I didn't _____ _____.

4. 어렸을 때, 우리는 주말마다 스키를 타러 가곤 했다.
   → _____ _____, we would go skiing every weekend.

5. 가능하다면, 내가 너에게 그 돈을 빌려 줄게.
   → _____ _____, I will lend you the money.

Grammar Tip

주절의 주어를 먼저 찾아보고 부사절에 「주어+be동사」를 시제에 맞게 추가한다.

A. possible 가능한

when, while, though, if 등이 이끄는 부사절에서는 「주어+be동사」를 생략할 수 있다.

B. would ~하곤 했다
　 lend 빌려주다

93 | 간접의문문

• 간접의문문이란 의문문이 다른 문장의 일부가 되어 간접적으로 물어보는 형식을 갖는 것으로 문장에서 주어, 목적어, 보어의 역할을 한다.

의문사가 있는 간접의문문	의문사+주어+동사	Do you know? + What does he want? → Do you know **what he wants**?
의문사가 없는 간접의문문	if(whether)+주어+동사	I don't know. + Can he play soccer? → I don't know **if(whether) he can play soccer.**
생각, 추측 동사의 간접의문문 (의문사가 think, believe, suppose, imagine, guess 등의 목적어로 쓰일 때)	의문사를 문장 맨 앞에 놓는다.	Do you think? + Who is he? → **Who** do you **think** he is?

Practice

A. 다음 문장에서 잘못된 것을 찾아 바르게 고쳐 쓰시오.

1. Do you know when the concert start? _____

2. I want to know if is he Chinese. _____

3. Do where you think he lived? _____

B. 다음 두 문장을 한 문장으로 바꿔 쓰시오.

1. Can you tell me? + Where is the bank?
   → _____

2. Do you believe? + How old is the old woman?
   → _____

3. Do you know? + Did Sarah loved him?
   → _____

4. I want to know. + Will you go on a field trip?
   → _____

C. 다음 우리말과 같도록 빈칸에 알맞은 말을 쓰시오.

1. 너는 누가 안전핀을 발명했는지 알고 있니?
   → Do you know _____ _____ the safety pin?

2. 너는 어디서 지갑을 잃어버렸다고 생각하니?
   → _____ do you think _____ _____ your purse?

3. 네가 내일 올 건지 나에게 알려 줘.
   → Let me know _____ _____ _____ _____ tomorrow.

4. 그는 나에게 그녀는 언제 그 도서관에 갔는지 물었다.
   → He asked me _____ _____ _____ to the library.

Grammar Tip

간접의문문은 직접의문문이 다른 문장의 일부로 쓰이는 것을 말하며 평서문의 어순을 갖는다.

A. concert 콘서트

B. field trip 현장 학습

의문사가 없는 간접의문문은 「if(whether)+주어+동사」의 어순을 갖는다.

C. safety pin 안전핀
purse 지갑

A. 다음 밑줄 친 부분을 강조하여 문장을 다시 쓰시오.

1. She doesn't think I love her, but I <u>love</u> her.
   → _____

2. She bought the scarf <u>two years ago</u>.
   → _____

3. You do <u>not</u> like her song.
   → _____

B. 다음 문장의 밑줄 친 부분을 바르게 고쳐 쓰시오.

1. Down <u>the rain came</u>. _____

2. Hardly <u>he does</u> work on the weekend. _____

3. I am proud of my parents. – <u>Neither do I</u>. _____

4. Do you know when <u>starts the train</u>? _____

5. <u>Do what</u> you think she wants? _____

C. 다음 부분부정은 전체부정이, 전체부정은 부분부정이 되도록 알맞은 말을 쓰시오.

1. I don't trust both of them. → I _____ trust _____ of them.

2. None of them will come. → _____ _____ of them will come.

3. I do not know both of them. → I know _____ _____ _____.

D. 다음 우리말과 같도록 빈칸에 알맞은 말을 쓰시오.

1. 그녀가 어렸을 때, 그녀는 키가 크고 예뻤다.
   → _____ _____, she was tall and pretty.

2. 가능하다면 너는 기름진 음식을 피해야 한다.
   → You have to avoid fatty food, _____ _____.

3. 그들은 휴가에 정말로 좋은 시간을 보냈다.
   → They _____ _____ a good time on holiday.

4. 나는 이것들 중 어느 것도 가지고 있지 않다.
   → I have _____ of these.

E. 다음 우리말과 같도록 괄호 안의 말을 이용하여 문장을 완성하시오.

1. 필요하다면, 난 어디든 갈 것이다. (necessary)
   → _____ _____, I will go anywhere.

2. 비록 졸렸지만 그녀는 연구를 계속했다. (sleepy)
   → _____ _____, she continued to do an experiment.

3. 나는 집에 머물고 싶었지만 그럴 수 없었다. (can)
   → I wanted to stay home, but _____ _____.

4. Emily는 빵 굽는 것을 좋아하고, 나 또한 그렇다. (so)
   → Emily likes to bake bread, _____ _____ _____.

Grammar Tip

일반동사의 강조는 「do+동사원형」이다. 이때 의미는 '정말로'이다.

A. scarf 스카프, 목도리

의견에 동의할 때 긍정은 「so+(조)동사+주어」로 표현하고 부정은 「neither+(조)동사+주어」로 표현한다.

B. proud 자랑스러운

부분부정은 not+both[all, every, always] 등과 같이 쓰인다. 전체부정은 none[neither, nobody, never] 등의 표현을 쓴다.

부사절과 주절의 주어가 같은 경우 부사절의 「주어+be동사」는 생략할 수 있다.

D. avoid 피하다
fatty 기름진
holiday 휴가, 방학

E. anywhere 어디에, 어디든
experiment 연구
bake 굽다

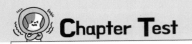

[1-2] 다음 빈칸에 알맞은 것을 고르시오.

1.
> Susan doesn't like sports. _____ do I.

① So
② Such
③ Either
④ Too
⑤ Neither

2.
> Never _____ such a thing would happen.

① he imagine
② imagined he
③ he imagined
④ did he imagine
⑤ did he imagined

3. 다음 밑줄 친 that의 쓰임이 다른 것은?
① It was at the corner that I met Sam.
② It was yesterday that they painted wall.
③ It was certain that he passed the exam.
④ It was James that left for New York.
⑤ It was the movie that we watched then.

4. 다음 대화의 빈칸에 알맞은 것은?

> A: I want to raise a cat.
> B: _____ do I

① So
② As
③ Both
④ Not
⑤ Neither

5. 다음 우리말과 같도록 괄호 안의 단어를 이용하여 빈칸에 알맞은 말을 쓰시오.

> 주말에는 그는 거의 일을 하지 않는다. (work)
> Rarely _____ _____ _____ on weekends.

6. 다음 밑줄 친 부분을 생략할 수 없는 것은?
① What an exciting game it is!
② When I was in my room, the bell rang.
③ She is much taller than her sister is.
④ While he was in London, he visited the palace.
⑤ I try to lose lots of weight if it is possible.

7. 다음 우리말을 바르게 영작한 것은?

> 그녀는 여기에 제시간에 온 적이 거의 없다.

① Seldom she was here on time.
② Seldom was here she on time.
③ Seldom here was she on time.
④ Seldom was she here on time.
⑤ Seldom did she be here on time.

8. 다음 문장과 의미가 같은 것은?

> There was a bus stop across the street.

① Across the street a bus stop was.
② Across the street did be a bus stop.
③ Across the street was a bus stop.
④ Across the street a bus stop did be.
⑤ Was a bus stop across the street there.

9. 다음 빈칸에 들어갈 말이 바르게 짝지어진 것은?

> · Penguins can't fly. _____ can ostriches.
> · He is very busy. _____ am I.

① So - So
② Neither - So
③ So - Neither
④ Neither - As
⑤ Neither - Neither

10. 다음 문장과 의미가 같은 것은?

> Some women can play the piano, but others can't.

① All women can play the piano.
② None of the women can play the piano.
③ Any women can play the piano.
④ Every woman can play the piano.
⑤ Not every woman can play the piano.

11. 다음 강조 문장 중 어색한 것은?

① It was a book that I bought yesterday in the bookstore.
② It was bought that I a book yesterday in the bookstore.
③ It was yesterday that I bought a book in the bookstore.
④ It was I that bought a book yesterday in the bookstore.
⑤ It was in the bookstore that I bought a book yesterday.

12. 다음 문장 중 생략된 부분이 없는 것은?

① He came here because he just wanted to.
② When young, I used to like the bands.
③ I think that the girl is very honest.
④ The baby sleeping in the bed is cute.
⑤ This is the watch given by my father.

13. 다음 빈칸에 공통으로 알맞은 것은?

> · Little _____ I dream of such a thing.
> · He spoke English better than she _____.

① can   ② be
③ do   ④ did
⑤ have

14. 다음 중 강조를 나타낸 문장이 아닌 것은?

① Here comes the bus.
② Never did I see her again.
③ I don't like Japanese music.
④ These are the very books I have been looking for.
⑤ The husband did love his wife forever.

15. 다음 중 문장의 전환이 잘못된 것은?

① He fell down.
   → Down fell he.
② She rarely said a single word that day.
   → Rarely did she say a single word that day.
③ The bakery is at the end of the street.
   → At the end of the street is the bakery.
④ Though he is small, he plays basketball well.
   → Though small, he plays basketball well.
⑤ I am not good at math. He isn't good at math, either.
   → I am not good at math. Neither is he.

16. 다음 중 부분부정의 문장이 아닌 것은?

① She does not know anything.
② Not both of his parents are alive.
③ Not every man is very diligent.
④ The people cannot do everything.
⑤ Not all of the students are present.

17. 다음 <보기>의 밑줄 친 부분과 쓰임이 같은 것은?

> <보기>
> I do know about the truth.

① When do you do your homework?
② I do call her, but she doesn't answer.
③ He does his best to finish the work.
④ Do they play soccer at the playground?
⑤ My brother swims better than I do.

167

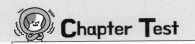 

18. 다음 두 문장의 의미가 같도록 빈칸에 알맞은 것은?

> I do not like either of them.
> = I dislike _____ of them.

① all   ② any
③ both   ④ none
⑤ neither

19. 다음 중 어법상 <u>어색한</u> 것은?

① Here comes the teacher.
② I do believe she is innocent.
③ He does wants to go on a picnic with us.
④ It was in the room where she lost a ring.
⑤ Not every bird succeeds in learning how to fly.

20. 다음 두 문장을 한 문장으로 바꿔 쓸 때, 빈칸에 알맞은 것은?

> Do you think?
> + What does he want to eat?
> → _____ to eat?

① What do you think he want
② What do you think he wants
③ What do you think does he want
④ Do you think what he wants
⑤ Do you think what does he want

<서술형 문제>

21. 다음 밑줄 친 부분을 강조하는 문장으로 바꿔 쓰시오.

> Denis had a car accident <u>on this road</u>.

= It _____

22. 다음 우리말과 같도록 괄호 안의 단어를 바르게 배열하여 문장을 완성하시오.

> 그 산 꼭대기 위에 큰 호수가 있었다.
> (a big lake, the top, of, the mountain, was, on)
> <조건> 부사구 도치 문장으로 쓰시오.

→ _____

23. 다음 두 문장을 한 문장으로 바꿔 쓸 때, 빈칸에 알맞은 말을 쓰시오.

> (1) Tell me. + Who did you play badminton last week?
> (2) Do you suppose? + Where are they going to go on a trip?

(1) Tell me _____.
(2) _____ on a trip?

24. 다음 주어진 내용을 참고하여 같은 의미가 되도록 빈칸에 알맞은 쓰시오.

> Tina goes to school by bus four days a week. She walks to school one day a week.

→ Tina does _____ _____ go to school by bus.

25. 다음 주어진 문장과 의미가 같도록 빈칸에 알맞은 말을 쓰시오.

> I don't want to be a soldier, and he doesn't want to be a soldier, either.

→ I don't want to be a soldier. _____ _____ he.

Student Book
Answer Key

Chapter 1. 부정사

Unit 01. 명사처럼 쓰이는 to부정사
Practice

A. 1. To understand 2. to lose 3. to be 4. to win
   5. not to leave
B. 1. It, to, go 2. It, to, use 3. It, to, ride
C. 1. to, do 2. to, walk 3. not, to, touch 4. To, make

Unit 02. 의문사 + to부정사
Practice

A. 1. how to use 2. when to order 3. where to put
   4. what to buy
B. 1. what, I, should, do 2. where, she, should, find
   3. when, I, should, leave 4. how, he, should, feed
C. 1. where, to, sit 2. who, to, invite 3. when, to, stop
   4. how, to, ride

Unit 03. 형용사처럼 쓰이는 to부정사
Practice

A. 1. to write with 2. to explain 3. to sit on
   4. to work
B. 1. a hotel to stay at
   2. time to charge my phone
   3. an important topic to talk about
   4. the best way to learn a new language
C. 1. to, play, with 2. money, to, buy
   3. first, woman, to, win 4. space, to, store

Unit 04. be동사 + to부정사
Practice

A. 1. to win 2. to enter 3. to observe 4. to open
B. 1. is, to, depart 2. were, to, get 3. are, to, submit
   4. are, to, be
C. 1. is, to, return 2. is, to, start 3. are, not, to, drive
   4. was, to, be, heard

Unit 05. 부사처럼 쓰이는 to부정사
Practice

A. 1. 그 진실을 안다면
   2. 그 파티에서 그녀를 보게 되어
   3. 4개의 언어를 말하다니
   4. 결정을 하기 위해
B. 1. only to find it closed 2. early not to miss
   3. easy to understand 4. sorry to hear
C. 1. to be 2. to climb 3. to pass 4. to wash

Unit 06. too ~ to, enough to
Practice

A. 1. so, clever, that, can, complete
   2. too, heavy, to, carry
   3. easy, enough, to, solve
B. 1. too cold to stay 2. tall enough to reach
   3. too icy to run
C. 1. too hot to drink
   2. too narrow, to pass
   3. loud enough, to hear
   4. smart enough to use

Review Test / Unit 01~06

A. 1. to preserve 2. to become 3. to tell 4. to return
B. 1. big enough 2. to see 3. to sit on
   4. are to succeed
C. 1. too, cold, to, sleep 2. is, to, have
   3. to, solve 4. when, to, send
D. 1. is, to, finish
   2. too, complicated, to, learn
   3. how, to, get

Unit 07. to부정사의 의미상의 주어
Practice

A. 1. for, her, to, bake 2. of, him, to, say
   3. for, them, to, obey 4. me, to, call
B. 1. of you 2. Julie 3. for her 4. for me
C. 1. you, to, tell 2. for, me, to, buy 3. me, to, park
   4. of, him, to, take

Unit 08. to부정사의 시제
Practice

A. 1. to, enjoy 2. to, have, had 3. to, be
B. 1. to, pass 2. to, have, been 3. to, have, been
   4. to, have, met
C. 1. to, know 2. to, have, broken, down 3. to, see
   4. to, have, started

Unit 09. 원형부정사
Practice

A. 1. pass 2. get 3. travel 4. crawling
B. 1. shake[shaking] 2. carry[to carry] 3. finish
   4. leak[leaking]
C. 1. the, accident, happening 2. me, stand
   3. me, apologize 4. him, go

Unit 10. 대부정사와 독립부정사
Practice
A. 1. exercise 2. try on this coat
   3. order Chinese food

B. 1. To be honest with you
   2. To make matters worse
   3. To be sure
   4. not to mention

C. 1. So to speak 2. To begin with 3. Strange to say

Review Test / Unit 07~10
A. 1. to, have, kept 2. to, have, been 3. of, you, to
   4. me, to, send

B. 1. wear[wearing] 2. of the boy 3. promise
   4. to have spent

C. 1. us not to touch 2. felt somebody touch
   3. so to speak 4. allowed me to use

D. 1. didn't, allow, to 2. makes, me, laugh
   3. To, make, matters, worse 4. to, have, been

Chapter Test / Unit 01~10
1. ② 2. ④ 3. ② 4. ⑤ 5. ② 6. ⑤ 7. ① 8. ⑤ 9. ①,
② 10. ① 11. ⑤ 12. ④ 13. to have taken 14. thirsty
enough to 15. ⑤ 16. ② 17. ① 18. ⑤ 19. to 20. ③
21. It's[It is] not easy to find a place to store the boxes
here. 22. Strange to say 23. to have had a lot of friends
24. where to go 25. to have → have

1. 문장에서 보어 역할을 하는 to부정사가 들어가야 한다.
2. '함께 말할 친구들'이 되어야 하므로 전치사 with가 오는 것이 자연스럽다.
3. to부정사의 부정은 to부정사 앞에 not을 붙인다.
4. ⑤는 목적을 나타내는 to부정사의 부사적 용법이고, 나머지는 형용사적 용법으로 쓰였다.
6. last는 과거를 나타내는 말이므로 완료부정사인 to have been이 되어야 한다.
8. '너는 다른 사람들을 놀려서는 안 된다.'는 뜻으로 의무를 나타내는 should나 must를 써야 하고 부정의 의미이므로 not을 붙인다.
10. ①은 사람의 성격을 나타내므로 of가 들어가야 하고, 나머지는 for가 들어간다.
11. ask는 목적격보어로 to부정사가 온다.
13. to부정사의 행위가 문장 전체의 시제보다 먼저 일어났으므로 완료형을 써야 한다.
14. '~할 만큼 충분히 …한'의 의미가 되어야 한다.
15. '그녀에게 혼자 긴 여행을 하지 말라고 말했다'의 의미가 되어야 하므

로 대부정사를 써서 not to가 되어야 한다.
16. ②는 to부정사의 행위가 문장 전체의 시제와 같은 때에 일어났으므로 단순형인 「to+동사원형」을 써야 한다.
17. 첫 번째 빈칸에는 보어 역할을 하는 to부정사가 들어가야 하고, 두 번째 빈칸에는 조건을 나타내는 「be+to부정사」의 형태가 들어가야 한다.
18. 〈보기〉는 원인을 나타내는 to부정사의 부사적 용법이고, ①③④는 명사적 용법, ②는 형용사적 용법, ⑤는 형용사를 수식하는 부사적 용법으로 쓰였다.

Chapter 2. 동명사
Unit 11. 주어, 보어로 쓰이는 동명사
Practice
A. 1. Protecting 2. watching 3. Traveling 4. eating

B. 1. is repairing vehicles
   2. Listening to classical music is
   3. is designing characters
   4. Reading e-books is becoming

C. 1. Driving, fast 2. going, fishing 3. Not, getting

Unit 12. 목적어로 쓰이는 동명사
Practice
A. 1. meeting 2. turning 3. being 4. taking

B. 1. living 2. purchasing 3. leaving 4. coming

C. 1. going 2. drinking 3. exploring 4. playing

Unit 13. 동명사의 의미상의 주어
Practice
A. 1. his 2. my 3. her 4. Their

B. 1. Chris staying up late
   2. her throwing away the old clothes
   3. your being so rude
   4. people killing animals for fun

C. 1. making 2. his, quarreling 3. his, student, breaking
   4. my, failing

Unit 14. 동명사와 현재분사
Practice
A. 1. a. 동명사 b. 현재분사
   2. a. 동명사 b. 현재분사

B. 1. 밤에 스키를 타러 가는 것은 매우 위험하다.
   2. 그들은 그의 개와 걷고 있는 남자를 안다.
   3. 우리의 계획은 시내에 가게를 여는 것이다.

C. 1. walking, stick 2. reading, glasses
   3. Playing, with, sand 4. wearing, a, yellow, cap

Unit 15. 동사의 목적어 1(동명사, to부정사 동사)
Practice

A. 1. doing 2. to skate 3. catching 4. shaking

B. 1. to, keep 2. breaking 3. interrupting 4. to accept

C. 1. reading 2. applying 3. to remember 4. to raise

Unit 16. 동사의 목적어 2(모두 쓰는 동사)
Practice

A. 1. a. 그는 소포를 보내는 것을 잊었다.
　　 b. 그는 소포를 보냈던 것을 잊었다.
　 2. a. 그들은 피자를 만들려고 애썼다.
　　 b. 그들은 시험 삼아 피자를 만들었다.

B. 1. saying 2. crying 3. to change

C. 1. making 2. to take 3. drinking 4. to turn

Unit 17. 동명사의 관용 표현
Practice

A. 1. camping 2. watching 3. seeing 4. preparing

B. 1. hearing 2. admiring 3. reading 4. skipping

C. 1. no, use, trying
　 2. spends, time, going
　 3. What[How], about, postponing

Review Test / Unit 11~17

A. 1. eating 2. our 3. to water 4. receiving

B. 1. arguing 2. winning 3. to go 4. to pass

C. 1. stopped using plastic bags
　 2. Lucy forgetting his address
　 3. give up inventing the time machine
　 4. Not wearing seat belts

D. 1. used, to, eating 2. Remember, to, call
　 3. forward, to, visiting 4. are, worth, collecting

Chapter Test / Unit 11~17

1. ③ 2. ② 3. ③ 4. ④ 5. ② 6. ② 7. ④ 8. ③ 9. ⑤
10. ⑤ 11. ③ 12. ⑤ 13. to take 14. my forgetting
15. have → having 16. ⑤ 17. ④ 18. ③ 19. ② 20. ③
21. Discussing the topics is necessary. 22. your appearing
23. is no living 24. We should stop throwing trash in the
river. 25. charging → to charge

1. 문장에서 주어 역할을 하는 동명사나 to부정사의 형태가 들어가야 한다.
2. give up은 동명사를 목적어로 취하는 동사이다.
3. ③은 현재분사이고, 나머지는 동명사이다.
6. 동명사의 의미상의 주어는 소유격으로 나타낸다.

9. decide는 to부정사를 목적어로 취하는 동사이다.
12. cannot[can't] help+-ing: ~하지 않을 수 없다, try+to부정사: ~하려고 애쓰다
13. '식사 전에 약 먹는 것을 기억해라'라는 뜻이 되어야 하므로 「remember +to부정사」를 쓴다.
14. '엄마는 내가 문 잠그는 것을 자주 잊어버리는 것을 싫어하신다'라는 뜻이므로 동명사의 의미상의 주어로 소유격을 쓴다.
16. 〈보기〉와 ⑤는 현재분사이고, 나머지는 동명사이다.
17. keep은 동명사를 목적어로 취하는 동사이고, '~할 가치가 있다'는 「be worth+-ing」의 형태로 표현한다.
22. 전치사 뒤에는 동명사가 와야 하고, 동명사의 의미상의 주어는 소유격으로 나타낸다.
23. There is no ~: ~하는 것은 불가능하다
25. '충전하는 것을 잊어 버렸다'라는 의미가 되어야 하므로 「forget+to 부정사」의 형태가 되어야 한다.

Chapter 3. 분사
Unit 18. 분사의 역할
Practice

A. 1. 서술적 용법 2. 한정적 용법 3. 서술적 용법
　 4. 한정적 용법

B. 1. falling 2. bored 3. written 4. wearing

C. 1. crawling, my, arm 2. very, satisfying
　 3. used, car 4. spoken, in, Canada

Unit 19. 분사구문
Practice

A. 1. Finishing 2. Seeing 3. Hearing 4. Not, having

B. 1. Being 2. listening 3. Turning 4. Entering

C. 1. Smiling 2. Not, feeling 3. Being

Unit 20. 분사구문의 의미1(시간, 이유, 조건)
Practice

A. 1. Eating 2. Being 3. Taking 4. Seeing

B. 1. If you do your best
　 2. when you cross the street
　 3. While he played soccer
　 4. Because he didn't receive an email

C. 1. Having 2. Listening 3. Changing

Unit 21. 분사구문의 의미2(양보, 동시, 연속)
Practice

A. 1. Approaching 2. Being 3. Waving 4. checking

B. 1. Though he is rich

2. and arrived here at nine

   3. As she drank hot coffee

   4. and paid for dinner

C. 1. Driving 2. Living 3. going

Review Test / Unit 18~21

A. 1. exciting, excited 2. baked 3. boiled 4. rising

B. 1. excited 2. made 3. Not, being 4. Finishing

C. 1. When we arrived 2. Holding

   3. Because he didn't feel 4. Listening

D. 1. something burning

   2. The novels written by

   3. Being interested in space

Unit 22. 완료형 부사구문

Practice

A. 1. Having spent 2. Having been written

   3. Having lost 4. Not having heard

B. 1. Having been painted 2. Not having eaten

   3. Having been born 4. Having met

C. 1. Having read 2. Having, been, made

   3. Having, been, destroyed 4. Not, having, slept

Unit 23. being, having, been의 생략

Practice

A. 1. Being, given, Given

   2. Having, been, born, Born

B. 1. Published 2. Seen 3. Bitten 4. Tired

C. 1. Sung 2. Taken 3. Covered 4. Injured

Unit 24. 독립분사구문, 비인칭 독립분사구문

Practice

A. 1. There being no bus service

   2. The sun having set

   3. It being a holiday

B. 1. It being 11 o'clock

   2. Chores being done

   3. There being a lot of traffic

C. 1. Judging, from

   2. Generally, speaking

   3. Frankly, speaking

Unit 25. with + 명사 + 분사

Practice

A. 1. shaking 2. turned 3. running 4. covered

B. 1. crossed 2. flying 3. watching 4. unlocked

C. 1. coming 2. hurt 3. hanging

Review Test / Unit 22~25

A. 1. Being, imported 2. Not, having, played

   3. his, eyes, closed 4. It, being

B. 1. Built 2. Having lost 3. Not having reviewed

   4. turned

C. 1. running 2. Pleased 3. Having, visited 4. Judging

D. 1. Frankly speaking, I'm disappointed at his rude manner.

   2. There being no seats, we waited for the next train.

   3. He sang along with his arms folded.

Chapter Test / Unit 18~25

1. ③ 2. ② 3. ⑤ 4. ④ 5. closing → closed 6. ③ 7. ⑤
8. ③ 9. asking 10. ② 11. ② 12. ③, ⑤ 13. ④ 14. ⑤
15. Not having ridden 16. and, reached 17. ② 18. ③
19. There being 20. Not meeting → Not having met
21. Though[Although] I heard the truth from her 22. Not knowing the road, she lost her way. 23. flying, with, crossed 24. Wanting to stay healthy, you should cut down on snacks. 25. her tears running down her cheeks

1. '떨어진 나뭇잎들'이라는 수동의 의미가 되어야 하므로 과거분사를 쓴다.

2. While he was watching a movie로 이루어진 부사절의 분사구문이 되어야 한다.

4. ④ Being lost → Having been lost

6. 수동의 의미를 나타내는 분사구문에서 being이나 having been은 생략할 수 있다.

7. 첫 번째 빈칸은 지각동사의 보어로 동작을 나타내므로 동사원형이나 현재분사를, 두 번째 빈칸은 명사와 분사의 관계가 수동이므로 과거분사를 쓴다.

8. 분사구문의 주어가 의미상의 주어와 일치하지 않을 때는 분사 앞에 의미상의 주어를 쓴다.

12. 수동의 의미를 나타내는 분사구문에서 being이나 having been은 생략할 수 있다. 분사구문의 시제가 주절보다 앞서므로 완료형으로 쓴다.

14. judging from: ~로 판단하건대

15. 부사절의 시제가 주절의 시제보다 앞서므로 완료형 분사구문으로 쓰고 부정이므로 not을 분사 앞에 쓴다.

16. '그리고 ~하다'의 연속 상황을 나타내는 분사구문이므로 and를 써서 연결한다.

20. 분사구문의 시제가 주절의 시제보다 앞서므로 완료형 분사구문을 쓴다.

21. '그녀에게서 진실을 들었지만 ~'의 양보의 의미가 되는 것이 자연스럽다.

23. fly와 bird는 능동의 관계이므로 현재분사를 쓰고, 동시동작을 나타낼 때는 「with+명사+분사」의 형태로 쓰는데 명사와 분사가 수동의 관계이므로 과거분사를 쓴다.

Chapter 4. 시제
Unit 26. 현재완료의 용법-완료, 결과
Practice

A. 1. 결과 2. 완료 3. 결과 4. 완료

B. 1. have, submitted 2. has, departed 3. has, spent
   4. has, stolen

C. 1. haven't, decided 2. has, lost 3. Has, finished
   4. has, gone

Unit 27. 현재완료의 용법-경험, 계속
Practice

A. 1. 계속 2. 경험 3. 경험 4. 계속

B. 1. Have, ridden 2. has, sung 3. has, read
   4. have, been

C. 1. have, donated 2. has, been 3. have, known
   4. haven't, heard

Unit 28. 현재완료 진행시제
Practice

A. 1. has, been, raining 2. have, been, flying
   3. have, been, learning 4. have, been, talking

B. 1. Has, been, waiting 2. have, been, building
   3. has, been, drawing 4. have, been, using

C. 1. have, been, living 2. have, been, discussing
   3. has, been, eating

Unit 29. 과거완료
Practice

A. 1. had borrowed 2. had written 3. had gone
   4. begun

B. 1. had, been 2. had, lived 3. had, seen
   4. had, taken

C. 1. had, ordered 2. had, finished 3. had, missed
   4. had, bought

Unit 30. 과거완료 진행시제와 미래완료
Practice

A. 1. had been waiting 2. had been writing
   3. will have stayed 4. will have remained

B. 1. will have visited 2. had been drawing

3. will have been married

C. 1. will, have, belonged 2. will, have, worked
   3. had, been, walking 4. had, not, been, feeling

Review Test / Unit 26~30

A. 1. has, been, working 2. has, lost
   3. had, been, waiting

B. 1. had known 2. will have lived 3. has gone
   4. had never seen

C. 1. had you been driving 2. will have finished
   3. had never been 4. have been decorating

D. 1. have, been, using 2. had, already, sung
   3. will, have, watched

Chapter Test / Unit 26~30

1. ③ 2. ④ 3. ④ 4. ① 5. had left 6. ④ 7. ④ 8. ②
9. ② 10. ① 11. ③ 12. ④ 13. ③ 14. have, been, running
15. will, have, stayed 16. ④ 17. ③ 18. ① 19. ④ 20. ③
21. They have never seen a rainbow till now. 22. had, used,
for, broke 23. The movie will have begun before five p.m.
24. has been wearing glasses since 25. ⓐ has learned
[has been learning] ⓑ will have mastered

1. 3월 이후 현재까지 동작이 진행되고 있으므로 현재완료 진행시제를 쓴다.

2. 과거 이전의 어느 시점으로부터 더 먼저 발생한 동작이므로 과거완료를 쓴다.

3. 미래의 어느 시점의 완료된 일을 나타내므로 have finished는 will have finished가 되어야 한다.

4. ①은 과거완료로 써야 하므로 had가 알맞고 나머지는 현재완료 시제이므로 have가 알맞다.

6. ④ has been crying → had been crying

7. 플랫폼에 도착한 것보다 기차가 떠난 것이 먼저 일어났으므로 과거완료로 쓴다.

8. 과거에 진행된 일이 현재까지 이어지고 있으므로 현재완료 진행시제를 쓴다.

9. 여기서 산지 얼마나 됐는지 묻고 있으므로 '작년부터'라고 답하는 것이 가장 적절하다.

13. 완료시제의 부정은 have[has/had] 뒤에 not을 붙이고, 부사 yet은 끝에 온다.

14. 과거에 시작된 동작이 현재까지 이어지고 있으므로 현재완료 진행시제를 쓴다.

15. 미래의 어느 시점까지 진행되는 상태나 동작의 완료, 계속 등을 나타낼 때는 미래완료 시제를 쓴다.

16. know는 진행형으로 쓸 수 없으므로 have known이 되어야 한다.

18. '인도에 가서 현재 여기에 없다'는 뜻이므로 결과를 나타내는 현재완료로 표현할 수 있다.

19. 〈보기〉는 현재완료의 계속 용법을 나타낸다. ① 결과 ② 경험 ③ 완료 ④ 계속 ⑤ 완료

22. 고장나기 이전부터 사용하고 있었으므로 과거완료를 사용해서 완성한다.

23. 미래완료 시제는 「will have + p.p.」의 형태로 쓴다.

25. ⓐ는 과거의 동작이 현재까지 계속되고 있으므로 현재완료 또는 현재완료 진행시제를 쓰고, ⓑ는 미래의 어느 시점에 동작의 완료를 나타내므로 미래완료 시제를 쓴다.

Chapter 5. 조동사

Unit 31. can, could
Practice

A. 1. can 2. can't 3. Could you 4. could

B. 1. can't see 2. Can I have 3. This cannot be
   4. wil be able to speak

C. 1. cannot, be, hungry 2. Could, you, turn
   3. couldn't, play 4. will, be, able, to, arrive

Unit 32. may, might
Practice

A. 1. Joseph은 병원에 있을지도 모른다.
   2. 그녀는 영화를 볼 수 있을지도 모른다.
   3. 너는 여기서 길을 건너서는 안 된다.

B. 1. may have 2. may be 3. May I use
   4. may not want

C. 1. might, come 2. may, not, like 3. May, I, see
   4. may, not, be

Unit 33. must, have to
Practice

A. 1. must 2. have to 3. had to 4. must

B. 1. must be 2. will have to study 3. don't have to work
   4. must not eat

C. 1. must, not, throw 2. don't, have, to, take
   3. must, be 4. had, to, walk

Unit 34. Should, ought to
Practice

A. 1. should wear 2. should offer 3. should walk
   4. should save

B. 1. not to 2. should 3. should not 4. exercise

C. 1. should, not, park 2. start 3. ought, to, recycle

4. ought, not, to, eat

Unit 35. had better, would better
Practice

A. 1. had 2. would rather 3. better not 4. stay

B. 1. would, rather, not, have 2. had, better, admit
   3. had, better, not, tell 4. would, rather, spend

C. 1. would, rather, travel 2. had, better, apologize
   3. had, better, not, buy 4. would, rather, wear

Unit 36. used to, would
Practice

A. 1. go 2. used to 3. would 4. be

B. 1. used to be 2. used to ride 3. used to think
   4. used to live

C. 1. used, to, be 2. would, go 3. used, to, be
   4. would, play

Unit 37. 조동사 + have + 과거분사형
Practice

A. 1. may 2. must 3. should have booked
   4. cannot have told

B. 1. must have touched
   2. can't have fallen asleep
   3. might have been

C. 1. can't[cannot], have, written 2. should, have, been
   3. must, have, felt 4. may[might], have, lost

Review Test / Unit 31~37

A. 1. could 2. ought not to 3. can't 4. would

B. 1. used to 2. had to 3. would rather
   4. should not have made

C. 1. should have arrived 2. can't have forgotten
   3. had better not watch 4. will be able to give

D. 1. should not[ought not to] have believed him
   2. don't have[need] to give a tip
   3. may[might] have called her mom

Chapter Test / Unit 31~37

1. ① 2. ③ 3. ② 4. ④ 5. ③ 6. ④ 7. ⑤ 8. ① 9. ③
10. will be able to 11. ①, ③, ⑤ 12. must, not, feed
13. may[might], go, camping 14. ② 15. ② 16. ③ 17. ⑤
18. ① 19. ② 20. ① 21. you, must, not 22. used, to, be
23. You had better work out regularly. 24. should, have, taken 25. might have forgotten

1. 의미상 '그는 잠든 게 틀림없다'라고 추측하는 내용의 조동사가 필요하다.

2. 의미상 '외투를 입는 게 좋겠다'라는 뜻이 되어야 자연스럽다.

3. ② ought to not → ought not to

5. ③은 허락의 의미로 쓰였고, 나머지는 추측의 의미로 쓰였다.

10. 조동사는 두 개를 함께 쓸 수 없으므로 can을 be able to로 바꾼다.

12. 금지를 나타내므로 must not으로 바꿔 쓸 수 있다.

14. 첫 번째 빈칸에는 과거의 불규칙한 습관을 나타내는 would가 들어가야 하고, 두 번째 빈칸에는 '~하는 게 낫다'라는 뜻의 would rather가 들어가야 한다.

17. had better의 부정은 뒤에 not을 붙인다.

18. 과거의 상태를 나타낼 때는 used to를 써서 표현한다.

20. 명령, 주장의 동사 뒤의 that절에서는 보통 should를 생략하고 동사원형만 쓴다.

21. 금지를 나타낼 때는 must not으로 표현한다.

24. 과거의 일에 대한 유감을 나타내므로 「should have+p.p.」의 형태로 바꿔 쓸 수 있다.

25. 불확실한 추측을 나타낼 때는 「may have+p.p.」의 형태로 나타낼 수 있는데, 과거의 일에 대한 추측이므로 might로 쓴다.

Chapter 6. 수동태

Unit 38. 단순 수동태

Practice

A. 1. is washed   2. by   3. Were   4. was not

B. 1. are caused by carless driving
   2. are employed by the company
   3. was not invited to the party
   4. is the word pronounced

C. 1. The man was bitten by a mosquito.
   2. The building was damaged by the typhoon.
   3. Is the wall painted by Anna?

Unit 39. 조동사가 있는 수동태

Practice

A. 1. can be used   2. should be   3. may not be
   4. must be

B. 1. Will, be, sent
   2. must[should], be, repaired
   3. may, be, published
   4. should[must], not, be, forgotten

C. 1. Food can not be taken into the library (by you).
   2. The dessert must be served soon by the waiter.
   3. Will a new computer be sold by them?
   4. The engine may be invented by him.

Unit 40. 진행시제와 완료시제 수동태

Practice

A. 1. is being filmed   2. being baked   3. had not been
   4. has been built

B. 1. Have the photos taken
   2. was being decorated
   3. is not being made
   4. had been prepared

C. 1. The orphans have been helped by David.
   2. Is the magic show being watched by kids?
   3. The missing dog hasn't been found by us yet.
   4. The thief was being chased by the policemen.

Unit 41. 4형식 문장의 수동태

Practice

A. 1. was given   2. was told   3. of   4. for

B. 1. were, sent, to   2. was, not, told   3. will, be, offered

C. 1. We are given lots of information in his blog.
   2. Special dinner was cooked for her by her husband.
   3. The letter was read to students by the principal.
   4. Ron was asked a question by the foreigner.

Review Test / Unit 38~41

A. 1. is held   2. will be posted   3. been built
   4. were composed

B. 1. can be used   2. been trained   3. being rescued
   4. will be given to

C. 1. have been remembered by us
   2. were shown to me by Ben
   3. was caught by the boy
   4. Are the coins being collected

D. 1. was, bought, for, me
   2. has, been, eaten
   3. should[must], be, paid

Unit 42. 5형식 문장의 수동태

Practice

A. 1. was elected   2. to shout
   3. was made   4. to turn

B. 1. were, seen, to, cross   2. was, kept, clean
   3. were, left, open   4. was, called, superman

C. 1. He was seen to drive a bus by me.
   2. She was made to follow the law by Bill.
   3. Their baby was named Becky by them.
   4. They were advised to exercise regularly by her.

Unit 43. 동사구의 수동태

Practice

A. 1. to 2. off 3. at 4. over

B. 1. will, be, dealt, with 2. was, brought, up
3. be, looked, down, on 4. be, put, off

C. 1. I was picked up by Daniel from the station.
2. My house was broken into by the robbery.
3. The lights were turned off by the staff in the hall.

Unit 44. 목적어로 쓰인 that절의 수동태

Practice

A. 1. It was believed that 2. It is thought that
3. are expected to finish 4. It is said that

B. 1. It, is, believed 2. is, said, to 3. was, thought, to
4. was, supposed, that

C. 1. was said that Brain was on vacation
2. was found to appear on the show
3. was reported that many people were homeless after the flood
4. is hoped to win the game

Unit 45. by 이외의 전치사가 쓰인 수동태

Practice

A. 1. with 2. from 3. at 4. in

B. 1. are, worried, about 2. is, filled, with
3. are, pleased, with 4. is, known, to

C. 1. is, known, for 2. was, satisfied, with
3. are, made, of 4. is, known, as

Review Test / Unit 42~45

A. 1. was broken into 2. is known that
3. was brought up 4. be covered with

B. 1. to wear 2. interested in 3. was bought for
4. seen to eat

C. 1. is, thought, to, be 2. was, given, to
3. was, heard, to, play 4. is, called, Sweetie

D. 1. was ran over by 2. is looked up to
3. It is believed 4. was asked to call

Chapter Test / Unit 38~45

1. ④ 2. ⑤ 3. ④ 4. ③ 5. ① 6. ④ 7. ⑤ 8. ④ 9. ③
10. ⑤ 11. made to stay 12. ③ 13. ① 14. ③ 15. ⑤
16. is being watched by us 17. was advised to quit
smoking 18. ③ 19. ② 20. ① 21. is, looked, up, to, by
22. have, not, visited, the, city 23. His name is being
written on the paper. 24. (1) is thought that James will
travel to Europe (2) is thought to travel to Europe
25. ⓐ is reported ⓑ be protected ⓒ be thrown

1. '기원전 400년경에 지어졌다'라는 의미이므로 과거시제의 수동태로 나타낸다.
2. '종이는 나무로 만들어진다.'라는 의미이므로 be made from이 알맞다.
3. ① can cooked → can be cooked ② was explaining → was being explained ③ tell → told ⑤ deliver → delivered
4. ③ found be → found to be
7. 의미상 수동태가 되어야 하고, 조동사가 있는 문장이므로 「조동사+be+p.p」의 형태가 되어야 한다. 조동사의 부정은 조동사 뒤에 not을 붙인다.
10. '울타리를 넘는 것이 목격되었다'라는 의미가 되어야 하므로 지각동사의 수동태로 쓰는 것이 알맞다.
11. 사역동사의 수동태는 목적격보어를 to부정사로 바꿔 준다.
14. 주어가 the cups이고 과거시제이므로 Yes, they were.가 알맞다.
15. 4형식 문장에서 동사 made는 간접목적어를 주어로 하여 수동태를 만들 수 없다.
16. 진행시제의 수동태는 「be동사+being+p.p」의 형태로 쓴다.
17. 5형식의 수동태는 목적어를 주어로 하고, 목적격보어는 동사 뒤에 그대로 쓴다.
18. '맛있는 파스타로 유명하다'라는 의미이므로 be known for로 써야 한다.
19. 완료시제 수동태의 의문문은 「Have+주어+been+p.p.~?」의 형태로 쓴다.
24. 목적어로 쓰인 that절의 수동태는 「It is ~ that ....」의 형태로 수동태를 만들거나 that절의 주어를 목적어로 하여 that절의 동사를 to부정사로 바꿔 쓸 수 있다.

Chapter 7. 비교구문

Unit 46. 비교급과 최상급

Practice

A. 1. shorter, shortest 2. bigger, biggest
3. happier, happiest 4. less, least
5. more useful, most useful 6. better, best

B. 1. hottest 2. more 3. longest 4. heaviest

C. 1. cheapest 2. more, interesting 3. later 4. highest

Unit 47. as + 원급 + as

Practice

A. 1. well 2. hard 3. yours

B. 1. as, early, as 2. as[so], dangerous, as
3. as, tall, as 4. as, much, as

C. 1. as, soft, as 2. not, smart, as

3. river, is, as, deep, as

4. not, as[so], difficult, as, I, think

Unit 48. 원급 비교구문과 배수 비교구문

Practice

A. 1. possible 2. many 3. times 4. could

B. 1. possible 2. more, than 3. twice, as, many

C. 1. three times as long 2. as soon as they could

3. twice as high 4. as much as possible

5. four times older than

Unit 49. 비교급＋than

Practice

A. 1. angrier 2. faster 3. happier

B. 1. longer, than 2. larger, than 3. earlier, than

4. younger, than, older, than

C. 1. more dangerous than 2. even harder than

3. still heavier than 4. much bigger than

Unit 50. 열등비교와 비교급 비교구문

Practice

A. 1. less, intelligent, than 2. less, popular, than

3. as, good, as

B. 1. faster → fast 2. than → as 3. larger → large

4. hot → hotter

C. 1. less busy than 2. getting smaller and smaller

3. The fresher, the better

Unit 51. 최상급 비교구문

Practice

A. 1. largest 2. of 3. artists 4. in

B. 1. men 2. the worst 3. by far 4. most

C. 1. the, shortest, of 2. the, largest, in

3. the, most, beautiful, of 4. one, of, the, liveliest

Unit 52. 다양한 최상급 표현

Practice

A. 1. No, planet, so[as], large, as, No, planet, larger, than, larger, than, any, larger, than, planets

2. so[as], important, as, Nothing, more, important, than, more, important, than, more, important, than

B. 1. as, important, Nothing, more, important, more, important, than

2. the, largest, clock, larger, the, other, clocks, No, other, larger, than

Review Test / Unit 46~52

A. 1. ② 2. ③ 3. ① 4. ④

B. 1. as 2. twice, as 3. three, times, more

C. 1. lighter, than

2. the, largest, city

3. less, expensive, than

4. as, she, could

D. 1. the, cheapest, shirt

2. less, interesting, than

3. one, of, the, best, players

4. The, longer, the, harder

Chapter Test / Unit 46~52

1. ② 2. ④ 3. ⑤ 4. ② 5. less easy 6. ③ 7. ⑤ 8. ①
9. ⑤ 10. one of the greatest 11. ② 12. ⑤ 13. ① 14. ③
15. ④ 16. more 17. ③ 18. ④ 19. ④ 20. ⑤ 21. Her school is twice as big as my school. 22. The earlier he leaves, the sooner he will arrive. 23. (1) as tall as (2) not as tall (3) less tall 24. (1) cheaper than (2) the cheapest (3) more expensive than 25. larger as → larger than

1. 두 대상의 성질이나 상태가 동등할 때 사용하는 원급비교는 「as＋원급 ＋as」의 형태로 원급이 와야 한다.

2. '가장 ~한'의 뜻을 가진 최상급 표현은 「the＋형용사/부사의 최상급」으로 나타낸다.

3. 비교급을 강조할 때는 much, still, even, a lot 등을 쓰며 원급을 강조할 때는 very를 쓴다.

4. 최상급을 만들 때, -ful, -ous, -less 등으로 끝나는 단어와 3음절 이상의 단어는 「the most＋원급」의 형태로 만든다.

5. 「not so(as) ~as」는 '~만큼 ~하지 않다'는 뜻으로 「less＋원급＋than」의 열등비교 문장과 바꿔 쓸 수 있다.

6. 「A ~ not so(as) ~as B」는 주어를 B로 해서 「B ~ 비교급＋than A」로 바꿔 쓸 수 있다.

7. 「비교급＋and＋비교급」은 '점점 더 ~한'이라는 뜻으로 비교급을 이용한다.

8. -ful, -ous, -less 등으로 끝나는 단어와 3음절 이상의 단어는 「more＋원급」의 형태로 비교급을 만들며 비교급을 강조할 때는 much를 비교급 앞에 쓴다.

9. 「not so(as) ~as」는 열등비교를 의미하고 나머지는 최상급을 의미한다.

10. 「one of the＋최상급＋복수명사」는 '가장 …한 것 중의 하나'라는 뜻이다.

11. than 앞에는 형용사/부사의 비교급이 온다.

12. 최상급은 정관사 the와 함께 쓰인다.

13. much는 수량을 나타낼 때 셀 수 없는 명사 앞에서 많음을 나타내며, 또한 비교급 앞에 쓰여 비교급을 강조하는 역할을 한다.

14. Kevin의 몸게는 84kg으로 Jane의 몸무게 42kg의 두 배이다.

15. ① 그녀의 목소리와 비교하는 것이므로 you 대신 너의 목소리(your voice) 또는 너의 것(yours)이 되어야 한다.

16. 「the+비교급」, 「the+비교급」: ~하면 할수록 더 …하다 / 같은 사람이나 사물의 성격이나 특성을 비교할 때는 「more+원급+than」을 쓴다.

17. 배수를 이용할 때는 「배수+as+원급+as」 또는 「배수+비교급+than」으로 나타낸다.

18. very는 원급을 강조할 때 사용하며 비교급 앞에는 사용하지 않는다.

20. 「the+최상급+in」 뒤에는 단수명사(범위)가 오고, 「the+최상급+of」 뒤에는 복수명사(대상)가 온다.

21. '~보다 몇 배 더 …한'은 「배수+as+원급+as」로 표현할 수 있다.

Chapter 8. 관계사

Unit 53. 주격 관계대명사

Practice

A. 1. who 2. that 3. that 4. which

B. 1. who, wears 2. which, are 3. that, lives

C. 1. This is the woman who[that] is a famous pianist.
   2. The bag which[that] was stolen belongs to Emma.
   3. The people who[that] are tourists have just arrived there.

Unit 54. 소유격 관계대명사

Practice

A. 1. whose 2. who 3. whose 4. whose 5. of which

B. 1. whose, cover 2. whose, hobby 3. whose, hair

C. 1. Alex has a friend whose name is Kelly.
   2. This is the hat whose price is very high.
   3. He is the man whose birthday is today.
   4. I have a neighbor whose brother lives in Germany.

Unit 55. 목적격 관계대명사

Practice

A. 1. which 2. who 3. that 4. whom 5. that

B. 1. which[that], I, wanted
   2. who(m)[that], she, is
   3. which[that], we, visited

C. 1. This is the music which[that] he likes the most.
   2. The songs which[that] he composed for her are so sweet.
   3. The man who(m)[that] they saw in my house is my nephew.
   4. What is the title of the novel which[that] you read recently?

Unit 56. 관계대명사 what

Practice

A. 1. What 2. which 3. what 4. that 5. What

B. 1. what → that 2. that → what 3. That → What
   4. what → that 5. that → what

C. 1. 그는 어제 무엇을 샀니?
   2. 이것은 그가 어제 산 것이다.

D. 1. what, I, advised
   2. What, he, says, what, he, does

Review Test / Unit 53~56

A. 1. which 2. whose 3. what 4. who

B. 1. what 2. who[that] 3. who[that] 4. What

C. 1. whose 2. which/that 3. what 4. who(m)[that]

D. 1. He wants a new car whose roof can be open.
   2. I read a magazine which[that] was full of exciting stories.
   3. We are looking for the man who[that] was called Jackson.

E. 1. who[that], suffer 2. what, you, have
   3. whose, mother, tongue

Unit 57. 관계대명사 that을 쓰는 경우

Practice

A. 1. that 2. which, that 3. that 4. who, that 5. that
   6. that

B. 1. the, only, person, that
   2. the, tallest, woman, that
   3. have, everything, that

C. 1. He is the first man that invented the phone.
   2. She is the smartest girl that goes to this school.
   3. You may borrow any book that you want.

Unit 58. 관계대명사의 용법

Practice

A. 1. who 2. who 3. which 4. whose 5. which

B. 1. for, he 2. but, it 3. and, it

C. 1. which, surprised 2. who, is 3. which, made

Unit 59. 전치사+관계대명사

Practice

A. 1. at which 2. in which 3. with whom 4. in 5. about

B. 1. in, which 2. with, whom 3. for, whom

C. 1. The music to which we listened was very good.
   2. I have found the data for which I was looking.

3. The colored pencil with which John is writing is red.

Unit 60. 관계대명사의 생략
Practice

A. 1. which 2. who is 3. who is 4. whom

B. 1. books, written 2. playing, the, guitar 3. to, which

C. 1. Look at the bright stars shining in the sky.
2. The bread he bought yesterday is delicious.
3. I have a watch made in Switzerland.
4. The girl surprised at the news is my cousin.

Review Test / Unit 57~60

A. 1. that 2. that 3. who 4. to which 5. at which

B. 1. and, it 2. for, it 3. but, him

C. 1. Look at the children holding balloons.
2. I will meet Jake we talked about yesterday.
3. Is this a drama written by Shakespeare?
4. Wastes carried from land to sea pollute water.

D. 1. only, person, that 2. anything, that
3. which, impossible 4. covered, with

Unit 61. 관계부사 when, where
Practice

A. 1. where 2. when 3. when 4. in which

B. 1. where 2. which 3. time 4. which

C. 1. The room where we slept was uncomfortable.
2. Friday was the day when they heard the news.
3. Winter is a season when we go skiing.
4. This is the river where the man often goes fishing.

Unit 62. 관계부사 why, how
Practice

A. 1. for 2. how 3. the reason 4. in which 5. why

B. 1. the, way 2. reason, why 3. way, in, which

C. 1. Tell me the way[how] you made this robot.
2. We knows the reason why he refuses to eat.
3. He shows me the way[how] airbags work.

Unit 63. 관계부사와 선행사의 생략
Practice

A. 1. how[the way] 2. why 3. place

B. 1. where 2. the, reason 3. the, time 4. the, way

C. 1. August 27th is the day when the second semester starts.
2. Tony wants to know the place where Julia lives.

3. She tells me the reason why Jay made such a decision.

Unit 64. 복합관계대명사
Practice

A. 1. whoever 2. whomever 3. Whoever 4. Whatever

B. 1. Whatever 2. whichever 3. No, matter, what

C. 1. Whoever 2. No, matter, what 3. anyone, who

Unit 65. 복합관계부사
Practice

A. 1. Wherever 2. whenever 3. However 4. when

B. 1. Wherever you go, you must exercise every day.
2. However fast he ran, he couldn't catch the thief.
3. Whenever the kid sees me, she bursts into tears.

C. 1. However 2. Wherever 3. No, matter, how, hard

Review Test / Unit 61~65

A. 1. where 2. which 3. how 4. when

B. 1. which/that 2. when 3. which 4. why

C. 1. whatever 2. However 3. wherever 4. whenever
5. Whoever

D. 1. when 2. whatever 3. No, matter, how

E. 1. Tell, me, how 2. Whoever, wins
3. Every, time, need

Chapter Test / Unit 53~65

1. ③ 2. ⑤ 3. ③ 4. ② 5. whatever 6. ③ 7. that 8. ②
9. ④ 10. ③ 11. ⑤ 12. ② 13. ③ 14. ④ 15. ⑤ 16. ①
17. ② 18. ① 19. ④ 20. ③ 21. Cathy is writing a book whose topic is about peace. 22. in which many people are interested[which many people are interested in]
23. However hard you may try 24. (1) What I want to eat (2) What I want to buy 25. (1) where I bought (2) why I bought

1. 선행사와 뒤의 명사가 소유 관계일 때는 관계대명사 소유격으로 쓴다.

2. the way how에서 the way가 생략된 형태이다.

3. who나 which는 선행사를 수식하는 관계대명사와 의문문을 이끄는 의문대명사로 쓰이는데 ③번은 의문대명사이다.

4. 관계대명사 what은 선행사를 포함하며 '~하는 것'으로 해석한다.

5. anything that은 복합관계대명사 whatever로 바꾸어 쓸 수 있다.

6. 관계대명사 that은 계속적 용법에는 사용할 수 없다.

7. 선행사 앞에 최상급이 있을 경우에는 관계대명사 that을 써야 한다.

8. 관계대명사 that과 what은 제한적 용법에는 사용하지만 계속적 용법에

는 쓸 수 없다.

9. 선행사가 시간을 나타내는 말일 때는 관계부사 when을, 장소를 나타내는 말일 때는 관계부사 where를 쓴다.

10. whatever가 '무엇을 ~하든'이라는 뜻으로 양보절을 이끌 때에는 no matter what으로 바꾸어 쓸 수 있다.

11. 선행사를 포함한 것은 what을 쓰며 소유격은 whose를 사용한다.

12. ②번은 의문사이고 나머지는 관계대명사이다.

13. 선행사가 방법일 때는 how를 사용하는데 the way와 how 중에서 하나만 써야 한다.

14. 전치사가 앞에 있는 경우 목적격 관계대명사는 생략할 수 없다.

15. 선행사가 시간을 나타낼 때는 관계부사 when을 사용한다.

16. '어디에 가든지'라고 할 때는 복합관계부사 wherever를 사용한다.

17. 「전치사+관계대명사」를 쓸 경우에는 who와 which를 사용하여 나타낸다.

18. 관계대명사가 주격으로 쓰인 경우에는 생략할 수 없다.

19. 종속절에 목적어가 없는 것으로 보아 관계부사 where가 아니라 관계대명사 which가 와야 한다.

20. '아무리 ~하더라도'라는 뜻으로 양보의 절을 이끌 때에는 however나 no matter how를 쓴다.

21. 선행사가 관계대명사절에서 명사와 소유 관계일 때는 소유격 관계대명사 whose를 이용하여 나타낼 수 있다.

22. 관계대명사가 전치사의 목적어일 때에는 전치사를 관계대명사 앞 또는 관계대명사절 끝에 둔다.

23. 「however+형용사[부사]+주어+동사」는 '(주어가) 아무리 ~해도'라는 뜻이다.

24. 관계대명사 what은 선행사를 포함하고 있으며 the thing that[which]으로 바꾸어 쓸 수 있다.

25. 선행사가 장소일 경우에는 관계부사 where를 사용하고, 선행사가 이유일 경우에는 관계부사 why를 사용한다.

Chapter 9. 접속사

Unit 66. 명사절을 이끄는 접속사
Practice

A. 1. that 2. that 3. whether 4. That 5. if
B. 1. that 2. if[whether] 3. That 4. It, that
   5. whether
C. 1. if → whether 2. I'm → It's 3. if → that
   4. whether → that

Unit 67. 조건의 접속사
Practice

A. 1. If 2. unless 3. don't 4. Unless 5. If
B. 1. Unless 2. If, don't 3. unless 4. if, doesn't
C. 1. Unless, will, fall 2. If, snows

Unit 68. 시간의 접속사 1
Practice

A. 1. when 2. while 3. as
B. 1. finish 2. While 3. As 4. when
C. 1. When(As) 2. while 3. As 4. While

Unit 69. 시간의 접속사 2
Practice

A. 1. before 2. since 3. until 4. since
B. 1. After, I, eat 2. before, I, left
   3. since, she, finished 4. until[till], he, goes
   5. As, soon, as, saw
C. 1. since → until 2. passed → has passed

Review Test / Unit 66~69
A. 1. that 2. whether 3. Unless 4. if 5. before
B. 1. I'm not sure whether the rumor is true.
   2. We don't know if he will invite us to his party.
   3. I'll tell her the truth when she comes this evening.
   4. They haven't seen him since he went to Paris.
C. 1. Unless 2. after 3. It, that
D. 1. If, it, is 2. until[till], the, rain, stops
   3. soon, as, they, saw 4. When, he, came

Unit 70. 이유의 접속사
Practice

A. 1. because 2. as 3. since 4. because of
B. 1. She was not happy since she didn't enjoy her work.
   2. Tom didn't go out because it was very hot.
   3. As my father grew older, he became less talkative.
C. 1. because, he, lost 2. As, he, often, lies
   3. As, you, know 4. Since, you, broke

Unit 71. 양보의 접속사
Practice

A. 1. Though 2. even though 3. Despite 4. Even though
   5. Even if
B. 1. Although we practiced hard, we lost the game.
   2. Even if the bag was light, she couldn't lift it.
   3. I couldn't sleep though I was very tired.
   4. Even though the man is old, he can do the project.
C. 1. Though[Although]
   2. Even, if[though]
   3. Even, if[though], he, failed

Unit 72. 상관접속사

Practice

A. 1. and 2. but 3. not, only, but 4. well, as

B. 1. Either 2. nor 3. but also 4. is

C. 1. Both, and 2. Either, or
   3. Not, only, am, as, well, as 4. Neither, nor

Unit 73. 접속부사

Practice

A. 1. Nevertheless 2. However 3. Therefore 4. Besides

B. 1. Otherwise 2. As a result 3. Besides 4. Moreover

C. 1. As a result 2. However 3. Nevertheless

Review Test / Unit 70~73

A. 1. Even though 2. because 3. not only 4. nor
   5. Thus

B. 1. Either you or you brother
   2. because there was no bus
   3. In addition, she is wise

C. 1. because 2. neither, nor 3. as, well, as
   4. Besides[Moreover]

D. 1. either a soldier or a police officer
   2. Both Sam's brother and Sam are traveling
   3. even if I didn't get an A
   4. As a result, many people died
   5. Since yesterday was a holiday

Chapter Test / Unit 66~73

1. ③ 2. ② 3. ④ 4. ⑤ 5. ② 6. ① 7. ④ 8. but 9. ①
10. ② 11. ② 12. ② 13. ④ 14. ④ 15. ② 16. ⑤ 17. ③
18. ③ 19. ④ 20. ⑤ 21. as soon as the baby wakes up
22. (1) Unless you return (2) If you lose 23. not, only,
Spanish, but, also 24. Neither Jim nor Hellen will go to
the party. 25. (1) and Kate can (2) has a cat (3) has a
dog

1. '비록 피곤했지만 그 일을 끝냈다'라고 해야 자연스럽기 때문에 양보의 접속사 though가 알맞다.

2. 「either A or B」 구문에서 인칭과 수는 B에 일치시킨다.

3. 명사절을 이끄는 접속사 that은 문장에서 주어, 목적어, 보어, 동격 역할을 한다. ④번은 관계대명사로 선행사 anything을 수식하며 형용사절을 이끄는 that이다.

4. '~인지 아닌지'라는 뜻으로는 if나 whether를 사용하는데, if는 or not과 함께 쓰지는 않는다.

5. 조건의 부사절에서는 미래시제 대신 현재시제를 쓴다.

6. because 뒤에는 원인이 오고, so 뒤에는 결과가 온다.

7. 'A와 B 어느 것도 아닌'이라고 나타낼 때는 「neither A nor B」로 쓴다.

8. 「not A but B」는 'A가 아니라 B'라는 뜻이다.

9. '~하는 동안'을 나타낼 때는 시간의 접속사 while을 쓴다.

10. 명사절을 이끄는 whether는 if로 바꾸어 쓸 수 있다. 단, 주어 역할을 할 때는 if로 바꾸어 쓸 수 없다.

11. ④번 if는 목적어절에서만 쓰인다. ⑤번 시간의 부사절에서는 현재가 미래를 대신하기 때문에 will arrive를 arrives로 써야 한다.

12. without으로 보아 Tom은 세수는 하지 않고 아침 식사를 했다.

14. ④번은 '~이래로' 나머지는 '~이므로'의 뜻이므로 원인, 이유를 나타낸다.

16. '비록 ~이지만'의 뜻을 갖는 양보의 접속사 though가 와야 한다.

17. 'A와 B 둘 중 하나'를 나타낼 때는 「either A or B」를 이용하여 나타낸다.

18. because 뒤에는 절이 오고 because of 뒤에는 명사나 동명사가 온다.

19. 의문의 내용을 가진 문장의 목적어는 접속사 whether나 if를 사용하는데 뒤에 or not이 있으므로 whether가 와야 한다.

20. since는 '~이래로'라는 뜻으로 과거시제를 이끌며 현재완료와 쓰인다.

21. '~하자마자'라는 동시적인 상황을 나타낼 때는 as soon as를 이용하여 나타낸다.

22. 첫 번째는 도서 연체 시 벌금을 내야 하므로 '책을 반납하지 않으면'이라는 뜻이 되어야 하고, 두 번째는 도서 분실 시 동일한 책을 구입해야 하므로 '책을 잃어버린다면'이라는 뜻이 되어야 한다.

24. '둘 다 아니다'라는 뜻의 상관접속사 「neither A nor B」를 이용하여 한 문장으로 만들 수 있다.

25. besides는 접속사처럼 문장과 문장을 연결하는 접속사로 첨가나 추가 사항을 나타낼 때 사용한다. 또한 「not A but B」는 'A가 아닌 B'라는 뜻이다.

Chapter 10. 가정법

Unit 74. if 가정법 과거

Practice

A. 1. were 2. would 3. had 4. did 6. helped

B. 1. weren't, could 2. were, could 3. don't, have, can't
   4. don't, know

C. 1. studied, would, pass 2. If, could, go
   3. If, were, could, buy

Unit 75. if 가정법 과거완료

Practice

A. 1. had been 2. had listened 3. would have gone
   4. had met

B. 1. didn't, see, didn't return

2. hadn't, been, could, have, talked

3. didn't, take, couldn't, recover

4. believed, could, succeed

C. 1. had practiced, would have won

2. had been, could have played

3. hadn't snowed, could have climbed

Unit 76. I wish+가정법 과거/과거완료

Practice

A. 1. am, not 2. had, gone 3. didn't, study

4. don't, hear

B. 1. knew 2. had gone 3. were

C. 1. learned 2. had, arrived 3. had had

4. hadn't lost

Unit 77. as if(though)+가정법 과거/과거완료

Practice

A. 1. is, not 2. were, not 3. as, if[though], read

4. were, not

B. 1. was → were 2. saw → had seen

3. were → had been

C. 1. had, visited 2. heard

3. as, if[though], had, passed, didn't, pass

Unit 78. without(but for), 혼합가정법

Practice

A. 1. If, it, were, not, for 2. But, for

3. If, it, had, not, been, for 4. Had, it, not, been, for

B. 1. would, fail 2. But, for, would, be

3. If, had, studied, would be

Review Test / Unit 74~78

A. 1. I could meet him.

2. we would have been happy.

3. I could live in a fairyland.

4. she knew everything about it.

B. 1. were 2. Without 3. had been 4. be 5. had known

C. 1. were, could, buy 2. don't, know 3. fact, didn't, see

4. But, for 5. If, it, were, not, for

D. 1. were, would, not, believe 2. Without, couldn't, live

3. as, if[though], knew 4. had, not, died, would, be

Chapter Test / Unit 74~78

1. ③ 2. ⑤ 3. ④ 4. ⑤ 5. ⑤ 6. ① 7. ④ 8. ② 9. ②

10. ④ 11. ⑤ 12. ③ 13. ④ 14. ④ 15. ③ 16. Had,

known, could, have, bought 17. ③ 18. ④ 19. ① 20. ③

21. If he were rich, he could build schools in poor countries. 22. (1) I played the piano well (2) I had taken piano lessons 23. (1) Were he your true friend, he would be here now. (2) Had I practiced more, I would have won the game. 24. Without, But, for 25. had studied, could have won

1. if절이 과거완료가 왔으므로 주절은 「조동사 과거형+have+p.p」가 와야 한다.

2. 시점이 과거이므로 과거 사실과 반대되는 가정법 과거완료가 와야 된다.

3. as if 가정법 과거완료는 과거 사실의 반대를 나타낸다. 직설법으로 바꿀 때 긍정은 부정, 부정은 긍정으로 바꾼다.

4. without은 but for로 바꾸어 쓸 수 있으며 '~이 없다면, ~이 없었다면'의 뜻이다.

5. 현재 비가 와서 나갈 수 없다는 것을 알 수 있으므로 가정법 과거가 와야 한다.

6. 현재 자신이 더 부지런해지기를 바라는 것으로 현재의 소망을 나타낸다.

7. 가정법 과거완료로 과거 사실의 반대를 가정한 것으로 직설법으로 바꾸면 과거시제와 부정으로 나타내야 한다.

8. 직설법이 과거시제이므로 「I wish+가정법 과거완료」로 나타내며 부정은 긍정으로 나타내야 한다.

9. 가정법 과거완료는 과거 사실의 반대를 가정하는 문장으로 '어제 일찍 일어나서 버스를 놓치지 않았다.'가 일치한다.

10. 두 번째 문장의 would have drunk으로 보아 가정법 과거완료 문장이다.

11. 시제가 couldn't have gone으로 가정법 과거완료이므로 If it had not been for ~로 바꾸어 쓸 수 있다.

12. If you hadn't advised me에서 If가 생략된 형태이다.

13. 직설법을 가정법으로 바꿀 때, 현재 사실의 반대는 가정법 과거로, 과거 사실의 반대는 가정법 과거완료로 나타낸다.

14. 주절의 형태로 보아 가정법 과거완료임을 알 수 있다. If it were not for는 가정법 과거에 사용된다.

15. 주절의 형태로 보아 '많은 돈이 있다면'이라는 가정법 과거가 와야 한다.

16. 과거 사실의 반대는 가정법 과거완료로 나타내는데, If I had known your birthday에서 If를 생략하고 주어와 동사의 위치가 도치된 형태이다.

17. 가정법에서 be동사는 인칭과 수에 상관없이 were를 사용한다.

18. '마치 ~인 것처럼'을 나타낼 때는 as if 가정법을 사용하며 현재 사실의 반대는 가정법 과거를 쓴다.

19. If절이 과거완료가 왔으므로 주절은 could have visited가 되어야 한다.

20. without 가정법은 주절에 가정법 과거나 과거완료가 온다.

21. 주어진 문장의 시제가 현재이므로 가정법 과거로 표현하며 긍정은 부정, 부정은 긍정으로 바꾼다.

22. 첫 번째는 현재의 희망이므로 가정법 과거로 나타내면 되고 두 번째는

가정법 과거완료로 과거의 아쉬움을 나타내면 된다.

23. If절의 동사가 were 또는 「had+과거분사」일 때 if를 생략하면서 주어와 동사 were 또는 had를 도치시킨다.

24. '~이 없다면/없었다면'의 의미로 나타낼 때는 without 또는 but for를 사용한다.

25. 과거의 사실과 반대되는 상황을 소망하며 유감이나 아쉬움을 표현할 때는 가정법 과거완료를 사용하여 나타낸다.

Chapter 11. 일치와 화법

Unit 79. 수의 일치(단수)

Practice

A. 1. is 2. is 3. means 4. likes 5. is 6. is 7. is 8. is

B. 1. have → has 2. were → was 3. are → is
   4. are → is 5. are → is

C. 1. Mathematics, is 2. Each, student, has, to
   3. Fifty, dollars, is

Unit 80. 수의 일치(복수)

Practice

A. 1. are 2. are 3. are 4. wear 5. like 6. are 7. are
   8. are

B. 1. number, sing 2. Leaves, of, begin
   3. Most, of, know 4. Half, of, are
   5. There, are, ten, men

Unit 81. 시제 일치

Practice

A. 1. made 2. has paid 3. could win 4. was

B. 1. O 2. can't → couldn't 3. O
   4. has had → had had

C. 1. could, do, anything 2. was, a, carpenter
   3. would, pass, the, exam 4. had, wanted

Unit 82. 시제 일치의 예외

Practice

A. 1. begins 2. discovered 3. rises 4. gets 5. broke

B. 1. He taught me that light travels faster than sound.
   2. The man said that Shakespeare was born in 1564.
   3. We knew that water boils at 100 degrees celsius.

C. 1. said, is 2. know, invented 3. learned, is

Review Test / Unit 79~82

A. 1. are 2. are 3. is 4. are 5. belongs 6. is 7. is
   8. is

B. 1. agree 2. needs 3. landed 4. would 5. sets

C. 1. I thought that he was diligent.
   2. Ten minutes is enough
   3. Bread with jam is my
   4. time flies like an arrow

D. 1. found, had, lost 2. Most, of, is 3. said, makes

Unit 83. 평서문의 간접화법

Practice

A. 1. said, was, then
   2. told, I, was, those
   3. told, he, wouldn't

B. 1. You have to study now.
   2. I saw the circus yesterday.
   3. I will watch the movie.

C. 1. arrived here, said, he had arrived, the day before
   2. will visit, she would visit, the next day

Unit 84. 의문사가 없는 의문문의 간접화법

Practice

A. 1. asked, I, was
   2. asked, I, had, gone
   3. asked, if[whether], she, would, be

B. 1. Do I have to take the medicine?
   2. Are you listening to me?
   3. Can you swim in the lake?

C. 1. asked, if[whether] she could have
   2. asked, if[whether] we knew

Unit 85. 의문사가 있는 의문문의 간접화법

Practice

A. 1. asks, who, my, coach
   2. asked, what, time, it, was
   3. asked, why, she, had, shouted

B. 1. what her address was
   2. who had sent him the present
   3. where he had bought the cap

C. 1. asked, where he wanted
   2. asked, who had broken
   3. asked, why she was angry

Unit 86. 명령문의 간접화법

Practice

A. 1. ordered, not, to, fight
   2. told, to, walk, my

3. advised, to, take, myself

4. asked, to, give, her

B. 1. to lend her ten dollars

2. asked me to open the door

3. advised him to stop smoking

C. 1. Don't play with the ball inside.

2. Get plenty of rest.

3. Don't tell them the truth.

Review Test / Unit 83~86

A. 1. if 2. was 3. not to touch

B. 1. before 2. would 3. who he was 4. to study

C. 1. told, could, play 2. asked, if[whether], I, can

3. asked, why, I, was 4. asked, to, brush

D. 1. told, she, looked 2. asked, where, he, lived

3. asked, if[whether], I, liked

E. 1. He asked judy if[whether] she was leaving that day.

2. He asked me if[whether] I knew her address.

3. He asked me when I had bought my watch.

4. Mom told me not to be late for school.

Chapter Test / Unit 79~86

1. ① 2. ④ 3. ① 4. ② 5. ④ 6. ⑤ 7. ① 8. ⑤ 9. ②
10. ④ 11. ② 12. ④ 13. ② 14. ⑤ 15. ④ 16. ②, ⑤ 17. ②
18. asked, where, she, wanted 19. ④ 20. ③ 21. he, was,
diligent 22. A number of, Most, The number of 23. She
asked me where I would study the next day. 24. asked,
When, passed, since, said, Ten, years, is 25. (1) what the
matter was (2) to take some medicine and get some rest

1. each, every, every-, any- 등의 부정대명사는 단수 취급한다.

2. 현재의 사실이나 습관은 항상 현재시제로 쓴다.

3. 시간, 거리, 금액, 학문명, 동일인 등은 단수 취급하여 단수동사를 쓴다.

4. and로 연결되어 복수처럼 보이지만 전체가 하나를 나타내는 것은 단수 취급한다.

5. 의문문을 간접화법으로 바꿀 때는 전달동사 ask를 사용하며 명령문의 경우 요청이나 부탁을 나타낼 때도 ask를 사용한다.

6. 의문사가 있는 간접화법은 「의문사+주어+동사」의 순서로 쓴다.

7. 명령문의 간접화법은 to부정사로 연결한다.

8. 의문사가 없는 의문문을 간접화법으로 전환할 때는 if나 whether를 사용하여 수와 시제를 일치시킨다.

9. 분수 표현 뒤에 단수명사가 오면 단수동사가 오고, 복수명사가 오면 복수동사가 온다.

11. the black and white dog은 검정색과 흰색이 있는 개(한 마리)를 의미하고 the black dog and the white dog은 검은 개와 흰 개(두 마

리)를 의미한다.

12. 역사적인 일이나 사건은 항상 과거시제로 나타낸다.

13. 부정명령문의 간접화법 전환은 not to부정사로 연결하며 전달동사는 의미에 따라 ask(부탁, 요청), tell(지시), order(명령), advise(충고)를 쓴다.

14. 직접화법을 간접화법으로 바꿀 때 부사(구)도 바꿔야 하는데 yesterday 는 the day before로 바꾼다.

15. 이전에 작업이 완료된 것을 표현해야 하는데, 주절의 시제가 과거이므로 과거완료시제가 와야 한다.

16. 주절의 시제가 과거일 때, 종속절에는 과거시제나 과거완료시제가 와야 한다.

17. someone은 단수 취급하므로 단수동사 was가 와야 한다.

18. 의문사가 있는 의문문을 간접화법으로 바꿀 때는 의문사를 이용하여 「의문사+주어+동사」의 순서로 쓰고 시제는 주절의 시제와 일치시킨다.

19. 평서문을 간접화법으로 바꿀 때 전달동사는 tell로 바꾸고 인칭과 시제를 일치시킨다.

20. 직접화법에서 간접화법으로 바꿀 때 부사 tonight는 that night로 바꾼다.

21. 주절의 시제가 과거로 바뀐 경우 종속절에는 과거나 과거완료가 올 수 있는데 when이 있으므로 과거시제가 와야 한다.

22. 「the number of 복수명사」는 단수 취급하고 「a number of 복수명사」는 복수 취급한다.

23. 의문사가 있는 의문문을 간접화접으로 전환할 때는 「의문사+주어+동사」의 순서로 쓴다.

24. 시간이나 거리가 하나의 형태를 나타낼 때는 단수 취급하지만 합쳐진 시간이나 거리는 복수 취급한다.

25. 의사는 감기에 걸렸으니 약을 먹으면서 쉬라고 말했으며 명령문을 간접화법으로 전환할 때는 to부정사로 나타낸다.

Chapter 12. 특수구문

Unit 87. 강조(동사, 명사, 부정어)

Practice

A. 1. does 2. in the least 3. themselves 4. the very

B. 1. herself 2. do, like 3. did, spend 4. at, all

C. 1. the, very, chair 2. himself 3. not, at, all

Unit 88. 강조(It ~ that)

Practice

A. 1. It was his client that(whom) Carol met at the station.

2. It was after school that(when) Billy played soccer.

3. It was the window that(which) I broke at that time.

4. It was in the library that(where) Susan wrote the report.

B. 1. was 2. that[which] 3. works

C. 1. It, health, that(which)
   2. It, last, Sunday, that(when)
   3. It, Eric, she
   4. It, this, dress, that(which)

Unit 89. 도치(장소 부사(구), 부정어)
Practice

A. 1. the table are the balls
   2. does it rain in the desert
   3. the window is the vase
   4. did we see him again

B. 1. did, he, know 2. did, I, see 3. stood, his, father.

C. 1. comes the taxi
   2. my head flew the ladybug
   3. was he late for school

Unit 90. 도치(So, neither+동사+주어)
Practice

A. 1. So, does 2. Neither, was 3. So, would 4. So, am
   5. Neither, do

B. 1. go to America, and so would she
   2. there next Sunday and neither will Jane
   3. a good lawyer, and so is Jimmy

C. 1. Neither, did, Mark 2. So, is, he 3. Neither, have, I
   4. So, will, I

Unit 91. 부분부정과 전체부정
Practice

A. 1. Nobody 2. both 3. Neither

B. 1. Neither 2. Not, all 3. doesn't, always 4. don't, any
   5. None 6. Not, all 7. No, one

Unit 92. 생략(공통부분, 주어+be동사)
Practice

A. 1. loves lakes 2. you can run 3. to go 4. can dance
   5. If I am 6. if it is

B. 1. Though, poor 2. the, theater 3. want, to
   4. When, young 5. If, possible

Unit 93. 간접의문문
Practice

A. 1. start → starts 2. is he → he is
   3. Do where → Where do

B. 1. Can you tell me where the bank is?
   2. How old do you believe the old woman is?

---

3. Do you know if[whether] Sarah loved him?
   4. I want to know if[whether] you will go on a field trip.

C. 1. who, invented 2. Where, you, lost
   3. if[whether], you, will, come 4. when, she, went

Review Test / Unit 87~93

A. 1. She doesn't think I love her, but I do love her.
   2. It was two years ago that(when) she bought the scarf.
   3. You do not like her song at all.

B. 1. came the rain 2. does he 3. So am
   4. the train starts 5. What do

C. 1. don't, either 2. Not, all 3. neither, of, them.

D. 1. When, young 2. if, possible 3. did, have
   4. none(neither)

E. 1. If, necessary 2. Though, sleepy 3. I, couldn't
   4. so, do, I

Chapter Test / Unit 87~93

1. ⑤ 2. ④ 3. ③ 4. ① 5. does he work 6. ② 7. ④
8. ③ 9. ② 10. ⑤ 11. ② 12. ③ 13. ④ 14. ③ 15. ①
16. ① 17. ② 18. ③ 19. ③ 20. ② 21. was on this road
that[where] Denis had a car accident 22. On the top of
the mountain was a big lake. 23. (1) who you played
badminton last week (2) Where do you suppose they are
going to go 24. not, always 25. Neither, does

1. 부정문에서는 「Neither+동사+주어」로 '~도 그러하다'라는 의미를 나타낸다.

2. 부정어를 강조하여 문두에 두고 주어와 동사가 도치된 문장으로, 일반동사의 경우에는 조동사 do를 이용하여 나타낸다.

3. It ~ that 강조구문에서 It is[was] ~ that의 세 단어를 빼고 다시 배열하면 완전한 문장이 된다.

4. 누군가의 말에 동감할 때 긍정이면 so를 이용하고 부정이며 neither를 이용한다.

5. He rarely works~에서 문두에 부정어가 도치된 문장이다.

6. 시간의 접속사 다음에 「주어+동사」를 생략할 때는 부사절과 주절의 주어가 같아야 한다.

7. 부정어를 도치한 문장으로 be동사의 경우에는 「부정어+be동사+주어」의 어순으로 쓴다.

8. 장소를 나타내는 부사(구)가 문장 앞에 오면 주어와 동사의 어순이 바뀌어 동사, 주어의 순서가 된다.

10. 몇몇은 피아노를 잘 치고 나머지들은 못 친다고 했으므로 부정어와 every를 이용한 부분부정의 표현이다.

11. It ~ that 강조구문은 강조할 내용이 주어, 목적어, 부사(구)일 때 사용한다.

12. 명사절이 목적어절을 이끌 때의 that은 생략이 가능하다.

13. 일반동사가 있는 문장의 부정어 도치나 일반동사를 줄여서 쓸 때는 do 동사를 이용하는데, 시제가 과거이므로 did가 공통으로 들어간다.

14. 부정문에서 부정어를 강조할 때는 at all을 문장에 넣어 '전혀[조금도] ~ 아니다'라고 표현할 수 있다.

15. 부사(구)를 문두로 도치시킬 때 주어가 대명사일 경우에는 「부사(구)+ 주어(대명사)+동사」의 순서로 온다.

16. 부정어가 any, any-, either와 함께 쓰이거나 neither, no, never 등의 어구가 있으면 전체부정을 나타낸다.

17. 보기 문장의 do는 강조의 뜻을 나타내는 조동사이다.

18. 전체부정으로 '둘 다 좋아하지 않는다'라는 뜻인데, 동사가 like가 아닌 dislike가 왔으므로 neither가 아니고 both가 와야 한다.

19. 동사를 강조할 때는 동사 앞에 do를 사용해서 나타내는데, 수와 시제에 따라서 do, does, did를 쓰며 뒤에는 동사원형이 온다.

20. 주절의 동사가 think, believe, guess, suppose 등이고 의문사가 사용된 간접의문문의 어순은 의문사가 문장 맨 앞으로 간다.

21. 'It ~ that' 강조구문은 강조하고자 하는 주어, 목적어, 부사(구)를 It is [was]와 that 사이에 넣어서 표현한다.

22. 장소 부사(구)가 문장 맨 앞에 오면 '장소 부사(구)+동사+주어'의 어순으로 쓴다.

23. 의문사가 think, believe, suppose, imagine, guess 등의 목적어로 쓰일 때 간접의문문의 의문사를 문장 맨 앞에 위치시킨다.

24. 일주일에 한 번은 걸어서 학교에 가기 때문에 '항상 ~인 것은 아니다'라는 뜻이 되어야 한다.

25. '~도 그러하다'라는 의미를 나타낼 때 긍정문에서는 「so+동사+주어」로, 부정문에서는 「neither+동사+주어」로 쓴다.